AF322726

# STUDY BOOK OF ESTHER

## ANALYSIS, ACCORDING TO GE'EZ MANUSCRIPT

BY

DR. YOHANNES TEKLE

TO...............................................................

...............................................................

.........................

FROM

...............................................................

...............................................................

.........................

# Dedication

First and foremost, I would like to express my immense gratitude and praise to my Lord Jesus Christ for every journey He has taken with me. Lord God, I praise You for not only the innumerable and immeasurably vast human, financial, and educational resources You have provided me with but also for equipping me to embark on the journey of conducting this manual.

My indebtedness extends to my beloved wife, Bizuayehu Zewude. She has been a living embodiment of the Lord's grace, presence, and generosity in my life. Bizuye, you have been my cushion, my partner, my friend, and my ever-reliable source of support and encouragement. You have been my solitary constant, compassionately lending an ear to my inquiries, supplying me with valuable suggestions, and, most of all, devotedly assisting me in developing myself as a writer through your insightful feedback.

My gratitude also extends to my two wonderful daughters, Raey Yohannes Tekle and Henon Yohannes Tekle, for their presence in my life, which enkindles a fire within my heart and guides me to shape and pursue my life aspirations.

I wholeheartedly wish to take this moment to express my deepest gratitude and appreciation. May the Lord continue to bless you all.

**Dr. Yohannes Tekle**

# SPECIAL THANKS

I would like to take this opportunity to express my immense gratitude to Pastor Mulualem Hagos for his encouragement and engagement throughout the development of my work. Whether by reviewing my drafts, participating in valuable dialogues during the writing process, or assuming a significant and proactive role in the monumental task of publishing my manual, I wish to recognize and appreciate his involvement in bringing this work into existence.

My heartfelt appreciation goes to my beloved siblings: Habtom Tekle, Birhan Tekle, Gebru Tekle, Sis. Kahsa Tekle, Tsadkan Tekle, Engineer Gebreegziabher Tekle, and Yosef Tekle for their unwavering moral support.

I would also like to express my sincere thanks to Reverend Dr. Kiros Lakew (former Vice President of the Ethiopian Evangelical Church Mekaneyesus and former President of the Ethiopian Evangelical Church Mekaneyesus Addis Ababa Synod), Evangelist Dr. Gebru Weldu, and Pastor Endashaw Kelkele (EECD Pastor) for their invaluable advice and unwavering guidance.

I am deeply grateful to Sosina for her assistance with typing. I also want to extend my thanks to all who contributed to the project, providing references, resources, and access to computer center facilities. I would like to acknowledge all the individuals and organizations I contacted for their readiness to assist and share information, offering their valuable input to this project.

A very special thank you goes to my daughter, Raey Yohannes Tekle, whose unwavering support and dedication in editing played a crucial role in the completion of this work. Your attention to detail and commitment to ensuring the quality of this manual has been a tremendous help, and I truly appreciate your contributions.

My deepest thanks go to my family for their sponsorship and support throughout the publishing process.

Finally, without the special guidance and help of the Holy Spirit, this manual would not have become a reality. Praise be to God.

# Personal Endorsement

The Book of Esther is a captivating story of courage, faith, and divine intervention set during the Persian Empire. It centers on Esther, a Jewish woman who becomes a queen and must navigate the complex political and cultural dynamics of the court. We see Gods interferance, with the guidance of her cousin Mordecai, Esther risks her life to confront the king and save her people. The book highlight's themes of providence, identity, and the power of individual action in the face of danger. Uniquely, the book of Esther does not explicitly mention God, yet it subtly demonstrates His influence through the unfolding events.

Dr. Yohannes Tekle, in his insightful work, walks us through the history and divine influence found in Esther, particularly through the lens of the Gé'éz manuscript. His deep understanding of the text reveals God's hand in the story in a way that is both scholarly and spiritually enriching.

Dr. Tekle's work is a magnificent contribution to the body of Christ, offering profound insights into the enduring power of faith and providence.

His piece is a sweeping call upon humanity to recognize, champion and embrace the high-principled and tenderhearted attributes of Esther—valiance, unflinching devotion, munificence and benevolence—and thus I implore readers to greet and entertain it with open arms.

**Pastor Mulualem Hagos**

# Author's Personal reflection

The major purpose of this book is to provide a Textual analysis, translation and commentary of the book of Esther according to the Ge'ez Manuscript. It's also to be well understood by the 21st Century contemporary Readers. The whole story of the book is summarized from the Holy Bible. The story of Esther is about a young Jewish woman and her uncle, who manage to secure the future of the Jewish people living under the Persian Empire. Their success explains the origins of a Jewish festival, Purim which has celebrated their victory ever since.

On the surface, God is absent from this great event of deliverance, In fact, God is not mentioned in the book at all! But a careful reading of the story shows us that from being absent, God is hidden in the story. If we take notice of the clues, we realize that God is the central character. At strategic moments, God is controlling presence and purpose need not be mentioned. In the light of this perspective, because the Lord is present with his people, Esther's uncle Merdocaios is certain that the Jews will be delivered (Esther 4:14).

Because God cares for his people, fasting has a purpose (4:3, 16). God is advisors hold the Jewish people in alive, (6:13). We can take if these assumptions are part of the midst of the original readers of the story. The writer does not need to tell them what they already know. Instead, the writer confirms foundation of all human experience, whether we choose to recognize it or not.

Despite, the book of Esther has not always been recognized as confirming and commending faith in God. Even the great religious peoples doubted whether it should be included in the old testament in contrast, the early Jewish scholars who translated the old testament from Hebrew into Greek added six new sections to the story, which specifically celebrate God's work which these translators show a certain lack of appreciation for the writers own perspective on the story they do at least indicate that very early God was recognized as the hidden and central characters in the story. They did not want to keep God hidden between the lines. They wanted to make explicit what the author implied.

Indeed, this book doesn't make sense without God. It confirms that God's purpose to bring relief and salvation to his people will not be the wanted thing by Haman.

This is why the book of Esther has many parallels to the exodus story. Circumstances have changed, but God has not just as He heard the cry of his oppressed people in Egypt (Exodus 6:5), now he hears the wailing of his people faced the terror of Haman (Esther 4:1-3). Once his people faced the terror of Egypt, now some of his people are experiencing a vindictive Persian official. But God's promises are unchanged. His people will always experiencing a vindictive Persian official. But God's promises are unchanged. His people will always experience deliverance and salvation because He remembers his covenant (Exodus 6:5) So God's actions in saving and delivering his people are worth remembering and celebrating. By so doing we recognize that God is active and pre-eminent in human affairs.

Esther's story is full of practical and spiritual help. It encourages us to believe beneath the surface of our circumstances to discover God's protecting using of refuge, (Ruth 2:12). This discovery brings relief, joy and celebration (Esther 9:22) as it transforms our restricted view of God into limit less wonder.

The Author of the book of Esther is not known, though it seems certain that he or she was a Jew writing between 460 and 330 BC. The Story is set on the reign of king Xerxes (486-465 BC), and therefore comes in the sixty –year gap presumed between the events of chapter 6 and 7 of the book of Ezra. During this time some of the exiled Jews returned to Jerusalem, but others remained is Mesopotamia under Persian rule. The Jews who remained were aware that their position was rather tenuous. In the person of Haman their fears were realized, for the threatened to destroy the Jewish people once again, in the light of the terror Haman represented to God is people it is remarkable that the role of a Jewish woman is so important. Esther co-operates with Mordecai and plays a crucial part in saving God his people. It is a role she alone can undertake. Esther in is not restricted by her gender, despite the lowly status of women in their culture. This manual appreciated that everyone has the opportunity to co-operate with God's purposes.

Finally, the Textual Analysis of this wonderful story and the important English translated Ge'ez book of Esther is done by using four different Manuscripts available in the Ethiopian national archive museum, referring libraries, internets and consulting different books and visiting local Churches. I have tried to do the best to collect available resources from different places. Thoughout this book, you will discover God's intervention and his unique ways of interacting with his people through his divine visitation. The leadership qualities of Esther and the wisdom of her uncle can also be a special challenge to contemporary readers. God cares for his people; His purpose is always to bring relief and salvation to his people. I encourage all readers to study more about the story of Esther, the beautiful queen inside and out, as well as the brave heart of her uncle Merdocaios, in which God our father used them as an instrument to help us changing our life journey.

**Thank you and God bless you all**

**Dr. Yohannes Tekle**

# Comments about the book



"As the pastor of the Ethiopian Evangelical Church of Denver (EECD), I am both honored and delighted to introduce Dr. Yohannes Tekle's insightful and exploration of the Book of Esther. In this work, Dr. Tekle artfully brings the ancient Narrative of Esther into the contemporary world, providing us with a fresh and practical Christian understanding. The Book of Esther, with its themes of courage, providence, and divine intervention, remains as relevant today as it has ever been. Dr. Tekle drew parallels between Esther's story and the challenges faced by Christians in today's world are remarkable. Through his work, readers will find not only a deeper understanding of the biblical text but also inspiration and guidance for their personal and spiritual lives. You will discover a wealth of wisdom and a renewed Appreciation for God's hand in our personal and communallives. Dr. Tekle's work is a gift to the church and a testament to the enduring power of Scripture. May it challenge, comfort, and inspire all who read it."

In Christ's service,

**Endashaw Kelkele**

**Pastor, Ethiopian Evangelical Church of Denver (EECD)**

"Dr. Yohannes Tekle Presented the book of Esther to Study in attractive way to understand it easily. This book Invites readers to trust in God's Sovereignty and to recognize His hand at work in all circumstances. In this Analysis,

· We can learn the leadership Quality of Meredoca's and Esther.

· We can learn how God works behind the scenes for those who trusted Him.

· We can learn How God protects His people from the enemy Destruction.

· We can learn God empowering ordinary people for extraordinary Purpose. I gladly recommended this book to read with great respect. Especially those of you want God's divine intervention when life under risk, and/or if you realy want to serve the Lord firmly in season and out of Season, I highly recommend reading this book."

**Pastor Demewez Abebe (EECD Family Pastor)**

"Dr Yohannes Tekle has excellently accomplished this great work of analysis, translation and commentary of the Book of Esther according to the Ge'ez Manuscript. It is a must-read for any one considering spiritual satisfaction. Read this book and learn a wonderful story about Esther, a young Jewish woman and her uncle, who managed to secure the future of the Jewish people living under the Persian Empire. Dr Yohannes has made the story easy to understand. The story encourages us to believe to discover God's protecting using refuge."

**Tewodros Gebremariam, MD.     Research Associate, Denver Health**

**Associate Professor of Medicine (visiting), University of Colorado School of Medicine**

"The Book of Esther is the story of God's purpose about advancing His kingdom. It invites us to see that God has a plan and purpose for each one of us. The book teaches us about obtaining wisdom and divine guidance on justice for the less fortunate. It is about love, advocacy, courage and triumph. Why did God remain silent? What is the Book of Esther relevant for us today? What is the main message?

To discover more about "The Book of Esther", Dr. Yohannes Tekle, has come up with a well-researched book. His book is educational, and you will find answers to your questions. Every Christian believer who is eager to attain a deep understanding of God's purpose for yourself and your family is encouraged to pick up and read this book. God bless, Dr. Yohannes and his family."

**Haftu Gebrehiwot, M.D, FAAFP**

**Assistant Clinical Professor, University of Colorado, School of Medicine.**

"Book of Esther, by Dr. Yohannes Tekle provides an insightful andthoughtful analysis of the biblical story of Esther. The author delves into themes of courage, faith, and divine intervention, offering a fresh perspective on the ancient narrative. Dr. Tekle's approach is scholarly yet accessible, making complex theological concepts understandable to a wide audience. Through careful examination of the text, he highlights the relevance of Esther's story in both historical and contemporary contexts. A compelling read for those seeking a deeper understanding of the Book of Esther."

**Mulualem Hagos**

**Pastor, Jubilee Evangelical Church (JEC)**

**Good Samaritan prison ministry (CEO)**

## About the Author

Dr. Yohannes Tekle is a licensed professional counselor candidate, lecturer on Psychology, counseling and marriage and family life courses. He has a Master of Art in Psychology counseling and a doctorate degree in biblical studies. More recently he was a high-level advisor to the state minister and general director in the ministry of industry and transport authority, with over a decade of experience. He also served as a Director of FTMSI (Director of the Federal transport management and safety institute) for longer years. He was assigned by government to be one of the specialized committees of the African union. He contributed a lot to the research studies to connect Africa to the energy, tansport, industry, tourism and infrastructure sectors. He devotedly serves the Lord in the Church being an elder, a counselor and on the teachings, preaching the word of God for several years.

Currently he is serving God's kingdom in his local Church. His insight reflects how the narritives reveal God's unconditional love and the divine interferance holds in our lives; he encourages readers to embrace the love of Lord, highliting the opportunity for repentence and acceptance of Jesus Christ as their personal savior.

# Table of Contents

# Study Book of Esther

# Analysis, According to Ge'ez Manuscript

**By**

**Dr. Yohannes Tekle**

## Chapter 1. Introduction; Understanding the Book:

### 1.1. Background:

Until the 20th century the development of textual criticism and analysis was inevitably dominated by classical and biblical studies. The systematic study and practice of the subject originated in the 3rd century BC with the Greek scholars of Alexandria. Albeit the prominent employment of printed publication in the 5th century, preceding this era, the conveyance of literature had been predominantly contingent upon oral transmission. Moreover, numerous texts had weathered grave degeneration due to the shroud of unfamiliarity surrounding the notion of accurate textual reproduction. Observing this conundrum, the Liberians of Alexandrina took it upon themselves to collect and systematize a consequential volume of pertinent texts in conjunction with their respective analytical commentaries. Several such editions and commentaries did in fact materialize.

Alexandrian editing was distinguished above all by respect for the tradition- the text was constituted from the oldest and best copies available and speculative commendation was rigidly confined to commentary, which was continued in a separate volume. A meticulous battery of critical signage was utilized to make transitions between textual copy and commentary text. The adoption of such techniques extended, although to a less grand and ambitious breadth to Roman scholars when marshaling and subediting Latin texts as well as a multitude of intellectuals in Africa.

Over the course of the past three decades, the history of Eastern Sub-Saharan Africa has overpoweringly and rather manifestly been structured around sources inscribed in European languages. In comparison, the employment of sources in Arabic and other languages like Gé'éz has been quite insubstantial, as has been the use of oral tradition, despite the indisputable emphasis bestowed on the latter. Historians of Africa have also been justly noted for incorporating evidence from other disciplines such as historical linguistics and epidemiology into their syntheses. In so doing they have more reasonable caution and have often sought out additional training, as benefits those who venture into unfamiliar waters. Comparatively, written sources in European languages, which are at the heart of the writing of African history, have excessively been put to use in a heedless and haphazard manner.

Among the languages of the world into which the Bible was translated during the first six centuries, two were African languages, namely Coptic and Gé'éz. Gé'éz literature blossomed in parallel with the Advent of Christianity and hence from the commencement of that era countless works originally put forward in foregein languages have been transcribed into Gé'éz.

Abysinia is one among the few countries who house a vibrant assortment of documents comprising of the most abundant written sources from 14$^{th}$ to 17$^{th}$ and 18$^{th}$ centuries in sub–Saharan Africa.

Dillmann considered the Gé'éz Bible as "the foundation of all Abyssinian literature and the standard to which all other writers conformed their style of writing. Many generations of Gé'éz writers have been nurtured and brought up on the Gé'éz Bible, and it has had a profound influence on both their language and their style. In shaping the language and terminology of Abysinian liturgical texts the role of the Gé'éz Bible is fundamental." (Dillmann, Auguest1907)

It is postulated that all the canonical and Apocryphal books of the Scripture were available in Gé'éz before the end of 6th century. (Ullendorff, 1968, pp.33-34). These represent the most notable literary achievements of the Aksumite Kingdom. (Ullendorff,1968, pp.33-34).

Until the 19th century Gé'éz was defacto the major written language of Abysinia. After the reign of Emperor Yohannes and, consequently, Tewodros (1855-1868) the language continued to be leveraged as a liturgical language in the Ethiopian Orthodox Tewahdo Church (EOTC).

Even in the contemporary era, Ge'ez Semitic languages and Cushitic languages continue to be seamlessly and inherently intertwisted. Hence, Gé'éz was influenced by its Cushitic substratum. The influence of Tigrigna and Amharic on Gé'éz is also visible after the incumbency of the Solomonic dynasty, being particularily prominent in the chronicles composed by the natives of the two languages as these were the figures who, during that era, took on the enterprise of consildating such literary pieces. On the other hand, Gé'éz as a classical language posseses a weighty bearing on the modern languages of Ethiopia as a considerable number of words and phrases of the nation are derivatives and by extension loan words springing from Semitic lanaguages such as Tigrigna and Amharic and a broad range of Cushitic languages.

## 1.2. The book of Esther in the Bible: -

In Easton's Bible Dictionary, the authorship of the Book of Esther remains unknown. It is widely accepted that it was written after the death of King Ahasuerus (the Xerxes of the Greeks), who passed away around 465 BCE. The detailed account of many historical events suggests that the writer was likely a contemporary of Mordecai and Esther. Therefore, it is reasonable to conclude that the book was written approximately between 444 and 434 BCE, with the author likely being a Jew from the Diaspora.

The Book of Esther stands out as one of the most historical books in the Bible, with the notable characteristic that the name of God is not mentioned anywhere in the text. Despite this absence, it has been rightly observed that "Though the name of God be not in it, his finger is." The book powerfully illustrates God's providential governance over the events, even without direct mention of His name.

Esther, the queen of Ahasuerus, is the central figure of the book. Born as a Jew named Hadassah (meaning "myrtle"), she is given the name Esther after entering the royal harem (Esther 2:7). Her story is one of courage, faith, and God's unseen guidance in the lives of His people.

The name "Esther" is thought to be a Syro-Arabian modification of the Persian word *Satarah*, which means "star." Esther was the daughter of Abihail, a Benjamite. Unlike many others, her family chose not to return to Jerusalem when Cyrus granted permission for the exiles to return. Instead, Esther remained in the Persian capital,

Shushan, with her cousin Mordecai, who held a position in the Persian king's household.

When Ahasuerus (the king) divorced his first wife, Vashti, he chose Esther to be his queen. Shortly after, he appointed Haman the Agagite, his prime minister, with the power to destroy the Jews across the Persian Empire. Esther's bravery and intervention led to Haman's downfall—he was hanged on the gallows he had prepared for Mordecai. The Jewish people then instituted the annual feast of Purim to celebrate their deliverance. These events took place about fifty-two years after the return from exile, around 479 BCE, during the time of the battles of Plataea and Mycale.

Esther is portrayed in the Bible as a woman of deep piety, faith, courage, patriotism, and caution. She is dutiful to her adopted father, Mordecai, obedient to his counsel, and determined to use her position to benefit the Jewish people. Esther's beauty and charm were instrumental in her winning favor in the eyes of those around her (Esther 2:15). She was raised up by God to avert the destruction of her people, to protect them, and to ensure their prosperity during their time in captivity. Esther's role in preserving her people is evident in the Scripture, making her one of the most beloved characters in the Old Testament.

However, the Book of Esther is often considered the least "Jewish" or "Christian" book of the Bible. The word "God" is never mentioned in the entire book, nor are there references to "Jerusalem," "the Temple," "the law of Moses," or "Palestine." The story takes place during the

Persian Empire when Jews were scattered across the vast empire. At this time, there was no central Jewish identity or homeland. The book thus reflects the disjointed nature of Jewish life during this period. Many Jews felt disconnected from their land, and possibly from God as well.

The events surrounding Queen Esther were written for Jews living in the early years of the Diaspora, a period that began with the Babylonian destruction of Jerusalem in 586 BCE and extended until the establishment of the modern Jewish state in 1948. Esther's story served as an example to Jews, showing them how to face injustice, bigotry, and prejudice. She embodied courage and integrity in the face of adversity, teaching Jews how to stand firm against anti-Semitism and to act in defense of their people.

### *1.3. The Book of Esther in the history of the Old Testament Canon:-*

The paradoxical absence of God's name and religious elements in the Book of Esther has long intrigued scholars, leading some to question its inclusion in the Old Testament canon. However, as part of the Holy Scriptures, the Book of Esther is recognized as the Word of God, with God being the ultimate author, the Creator, and Lord of Israel's history. The canonization of Esther has granted it the same status as the other biblical narratives that document the sacred history of Israel. In this way, the book reveals God's will as manifested in historical events.

Given these considerations, we deem it necessary to explore the process through which the Book of Esther was canonized. This process allows us to trace the moment when the book was officially included in the canon, highlighting the theological and ideological reasons behind its acceptance, as well as the reception it has received over time. For a comprehensive understanding of the factors leading to the canonization of the Book of Esther, we examine relevant ancient sources and various studies on the subject. The issue is analyzed diachronically, contextualizing the Book of Esther's canonization within the broader formation of the Old Testament canon, with particular attention to the canonization of its final section—the Writings—of which Esther is a part, according to the Hebrew tradition. Consequently, we provide detailed information for each step in the canonization process, offering insights into the rationale for the inclusion of Esther in the Hebrew canon.

## 1.4. WHO IS ESTHER?

Among the most inspiring and imposing female figures of the bible, Esther unequivocally assumes a pivotal and unparalleled position. Her life and ministry were so prominent and of such consequential value that she is one of only two women who have a book of the Bible that bears her name. Esther is an ordinary woman that God chose to use for His purposes. In a nutshell, the book of Esther details the story of a young Jewish girl who grows to shoulder the far-reaching authority coupled with momentous responsibility of a queen. However, it does not merely serve chronological functions but also supplies a keen threshold into the life of Jewish people living under Persian dominion. During Esther's period of existence, the Persian Empire was immensely vast and extended over astronomical geographical landscapes, with its eastern bounds encircling modern-day India and its western peripheries stretching to Turkey and Ethiopia. Albeit the lack of explicit mentions of God's name in this book of the Bible, the story of Esther is absorbed into the canon of scripture on account of its pertinence to mankind and embodiment of God's providential work. Based on these grounds, even though the narrative of Esther is a historical account centered around Esther's life and the lives of Jews residing in Persia between the late 5th and early 4th century BC, its applicability and weight is not solely constrained to the perimeters of that particular spatiotemporal realm but rather transcends it, being germane to Jews and Christians across all contexts. In this paper, Esther's life, ministry, and leadership qualities will be examined, dissected, and scrutinized as follows.

## *Esther's life*

Esther was no different than any other young lady. She bore the same desires and sentiments that would be deemed par the course for a young adult of her milieu. On a rudimentary level, it can be posited that Esther's early life plausibly mirrors that of many women in contemporary society. She was orphaned at a young age and raised by her male cousin, Mordecai. Premature parental loss not only precipitates deep-seated grief compounded with irremediable psychological scarring and trauma but also induces a range of detriements to a child's daily activities. Therefore, Esther's life and attitudes were certainly impacted by her strained and disheartening familial status. However, just as anyone struggling with a devastating obstacle in life, this was an impediment that the future queen had to contend with and ultimately surmount.

During the stretch of time the events in this book transpired, Esther resided in the Persian city of Susa with her cousin. The events recorded come to pass fifty years after King Cyrus proclamation countermanding sanctions that exiled Jews in Babylon, permitting them to return to Jerusalem and twenty-five years before Ezra's return to Jerusalem to reconstruct the temple. This information puts Esther and her life into context. Despite possessing the latitude to depart from Persia, she and Mordecai made the proactive choice to stay. This may be an indication of how actively they were adhering to their Jewish faith and how deeply they have assimilated into the Persian culture. Nevertheless, scripture asserts that God, in his predisposition, is indeed a jealous God--"For the Lord your God is a consuming fire, a jealous God." (Deuteronomy. 4:24) -- pursuing His people relentlessly so they will turn to Him alone.

Esther was lovely woman. She was so strikingly beautiful that she won the king's favor through a beauty contest that was held for all of the young maidens in the land. This propelled her to the position of Queen of Persia. It is possible the king observed more than just outward beauty when he looked at Esther. As most scholars said, "He must have seen intelligence, integrity, and courage in Esther-not a fawning but a queenly character. These are qualities that would certainly attract a king."

Exterior beauty was a desirable attribute in Esther's time, just as it is in today's world. When physical attractiveness is considered extremely important, it is easy for any woman to fall prey to this much sought after trait in life. Beauty and beauty rituals were all Esther needed to concern herself with. This was her life, a life devoted to pleasing King Xerxes.

Esther had to contend with the baggage of losing her parents, the societal priority of physical beauty, and the inferior place of women within the culture. However, in the face of these social conformities and psychical millstones, God divinely placed her as a leader and tool for His glory. Only God can equip and establish a person as an instrument to accomplish His will. God chose Esther to be such a device. If God can utilize an unlikely candidate like Esther, surely, he can use any woman who desires to surrender herself to His plans and purposes. God can leverage any entity, whether living or otherwise, as a vehile to catapult His will into fruition; notwithstanding one's depth of faith in Him. It does not matter how little one has to offer God; he takes whatever is given and makes it enough. It is not what we possess, but who possesses us, that constitutes the difference.

Esther found herself submerged in a life she knew nothing about. She went from being a carefree young girl in Mordecai's household to the courts of the king. She was in an unfamiliar territory. Many times, as leaders, we find ourselves engulfed in unfamiliar territories striving to effectuate and actualize tasks and ventures that in their essence are alien to us. These circumstances necessitate that we, analgous to Esther, not only foster the ability to enter a flexible and perceptive frame of mind but also cleave to the assurance that God is present and working regardless of our situation.

God formed Esther into the woman she was, and she continued to rely upon the characteristics He had instilled in her. Esther continued to be respectful of others and humble, even though her social position in life had changed dramatically. Respectfulness of others and sincere humility are leadership qualities that will positively alter our trajectories and launch us into dimensions beyond the realm of reason and comprehension.

God puts into effect a miscellaneous reservoir of mechanisms and mediums to contour a leader. The cultural and communal backdrop ringing the younger years of a leader extensively sculpts the configuration of the latter years of the leader's life. Many times, attitudes are formed and instilled during early years, and these can either benefit or hinder the leadership qualities of an individual. It is evident that Esther did not allow the fact that she was an orphan to dictate the outcome of her life.

She chose to ascend above her less-than-perfect situation. As present-day leaders, we must learn to overcome our past circumstances and difficulties. We must not allow them to tyrannize our future. Esther is a paramount epitome of this type of overcoming attitude, resolve and fixity of purpose.

A casual observance of Esther's life does not seem to reveal that she had any desire or motivation to be in any type of service or ministry for the Lord. She was content with life in Mordecai's house and then became content with the day-to-day concerns of life in the courts of the king. She never ventured to serve God in any grand manner or vociferously requested be assume an instrumental role in enabling His will materialize. However, God had strategically placed Esther to be His divine tool even though it was not sought after or understood by her.

We may not make the point of journeying to be in ministry for God or have any ambitious and elaborate aspirations, but God knows why He has created us and what He has ordained as the purpose our lives will fulfill. We may not feel as though we have any unique skill set, gifts, talents or qualities. But whatever God has developed and poured into our lives is more than enough to accomplish the task when anointed by the Holy Spirit.

Esther was an unlikely leader in God's army. However, God chooses, divinely prepares, and establishes whoever He desires to fill the assigned standing He ordains. He brings to pass His will through surrendered vessels. Just as He used Esther, He is able to use any woman that surrenders herself to Him.

Esther placed her own life at peril to salvage and reinstate the sustained vitality of the Jewish population. She was enveloped with sufficient stoutheartedness to bear a responsibility that in the eyes of the commonality would have been regarded as too arduous or daunting to assume. Because of the actions of this young Jewish girl, the lives of entire chains and successions of generation were spared. Esther's life is inspiring.

Thirty years after Esther's actions saved the Jewish people, Nehemiah rebuilt the walls of Jerusalem. This cardinal milestone would have been unatteniable without the intervention of Queen Esther. God consistently uncovers means and routes to execute His will. However, scrutinizing this situation through the lens of a human eye, it may appear that without Esther there would not have been a Jewish nation from which the Messiah can ascend. Esther, without absolute knowledge of the forthcoming reverberations of her valor, paved the way for the coming of Christ. Through her God has also indicated that His guidance is available to His followers for making decisions. These decisions should be based upon the Word of God, tested by prayer, and the counsel of others, dependent upon an inner assurance and upon God-opened doors. God desires to use each one of us. He will guide and direct us, as we wait on Him. We can also be used by Him as His instruments in the world.

## *Leadership Qualities of Esther*

A young inexperienced woman blossomed into the queen of the great Persian Empire. She was the chosen vessel of God for delivering the Babylonian Jews from their impending destruction and demise.

However, this young queen was subject to the laws of the land. She was only able to enter the presence of her husband, the king, when summoned by him. To enter without an invitation could mean death for her. However, despite these earthly stipulations and conventionalities, the leadership qualities that God had deposited within Esther would eventually surface for all to see.

Esther, isolated from society by her royal home, did not realize that a decree had been announced issuing the death of the Jews. She was informed of this serious situation by information received from Mordecai through her attending eunuch, Hathach. Upon receiving this information, Esther was shocked but did not realize the gravity or looming implications of such a decree. A challenge was issued to her by Mordecai to be strong and defend the Jewish people. He said, "… Do not think to yourself that in the king's palace you will escape any more than all the other Jews. For if you keep silent at this time, relief and deliverance will rise for the Jews from another place, but you and you father's house will perish. And who knows whether you have not come to the kingdom for such a time as this?" (Esther 4:13-14)

In her exchange with her cousin, Esther channels and personifies a monumental leadership attribute. She exhibits a receptive frame of mind along with an amenable spirit: one capable of garnering counsel and advice. She did not allow her aristocratic stature and preeminent locality in the socio-economic spectrum monopolize and engross her nor steer her to the ill-guided presumption that she is omniscient and thus above seeking counsel. A good leader is open to the advice of others and requests input and suggestions for consideration.

Fear is a great hindrance to any leader. A leader must learn to overcome fear, which is exactly what Esther did. Coming before the king without a summons could result in her death. The matter at hand was of such vital importance the Esther risked her own life to save the lives of her people, the Jews. This undeniably called for courage. She was willing to put her position and more importantly her life at jeopardy by entering the king's presence without invitation. She could never have mustered the courage for such a courageous feat unless she leaned on another attribute that ought to take up residency in the internal makeup of a leader; a dependence upon God revealed through a reliance on prayer.

Esther perceived her lack of ability to perform what was being asked of her or survive the ordeal that spawns from it by banking on her own strength and resiliance. Therefore, she called upon the Jewish people to come together in communion to fast and pray for three days. A good leader must recognize their need for God. Prayer invites God into the situation. Time spent in fasting and prayer demonstrates a dependence upon God and His intervention and presence in our circumstances. A good leader must be a person of prayer.

Esther was a woman of patience, another indispensable necessity for a leader. Too often we rush into situations without counting the cost or examing the circumstances from every plausible vantage ground. We, as humans, manifest the proclivity for seeking prompt remedies to diffuse the complications and drawbacks we encounter. However, Esther knew the importance of timing and allowing God's calculus to take effect before charging forward. Esther allowed God time to work through the prayers of the people, and in the heart of King Xerxes, before embarking on her quest.

Proper timing is an important element of leadership. Even when Esther burst into the presence of the king without being summoned, she did not immediately verbalize her request. Esther invited the king and Haman to a banquet. Yet, at the banquet she was not hasty to divulge her request. Instead, Esther invited them both to a second banquet. She unabatingly awaited the proper time. She used wisdom to determine the proper timing to put forth her request. Improper timing can thwart the best laid plans and ideas. As we follow God, we must stay in tune with His temporal layout and not get a head of Him or behind Him.

Esther found favor with the king and Haman's plot was unraveled. What was previously a death sentence for Esther, Mordecai, and the Jews was revoked. Esther's request was granted and the Jews were given ample opportunity to defend themselves rather than acquiesce to their annihilation. These events all transpired because Esther chose to take time to seek the face of God and then patiently follow His direction. In the end, the Jews gained support from the government officials employed by the king. God turned things around completely.

It is important as leaders to never forget we must depend upon God. Our trust cannot be in our own talents, gifts, knowledge and insight to accomplish desired objectives. God is the one who will guide us through difficult times and decisions. It may even be possible to avoid difficulties when we spend time seeking Him. Dependence upon God must be our motto.

Esther was a loyal woman. She was loyal to Mordecai and cared about what he was concerned about. She acted when he prompted her to act. Loyalty is a quality that is scarce in today's world. Mordecai knew he could rely on Esther to listen to his advice and concerns. As a leader, loyalty to others and from others is extremely important. A person who displays loyalty and respect will also receive it in return from others.

To conclude the above idea, when reading the book of Esther, we are tempted to believe situations like this only happened during Bible times. However, there are many opportunities that lie before each one of us. We must not let the busyness of life and things of this world blind us to His divine appointments. God is still on the throne and looking for people he can use in variety of circumstances to be His instrument in the world.

Esther came to what many would call her 'defining moment. Esther could never have imagined she would be placed in such circumstances. At the time of Esther's reign as queen and her intervention for the Jewish people, she probably never realized the importance of her decisions. This was Esther's defining moment. It is times of pressure we discover the truth of our framework. Esther never saw herself as a heroine for the Jewish people or having a pivotal place in history, yet this is where God placed her. She was an unlikely candidate for the job.

Many times, we see ourselves as unlikely candidates for what God has called us to do. It is easy to feel inadequate for the task. However, realizing Esther was an ordinary person who dealt with human struggles (an orphan, young, Jewish, woman) should make us very aware of her humanity. If God can use Esther, He can use anyone.

Esther's life is an example of what God can do with a life submitted to Him. He can take what little we have and multiply it and use it for His glory to accomplish exploits.

Esther is an encouragement and inspiration for women everywhere to pursue and develop leadership qualities. We must be women who recognize the necessity of total dependence upon God, living a life open to godly counsel and advice, committed to prayer and fasting, fearless, patient, and loyal.

Because of Esther's selfless actions in securing the deliverance of the Jews, she is now remembered annually at the Jewish Feast of Purim. A young ordinary woman became the heroine of the Jewish nation and will be remembered throughout time.

Esther was God's instrument for the saving of many lives. In many ways, Esther depicts the person that is standing in the gap in the following verse: "And I sought for a man among them who should build up the wall and stand in the breach before me for the land, that I should not destroy it, but I found none." (Ezekiel 22:30) Esther was a woman who was willing to stand in the gap for the Jewish nation and God used her mightily.

## 1.5. Definition of Terms

- Textual criticism: - The technique of restoring texts as nearly as possible to their original form (Encyclopedia Britannica, 2009).

- Textual analysis: - A discipline, which is associated with the discovery, description, transcription, editing, glossing, annotating and commenting upon texts. (Encyclopedia Britannica, 2009).

. Manuscripts: - Old written texts

- Gé'éz:- Is afro Asiatic language family, which is Semitic group and is a classical Ge'ez, an ancient language used by Church scholars in Abysynia, Tigray and Eriteria. It was a national tongue of Abysyinia during the Axumite age (100-900 AD).

## 1.6. Ethical considerations

Ethical considerations are more relevant due to the text writings other than formal documents, inscribed or printed on paper, papyrus or similar materials. These belong to the history of specific countries, which can be transmitted in print to the next generation or to the contemporary readers.

The Actual author's original may have been a manuscript or a typescript or recording in the process of publication it has passed through several stages of transmission, including possibly storage in computer at any one of which errors have necessarily occurred. Experience teaches that some errors will survive uncorrected in the published version. Further errors are likely to occur if a book is reprinted. Even an edition revised by the author is not to be regarded as textually definitive. Errors committed and overlooked by the author himself may be corrected by the critic in appropriate cases. Special problems are posed by an author's second thoughts; whether preserved in his books and papers or incorporated in editions revised by him. In other hand, nearly all classical and patristic texts and great many medieval texts, fall into the category of books transmitted in manuscript, every hand written book is textually unique, and to that extent represents a separates edition of the text.

Though the text appears to have been transmitted from the first in writing, the textual variations are in many ways analogous to those of an oral tradition, and it is commonly held that the essential task of the critic is not to try to reconstruct the "original" but to isolate those forms of the text that were current in particular centers in the ancient world.

# Chapter 2.  History and Related Literature: -

## *2.1. History of Research on the Ge'ez Bible: -*

Several books deal with specific regions of the country consider coverage by written sources in terms of periods, geographical areas, much contribution of the Aksumite to the flowering of  Gé'éz literature is indicted as a significant one.  The birth of Gé'éz literature have taken place in the country following the official introduction of the Christianity (August, Dillman, 1907, pp1-7). Many biblical texts and many hagiographies were translated directly from Greek and Arabic languages to Gé'éz.

The Ge'ez writing system is the product of reduction of the Sabaean alphabet that was a thorough and deliberate reform under king Ezana (Paul D. Wanger, 1999). So, we can assume that it reflects the structure of the languages of the 4$^{th}$ century quite well.

Christianity was introduced in Abysinia before the 4$^{th}$ century AD and it was the state religion during this period. Following this, it expanded into the interior. Historians argue that Christianity led to the making of books because the bible and other religious books had to be translated. Therefore, the birth of Gé'éz literature is supposed to have take place in the centuries following the official introduction of the religion.

The Translation of Bible and various doctrinal and liturgical texts into Gé'éz were made during the Axumite period and after the decline of the Axumite civilization. The language contributed to retaining its full importance as literary language, in which all books and even official documents were written. Many Christian- Arabic texts of the Coptic Church of Egypt were translated, some adapted into Gé'éz and original texts were also composed. It was a spoken and literary language by then, inscriptions (at Axum, metera, Adulis, Yeha, Keskese, Pentelewon…) are inscribed in Epigraphic Gé'éz. Still, they are the only direct evidence of original and non translated texts done by native speakers.

Since recent years, scholars have produced many different articles, books and texts on the Ge'ez Bible. Some written Old Testament text editions and critical Analysis of books like Genesis, Psalms, Proverbs, Micah, Hosea, Enoch, Jubilees etc. (Rochus Zuurmond ,1992. pp 808-810) (Ullendorff, 1968.pp 31-56).

Some of the Old Testament written editions by different scholars is indicated below.

An updated critical analysis on the text of Genesis (Blain Alan Edele 1995), H. F Fuhs prepared Ge'ez editions of Micah And Hosea (H.F Fuhs,1968), Hugh Pilkington edited a Ge'ez text of proverbs (H.A. W Pilkington 1978), M. Bezemer edited Portions of exodus for his doctoral dissertation (M.Bezemer, 1982). And from the Apocrypha or pseudepigrapha, Michael knibb prepared a critical edition of the Ethiopic version of Enoch (Michael A. Knibb 1979). James C.Vander Kam edited the text of Jubilees (Jame C.Vander Kan 1989) .

We have also some more from the new testament text editions in Ge'ez like Revelation by Hofmann (1969) catholic Epistles by Hofmann and Uhlig (1993), Zuurmond on Mark (1989), Mathew (2001), Romans by Tedros Abraha (2001), He also produced a book on the Gé'éz letter of Hebrews, The Gospel of John by Michael G.Weshsler (2005), C, Niccum on the book of Acts (2000). And letter of captivity (prison Epistles) i.e Eph., phil., col. and Philemon) by Uhlig and Maehlum (1993), Cf, Weninger 1995 and Kinbb 1996.

The above mentioned are some of the editions which are on hand to give us highlight to do our text edition or analysis, even though some meet the academic standard and others need a re-edition because of the newly available Gé'éz manuscripts.

Traditionally Abysinia has formed a bridge between Civilizations of Africa and Asia. Many of her inhabitants came from South Arabia introducing their language, writing system and other aspects of their cultural heritage. Jerusalem becomes as vital as Aksum in the national consciousness of the Abysinians.

In the book of 'Ethiopia and The Bible', Professor Ullendorff, the first incumbent of the only chain of Abysinian Studies in Great Britain, investigates the relationship of Abyssinia to the Bible, He considers the historical background of religious manifestations in the country, Translations of the Bible in to Ge'ez languages and the impact of the Old Testament, which goes beyond anything experienced in the other Oriental Christian Churches.

The book concludes with an examination of the story of Queen of Sheba, based on the Bible account of the queen's visit to King Solomon, which has undergone extensive Arabian Ethiopia, Jewish and other elaborations and has become the subject of one of the most ubiquitous and fertile cycles of legends in the Near East, from a large and confused skein of traditions and tales professor Ullendorff  has disentangled some basic features which are common to all stories about the famous encounter between the Queen of the South and the greatest of the kings of Israel.(Edward,Ullendorff,1968,pp.56-77).

## *2.2. History on the Ge'ez book of Esther: -*

### *2.2.1.  The Geez Script:*

Gé'éz (ግዕዝ Gé'éz), is a script used as an abugida for sercral languages of Northern Ethiopia, Tigray and Eritrea but originated in an abjad used to write Gé'éz, now the liturgical language of the Abyssinian Orthodox Church. In Amharic and Tigrinya, the script is often called fidal (ፊደል), which means "script" or Alphabet"

The Gé'éz script has been adapted to write other, mostly Semitic, languages in Northern Ethiopia such as Amharic and  Tigringa.  It is also used lately for sebatbeit, me'en and most other languages of Ethiopia. In Eritrea it is used for Tigre, and it has traditionally been used for Bilen, a Cushitic language. Tigre, spoken in western and Northern Eritrea and eastern Sudan, is considered to resemble. Some other languages in the Horn of Africa, such as Oromo, used to be written using Gé'éz but have migrated to Latin based orthographics. (Wikipedia, the free Encyclopedia).

For the representation of sounds, this article uses a system that is common (through not universal) among linguists who work on Abyssinian Semitic languages. This differs somewhat from the conventions of the International Phonetic Alphabet.

### 2.2.2. History and Origine of Ge'ez:

The earliest inscriptions of Semitic in Tigray, Eritrea and Amhara date to the 9th century BC in Epigraphic south Arabian (ESA), An Huruf Abjad (the Arabic Alphabet) shared with contemporary kingdoms in south Arabia.  After the 7th and 6th centuries BC, However, variants of the script arose, evolving in the direction of the Gé'éz abugida (a writing system that is also called an alpha syllabory). This evolution can be seen most clearly in evidence from inscriptions (mainly graffiti on rocks and caves) in Tigray region in northern Ethiopia and the former province of Akele guzay in Eritrea by the first centuries AD, what is called the "old Gé'éz ' alphabet arose, an objad written left to right (as opposed to boustrophedon like Epigraphic kingdoms in south Arabia)  with letters basically identical to the first order forms of the modern vocalized alphabet (eg "k" in the form of "ka"). There were also minor differences such as the letter "g" facing to the right, instead of to the left as in vocalized Gé'éz, and a shorter left leg of "I" , as in ESA, instead of equally long legs in vocalized Gé'éz (resembling the Greek letter lambda, some what) . Vocalization of Gé'éz occurred in the fourth century, and through the first completely vocalized texts known are inscriptions by Ezana, vocalized letters predate him by some years, as an individual vocalized letter exists in a coin of his predecessor wazeba. Other scholars have also pointed out (in an early 1990s unpublished paper) anomalies with known inscriptions of Ezana that imply he was consciously employing an archaic style during his reign, indicating that vocalization could have occurred much earlier. As a result, some believe that the vocalization may have been adopted to preserve the pronunciation of Gé'éz texts due to the already moribund or extinct status of Gé'éz, and that, by that time, the common Language of the people was already later Ethio-semitic languages. At least one of wazebacoins form the late $3^{rd}$, early $4^{th}$ century contain a vocalized letter, some 30 or 50 years before Ezana, Daniels and others have suggested possible influence from the brahmic family of Alphabets in vocalization, as they are also abugidas, and Aksum was an important part of major trade routes involving Indian and the Greco- Roman world though out the common era of antiquity.

According to the beliefs of the Ethiopian Orthodox Tewahedo church, the original consonantal form of the Gé'éz fidel was divinely revealed to Henos "as an instrument for codifying the laws" and the present system of vocalization is attributed to a team of aksumite scholars led by Furmentius (Abba Selama). The same missionary said to have converted king Ezane to Christianity in the $4^{th}$ century AD (http://www eotc-patriarch. org). A separate tradition, recorded by alequa Taye, holds that the Gé'éz consonantal alphabet was first adapted by Zegdur, a legendary king of the Agazyan sabaean dynasty held to have ruled in Ethiopia C.1300 BC (Alequa Taye, 1914.)

Gé'éz has 26 consonantal letters, compared to the inventory of 29 consonants in the south Arabian alphabet, continuants of g, z and the interdental fricatives (d,t) are missing, as well as south Arabian $5^3{}_x$ (Gé'éz sawt W-being derived from south Arabian $5^2$ 3) On the other hand, emphatic paint ቆ, a Gé'éz innovation, is a modification of sa'dai, while pesa T is based on Tawe ተ (Ethiopic grammar) thus, there are 24 correspondences of Ge'ez and south Arabian Alphabet.

**Table A:** Gé'éz and South Arabian Alphabet

| Translit | H | l | h | m | S(SA s$^2$) | r | S(SA s$^1$) | k | b | t | h | n |
|---|---|---|---|---|---|---|---|---|---|---|---|---|
| Gé'éz | ሀ | ለ | ሐ | መ | ሠ | ረ | ሰ | | ቀ | በ | ተ | ኀ | ነ |
| South Arabian | | | | | | | | | | | | | |

**Table B:** Gé'éz and South Arabian Alphabet

| Translit | ' | k | w | ' | Z(Sad) | y | d | g | t | s | d | f |
|---|---|---|---|---|---|---|---|---|---|---|---|---|
| Gé'éz | አ | ከ | ወ | o | H | የ | ደ | ገ | ጠ | ጸ | θ | ፈ |
| South | አ | ለ | ወ | O | H | | | | | | | |

| *Arabian* | | | | | | | | | | | |
|---|---|---|---|---|---|---|---|---|---|---|---|

### 2.2.3. Ge'ez Biblical Canon: -

The canon of the Ge'ez bible differs both in the old and New Testament from that of any other Churches list all books, As a whole, Books written in the Gé'éz Language and on parchment are numerous. The Ethiopian Orthodox Church has 46 books of Old Testament and 35 books of the New Testament that will bring the total of canonized books of Bible to 81.

The Ge'ez version of the old and New Testament was made from the Septuagint. It includes the book Enoch, Baruch, and the third and fourth esdrus. In the international Bible studies, there are certain books belonging to the class usually designated pseudepigraphic, the whole Christendom and whole- learned world owes a debt of gratitude to the church of Ethiopia for the preservation of those documents.

Among these books is the book of Enoch which throws So much light on Jewish thought on various points during the centuries immediately price during the Christian era. The book of Jubilee (Kufale, i.e division) otherwise known as the little genesis has also been preserved entirely in the Ethiopic version. The preservation of yet one more book in its entity, namely, the ascension of Isaiah, is to be remembered to the credit of the Ethiopia Church.

(A short history , faith and order of the Ethiopian Orthodox Tewahdo Church, published by the Ethiopian Orthodox Tewahdo Church Holy synod, Addis Ababa 1983,- edited by Aymero Wand Joachim M. The Ethiopian Orthodox Church, published by the Ethiopian Orthodox Mission, Addis Ababa 1970).

### 2.2.4. Ge'ez Version: -

The beginning of the Abyssinian Kingdom emerged into the history immediately upon its conversion to Christianity in the 3 rd century, and with increasing clearness to Christianity into the seventh, and from that time foreword, all through the middle age and up to the commencement of the 17th century, it occupied an important position in the midst of the bordering populations of Africa and Arabia. (August, Dillman1907, p1).

In the kingdom once flourished the language commonly called Ge'ez, and it is to the description of that language that the present work is devoted. Originally one only of the manifold dialects into which the Arabic-Africa branch of the Semitic tongue split up. Though one of the noblest among them, it gained, through the tribe by which it was spoken, the position of being the leading speech in the Kingdom, starting as it did from their country of Tigre and its chief town Axum, and keeping pace with the development of the Kingdome, while the modes of speech native to other tribes in the land lived on alongside of it merely as vulgar dialects. Further, by means of the numerous writings, chiefly of Christian contents, which were speedily composed in it, it becomes bound up in the most intimate manner with the life of the Church and the whole culture of the people. (August, Dillman1907,p.2).

From that time on the Ge'ez version started to be translated and known specially in the northern part of the country during the first six centuries.

The flourishment of Gé'éz literature is directly attached with Christianity, in this time the Kingdom remained in Tigre, Axum. It is true that when the southwestern province grew in to importance ,and the seat of government was transferred to the district south of Takazze towards LakeTana, another dialect the Amharic, come into fashion as the ordinary speech of the court and of the officials of the country, but Ge'ez even then continued to retain its full importance as the literary language, in which all books , Ethiopic versions, official documents were written and the three centuries of this period may be regarded indeed as the age of the second bloom of the Ethiopic speech . (August Dillman, 1907.pp2-3).

To be sure Ge'ez has remained the sacred language and the ecclesiastical language up to the present day. As late even as last century many nobles and even such men preferred to write in Tigrigna and Amharic.

The earliest Printed Text in Gé'éz were done by a small group Ethiopian Monks at Santo Stefani dei mori in Rome: The Psalms in Gé'éz were published in 1513 and the New Testament in 1549 (Ullendorff, Edward, Ethiopia and the Bible. 1968, pp.8).

During the time Gé'éz was no longer in use as a vernacular language in Ethiopia and the official language was Amharic. However, Gé'éz continues to be used as the liturgical language and the language of scholarship. Gé'éz was called "The language of the books".

The Gé'éz version of the Bible has attracted the attention of scholars on several topics. Rochus Zuurmond summarizes them as follows (Rochus Zuurmond, 2001, p.142).

-When, where and why did this version originate?

-Was there one original translation only? Or were there several ancient   independent attempts to translate.

-It is obvious that the Ge'ez version as we know it from the extant manuscripts has been revised several times. When and on what basis was these revisions made and can they be traced in the manuscript's tradition.

-Have all the books of Gé'éz the same history to transmission or are there significant differences?

-Was the earliest text of the Old Testament and New Testament translated from the Greek or from other languages for example, Syriac?

Finally, given a reliable analysis, what is the value of the Ge'ez version for the Textual criticism of the Greek OT?

However, it is impossible to clearly separate this issue, All of the above should be answered and this mannual may try to contribute to fill the gap to understand better the book of Old Testament by providing this Mini research based manual " Study Book of Esther: Analysis, According to The Ge'ez Manuscript ".

### *2.2.5. Translation History: -*

The Translation history of the Bible from Greek to Gé'éz has long history going back to the Aksumite period. Most scholars conclude that the "original" translators of the Gé'éz Bible employed Greek texts.

Uhlig says the following about the translators of the Gé'éz Bible "the personalities of ancient translators of the Ge'ez Bible remains hypothetical (Seegbert, Uhlig,"Gé'éz Bible, Encyclopedia Aethiopia", vol.1, 564). However, translation argues, the Nine Saints translated the Bible into Gé'éz probably using the Septuagint for the Old Testament and the original Greek for the New Testament. They also translated some extra books as well as monastic writings. As a result, the Abyssinian Canon is much more extensive than that of any other Church.

The Abyssinian canon includes works such as Enoch and Jubilees, Shepherd of Hermas, and sometimes also Ascension of Isaiah (Added to the Old Testament). (G.A.Mikre-Sellassie, 2000 E.C. pp.111-123).

As with some other Orthodox Church, there is no definitive text of scripture. It raises interesting questions about whether the canon of scripture is closed or open, at least potentially, to further development as said above, the question of translators, the exact time and the base text are still unresolved. Some traditional Church scholars basing their argument on the Judaic influence/Old Testament on Orthodox Christianity have argued that the Old Testament as a whole or portions of it were translated before the Christian era. (G.A. Mikre Sellassie, 2000 EC. p.59)

# Chapter 3. Textual Criticism: -

By Textual criticism is meant any methodical and objective study which aims to retrieve the original form of a text or at least the form closest to the original. (Encyclopedia Britannica, 2009)

The technique of restoring texts as nearly as possible to the in original form, Texts in this connection are defined as writings other than formal documents, inscribed or printed on paper, parchment, papyrus or similar materials.

Textual criticism, properly speaking, is an ancillary academic discipline designed to lay the foundation for the so-called higher criticism which deals with questions of authenticity and attributions, of interpretation, and of literary and historical evaluation (Encyclopedia Britannica 2009)

An acquaintance with the history of texts and the principles of textual criticism and analysis is indispensable for the student of history, literature or philosophy. Written texts supply the main foundation for these disciplines and some knowledge of the processes of their transmission is necessary for understanding and control of the scholar's basic materials. For the advanced student the criticism, analysis and editing of texts offers unrivalled philological training and a uniquely instructive avenue to the history of scholarship, it is broadly true that all advances in philology have been made in connection with the problems of editing texts. This is to recognize that the equipment needed by the critic for the task includes a mastery of the whole field of study with which his text lies.

It would be wrong, however, to paint a picture too black. The great majority of the divergences in reading are to do with details of spelling, grammar or style and do not affect in any way the meaning of the text. True, these Minor differences aside, there are a good number of variants which arouse the reader's curiosity by reason of some detail omitted or added to the text. Some are particularly interesting either because they involve a considerable portion of the text or because of their theological significance. In the letter case, though as would be expected, the substance of Christian doctrine is never affected, rather such variants reflect the diversity of the text as it was known in the first Christian communities. The early papyri attest the overall integrity of the text. The alternations of the most daring revisers are proof of the limits they set themselves. Nevertheless, between these general sounders on which historical and theological deductions rely and a text which is perfectly identical to the original one, there is perfectly identical to the original one, there is quite a considerable gap' (encyclopedia Britannica 2009).

Generally, textual criticism is the traditional term for the task of evaluating the authority of the words and punctuation of a text is often considered an understanding preliminary to literary criticism; many people believes that the job of textual critics is to provide reliable texts for literary critics to analyze G. Thomas Tanselle argues on the contrary, that, the two activities can it be separated.

The textual critic, in choosing among textual variants and correcting that appear to be textual errors, inevitably exercises critical judgment and reflects a particular point of view toward the nature of literature and the litrary critic, in interpreting the meaning of a work or passage, needs to be (though rarely is) critical of the makeup of every text of it, including those produced by scholarly editors.

## 3.1. Descriptions of Manuscripts (Texts): -

**The Manuscripts in general**

All kinds of materials have been used for writing on, stone, metals, terracotta, waxed tablets of wood and ivory, even pottery remains. But the main materials are papyrus, parchment and paper and it is for writings on these that the term "manuscript" is reserved.

The papyrus plant is a fibrous reed which used to grow in abundance along the marshy banks of the river Nile. The Egyptians were using it for writing before 2000 BC, and it appears to have been known to the Greeks in the seventh century BC. It was however, until the fifth century BC that is entered into general use, first among the Greeks, and then among the Romans. In the writings, there are some indications as to how papyrus was made. The inside of the reed (the pith) was cut length wise into their strips which were laid across each other in two layers at right angles and then pressed together. When the fabric was dry, it was polished and then coated with wax to be ready for writing on. Papyrus remained in general use until the Arab conquest of Egypt in the seventh century AD when its importation becomes practically impossible. The first discoveries of papyrus manuscripts were made in the eighteenth century, since when large numbers of these literary treasures have been found, mostly in Egypt where the dry climate favors the preservation of such fragile materials.

The age of papyrus was succeeded by the age of parchment, hides of animals had been used for writing since very early times and outside Egypt, were the chief writing material until papyrus become common in the fifth century BC. The oldest Greek parchment known dates from the end of the third or the beginning of the second century BC and was found at Dur- Europes in the Euphrates valley some seventy years ago. Tradition has it that when one of the Ptolemaen kings refused to send papyrus to the people of Pergamun it was they who invented a method of preparing skins that made writing on them less arduous than it had been previously. The animal skin, usually a sheep's, instead of being tanned was softened in a solution of lime and then scraped with a knife to take off the hairy or greasy parts, before being finally polished with a pumice  stone. This is how "parchment" or skin of Pergamun, got its name, permanent also know as membrane, and it was then that this new material, being strong enough to allow for mistakes to be scratched away, began to compete both with tablets and with papyrus for things like rough work, sketches and anything needing retouching later as if become less expensive, parchment was preferred for literary texts, and for other important work generally. Finally, form around AD 650, when papyrus becomes rare, parchment predominated until the fourteenth century.

Then it was the turn of paper to take over. Its place and date of origin are somewhat uncertain; it does not seem to have been known in Syria or Egypt until after the taking of Samarkand by the Arabs in AD 707. Distinction can be made between, on the one hand, oriental paper or "bumbycine" which is of Arab invention and manufacture, and, on the other hand, paper of different sorts manufactured in the west. Of the latter, the earliest was that made in Spain form the tenth century, which resembles the paper of Arabic origin, but later types have their own characteristic format (eg Catalan paper, mid-twelfth century). The Italian paper (early in fabriano) replaced all the other western papers from the fourteenth century. The fragile nature of paper, its high cost and its Arabic origin prevented it from being widely known for a long time. It was parchment which continued to be generally used for finer copies, particularly for the sacred books. Paper finally took over completely with the invention of printing.

Towards the end of the first century AD the codex entered use. It had already been customary to fasten several waxed tablets together with one or more threads and this practice was later extended to the typing together of sheets of parchment or papyrus. These would be folded and sewn together in quires. This is the origin of the modern book. It was much easier to handle a codex than a scroll and in addition, a codex could hold more than a scroll, yet despite this advantage it was only gradually that it replaced the scroll, such is the force of habit. It is interesting to note that the Christians were among the first to use the papyrus codex, when they came to write then sacred books. The oldest New Testament papyrus fragment dating from the first half of the second century comes from a codex. From the same period, there is a copy of Numbers and Deuteronomy which is a combination of a papyrus scroll and a parchment codex. From the fourth century onwards, the codex form becomes general.

Expatriate scholars such as, August.Dillmann(1874), E. Cerulli (1942), Edward Ullendorff (1951), S. Wright (1961), work on Ge'ez texts and produced an extensive list of documents on the culture, history and language of the Abyssinian people.

So far, the Writer has discovered different manuscripts from national archive library and other parts of the country specifically, on the Ge'ez Book of Esther.

### 3.2. Sample Manuscript Discription of the Ge'ez Book of Esther: -

Five different sample manuscripts were discovered from varying geographical sites. The following are identified to provide hint for our readers with an enhanced comprehension of the overarching characteristics and the underlying configuration of such manuiscripts. The 1ˢᵗ (A) is one of the pivotal and rather most benefical reference text and the next (B to E) are the four other examples of the old manuscripts of the Ge'ez book of Esther.

**Five discovered different manuscripts**

## (A)-NAL  09 /code 01/ reference text/

- The Subject is: - The Ge'ez Book of Esther/metshafe Sirak, Eyob, Tobit, Aster and Yodit/

- Language: - Gé'éz
- Property: - National Archive Library
- District: - A.A
- Date of publication: - Unknown (Will be Identified if possible )
- Material: - Parchment
- Size: - 23X21 cm
- Column: - 3
- Thickness: - 0.6 cm
- Pages: - 21
- Lines: - 28
- Folios: -260
- Written by: - 16th and 17th century
- Ordered By: - Unknown
- Binding and condition of the book and other remarks. Wooden boards covered with stamped leather.

## (B)-NAL 015 /code 02/

- The Subject is: - The Ge'ez Book of Esther/Tobit, Aster Yodit and Ezra/

- Language: - Gé'éz
- Property: - National Archive Library
- District: - A.A
- Date of publication: - Unknown (Will be Identified if possible )
- Material: - Parchment
- Size: - 22X17 cm
- Column: - 2
- Thickness: - 0.6 cm
- Pages: - 27
- Lines: - 26
- Folios: -330
- Written by: - 16th and 17th century
- Ordered By: - Unknown
- Binding and condition of the book and other remarks. Wooden boards covered with stamped leather.

## (C)-NAL 018 /code 03/

- The Subject is: - The Ge'ez Book of Esther /Tobit, Aster, Yodit, Ezra and Nehmia/
- Language: - Gé'éz
- Property: - National Archive Library
- District: - A.A
- Date of publication: - Unknown (Will be Identified if possible)

+ Material: - Parchment

+ Size: - 18X15 cm

+ Column: - 2

+ Thickness: - 0.6 cm

+ Pages: - 24

+ Lines: - 26

+ Folios: -246

+ Written by: - 16<sup>th</sup> and 17<sup>th</sup> century

+ Ordered By: - Unknown

+ Binding and condition of the book and other remarks. Wooden boards covered with stamped leather.

## (D)- EMML 57 /code 04/

+ The Subject is: - The Ge'ez Book of Esther. /Tobit, Aster, Yodit, and Mekabian/

+ Language: - Gé'éz

+ Property: - EMML 57 /ST. Paulo's Church/

+ District: - USA

+ Date of publication: - Unknown (Will be Identified if possible)

+ Material: - Parchment

+ Size: - 21X17 cm

+ Column: - 2

+ Thickness: - 0.6 cm

+ Pages: - 31

+ Lines: - 21

- Folios: -142
- Written by: - late 15th and early 16th century
- Ordered By: - Unknown
- Binding and condition of the book and other remarks. Wooden boards covered with stamped leather.

**(E)-ASM version /code 05/**

- The Subject is: - The Ge'ez Book of Esther. / Tobit, Yodit, Aster and Nehmia/

- Language: - Gé'éz
- Property: - AAU
- District: - A.A
- Date of publication:- Unknown (Will be Identified if possible)
- Material: - Paper
- Size: - 35X25 cm
- Column: - 2
- Thickness: - 0.4 cm
- Pages: - 22
- Lines: - 21
- Folios: - 430
- Written by: - Asmara Printing Press
- Ordered By: - Unknown
- Binding and condition of the book and other remarks. Paper covered with stamped leather.

The above manuscripts and other texts have been refered in the preparation of the textual analysis, Ge'ez book of Esther.

The selected texts included the tradition, geography and time of production ranging in age from 14-17$^{th}$ century. Extra efforts were done in reading the oldest manuscript of the Ge'ez Book of Esther, other than the text which is now placed on the national archive agency library.

One cannot fully be accurate in dating Gé'éz manuscripts. For this reason, this book was not intended to provide absolute dating for this textual analysis, unless such dating was stated in the manuscripts and is confirmed by paleographic analysis.

# Chapter 4. Historical and Theological analysis of the book:

## 4.1. Historical Overview of the Text:

ESTHER

IS IT HISTORICAL?

Is the Esther Story, history or fiction? Until the eighteenth century this was not a lively issue: it was assumed that the events described were historical. Then historians suggested that the story was more in the nature of a romance – a suggestion much in line with the scientific spirit of the Enlightenment. And this is the view that has largely prevailed since. Important 'Introductions' to the old Testament by Eissfeldt and Pfeiffer, for example, describe Esther as a historical novel and, as clines (Esther) has argued, it is not satisfactory to gloss over this issue by saying (as Myers did in The World of the Restoration, 1968) that the accent is more on the adjective 'historical' than on the noun 'novel'. A novel is a work of fiction, and to describe a novel as historical is merely to say that it is decked out with historically plausible details. A claim to historicity must be based on a higher degree of correspondence with externally verifiable events than that. (The 'annals of the kings of Media and Persia' mentioned as an independent source in 10.2 are unknown to us and are unlikely to have been any more than a Jewish midrashic source). (Clines,1984)

However, it would be wrong to give the impression either that Esther does not stand up well to certain kinds of verification, or that scholars are all of one mind in the conclusions they draw. The arguments for and against the historicity of Esther can be summarized as follows.

Arguments in Favour of Historicity

There are three main lines of argument in favour of the historicity of Esther, namely (1) that it is supported by the accounts of ancient historians, principally Herdotus; (2) that it is supported by the findings of archaeology, particularly at the ancient Persian capital of Susa where the story is set; and (3) that the existence of Mordecai in particular becomes plausible in the light of ancient epigraphic evidence.

1. The Evidence of Ancient Historians

First, it should be explained that although the Jewsish historian Josephus, thought that the monarch Ahasuerus was the king known to the Persians as Artaxerxes I (465-424 BC), the decipherment early in this century of trilingual inscriptions found on Persian monuments has made it almost certain that Ahasuerus (the name in this form is Hebrew) can be identified with Xerxes (this is a Greek name corresponding to the Persian name Khshayarsha). Most of the statements made about Ahasuerus in Esther fit the events of Xerxes' reign (486- BC) and do not fit those of any other Persian monarch. Even his character agrees with the portrayal of him by Herodotus and other classical historians. (Clines,1984)

Intriguingly, Ezra says that in the year of Ahasuerus's accession 'they wrote an accusation against the inhabitants of Judah and Jerusalem' and the context implies that this accusation had to do with the rebuilding of the temple, although that had in fact been completed much earlier, in  BC. Controversy did occur over the rebuilding of the city walls, but later under Artaxerxes I (Ezra). The chronological sequence at the opening of the book of Ezra is notoriously confusing. The historian Morgenstern has suggested that in 486 BC, the year of Xerxes' accession, the Jews joined a rebellion led by Egypt against the Persians, which was not put down until 483. It is not possible, however, to demonstrate that this underlies the book of Esther.

The author correctly describes some Persian customs of the time (so far as they are known to us from other sources), such as the existence of a council of seven to advise the monarch, the use of a postal system in the empire, and so on. He even uses ten Persian terms for Persian objects (all from the language of government and trade) and some thirty-five quasi-Persian names, although the authenticity of these has come under fire.

2 Macc. 15.36 specifies that the defeat of Nicanor by Judas Maccabeus should be commemorated each year on the 'thirteenth day of the twelfth month-which is called Adar in the Aramaic language – the day before Mordecai's day'. This certainly shows

that the Diaspora festival which is the subject of Esther was accepted in Palestine at an early date, although under a different name, and it has been suggested that the essential historicity of Esther must be assumed if we are to explain the fact of the observance of the festival. None of this, however, really proves the historicity of the story that accompanies the festival; bearing in mind the problems concerning the acceptance of Esther in to the canon it is more likely that the story was not believed or valued in some quarters, and that it was fabricated to justify and commend the observance by all Jews of a feast that was originally observed only by a certain community of Diaspora Jews around Susa, and had pagan roots. (Clines,1984)

2.  The Evidence of Archaeology

There was indeed a royal palace at Susa (though it belonged to Artaxerxes Mnemon, not Xerxes). The French archeologist Perrot who was excavated the gate and the square before it (4.6) was impressed by the accord between archaeological findings and the biblical account. Support has also been claimed from the finding of the Lachish cosmetic burner for the practice attested in 2.12-13 of perfuming the whole body and clothes. Such verisimilitude, however, is to be expected in any historical novel and is not in itself a guarantee of historicity. (Moore,1977)

3.  The Name of Mordecai

In two articles which appeared between 1941 and 1943, scholar A. Ungnad published a tablet of uncertain date and provenance, but probably from fifth century Borsippa (so Clines, Esther), containing a reference to a finance officer called Marduka visiting Susa on a tour of inspection in the reign of Xerxes. This, he claimed, could be the biblical Mordecai. The suggestion has been taken up and approved by a number of scholars such as Gordis, and (more cautiously) by Moore (who noted that the existence of the biblical Mordecai could not actually be proved by such means) and Anderson (who was less interested in the historicity of Mordecai than in the fact that the name was attested for a human being, since it is also reminiscent of the name of the Babylonian god Marduk). (Clines,1984)

Clines, however, has objected that the tablet has been over interpreted. It refers to Marduka only as some kind of administrator (his office is unspecified) belonging to the satrapy of Ushtannu, otherwise known to the Bible as the province of 'Babylon and Beyond the River', and does not specify that he personally visited Susa, but only that he received monies from Susa. Yamauchi has responded by accepting Clines's criticisms, which he reinforces by stating that a full survey of Persian and Elamite tablets from Persepolis at this date reveals the existence of at least four Mardukas! But he adds that his survey has also added verisimilitude to Esther by turning up parallels to other names it contains, such as those in 1.10, 14; 3.1 and 9.7-9. None of this can really remove the force of Clines's objection that fictitious characters usually do bear names attested for real people, so that the presence of a Marduka at Xerxes' court is not relevant to the historicity of Esther. (Moore,1977)

## Arguments against Historicity

A preliminary distinction should be made between evidence that damages a claim to historicity and evidence that just points to fiction-like traits in Esther (Clines, Esther). There is much in Esther that is not corroborated by the classical historians. Vashti, Esther, Haman and Mordecai are nowhere mentioned. In fact, Xerxes' queen from the seventh to the twelfth year of his reign (Est. 2.16; 3.7) was Amestris, daughter of a Persian general. And during part of this period Xerxes was away fighting his Greek wars and was not in Susa at all. Esther is supposed to have arrived at court in 480 while Xerxes was still away. It may strain credulity that the Persian Empire should have had two non-persian viziers one after another as well as a non-Persian queen. And the author is sometimes incorrect about Persian laws and customs. In particular, the notion of a Persian decree being unalterable one promulgated is not attested by ay of the ancient historians, and its very impracticality in real politics makes its existence unlikely. (Moore, 2008)

The account of the origin of Purim given in Esther is historically improbable. If the feast really originated in a historical event in Persian times and was accepted in to the Jewish calendar in Persian times it is remarkable that it is not mentioned in the late

Priestly strand of biblical law. Furthermore, the word 'Purim' is neither Hebrew nor Persian and the meaning 'pur' = 'lot' suggested for it in 3.7 and 9.26 seems arbitrary; the plural form 'purim' is not accounted for. In fact, all the occurrences of the word in the book (3.7 and 9.20-10.3) could be secondary.

There are some historical implausibilities which can be explained away. For example, although it was until recently often objected, following Herodotus, that a Persian king could not have had a foreign queen because he would have been required to seek a wife within one of seven prominent Persian families, Clines has shown that a survey of who the Persian queens actually were does not support the existence of such a restriction. At first sight Est. 2.5-6 seems to say that Mordecai had been one of the Jews deported from Jerusalem in the time of Jeconiah, which would have made him 120 years old when the story opens – unless the text means (on a rather less natural reading of the Hebrew) that Mordecai's grandfather Kish was the deportee.

More serious is the question whether it is plausible that Xerxes authorized the extermination of the Jews, or that, having done so, he should have announced the massacre eleven months in advance. It has to be remembered that although pograms are known to both ancient and modern historians (and even a delay of four months is instanced by Gordis) this slaughter of Jews by Persians is no more or less likely than the slaughter of Persians by

Jews which is also a feature of the book, and which is also unknown to history. (Moore,1977)

As Clines emphasizes, we should not overlook the fact that the book does have notably novelistic qualities, such as the very frequent use of hyperbole, and that (even though it appears to be a tightly knit account, with no secondary material in the main body of the story), the author is indifferent to internal inconsistencies such as the fact that Esther hides her Jewishness yet Mordecai who is known to be a close relative does not. It is a romantic story, like Daniel 1-6, Tobit, Judith, and Ahikar. With its location in an exotic court, its constant banquets, its extravagance, its bloodshed and its constantly plotting courtiers and even with its reversal of the expected disaster for the underdogs) it has a strong flavor of the Arabian Nights. Even the opening words have an air of 'once upon a time' about them.

While therefore it is not impossible that Esther has an historical core, it is very improbable – especially in view of the literary characteristics of the book- that it is primarily a historiographic work. It has much authentic colouring but may be no more than one should expect from a historical novel. Fox reckons that the author intended his work to have verisimilitude, since historicity was desirable in order to underpin the celebration of Purim and to ensure its acceptance in the canon; he did, in short, want his book to be classed with the works attributed to Ezra, Nehemiah and the Chronicler (cf. Clines, Myers), and this self-presentation as history is not necessarily falsification. What, in any event, is history? As Halpern points out in The First Historians, anyone can present material which contains distortion (unwitting or otherwise) as 'history' and still be engaged in history writing. The ancient author of Esther may not have realized that he was leaving any clues to enable the modern historian to judge him unhistorical. Any real historical core in Esther is likely to be, in Clines's words, very tiny'. Rather, Esther is best understood as typological treatment of anti-Semitism. (Fox,2001)

**What is the Real Origin of Purim?**

This question is fully discussed by Paton in his ICC commentary, and his discussion is still of interest as so little solid fresh evidence has come to light.

It has been argued that the origin of Purim must be Jewish because its admission to the calendar is otherwise hard to explain. Thus, Michaelis in 1772 suggested that it referred to the victory of Judas Maccabeus over the Syrian general Nicanor (1 Macc. 7.39-50; 2 Macc. 15.20-36 etc.), and that the name Purim is derived from the word 'pura' meaning wine press, as an allusion to the crusing of the grapes of wrath by the victors. But this etymology has been severely criticized, and the theory faces several serious problems namely (a) that the Maccabean victory was celebrated on 13th Adar whereas 'Mordecai's day was apparently already established at that time as feast on 14th-15th Adar; (b) the theory cannot account for the prominent role given to a woman in the story; and (c) no reason is given for the connection of a Pesian story with a Jewish event having and entirely different meaning. Paton rightly observes that a true story to go with it, whereas one from a pagan origin would have a fiction such as Esther appears to be. (Moore,1977)

Another possibility which has long been discussed is that Esther has older Gentuile material standing behind it, and perhaps relates to the Persian New Year fesstiva held at the spring (vernal) equinox. The word Purim, which has never been successfully related etymologically to any Hebrew tem, could then derive from and old Persian equivalent of the Vedicpurti 'portion' in the sense of 'gift', originally denoting the gifts exchanged at the festival and now reflected in the gifts Jews give to each other at Purim (9.19). One could envisage Diaspora Jews adopting such a feast on a secular basis, as a holiday, in much the same way as they have adopted Christmas in more recent times. Alternatively, it could be a disguised feast of all souls, which took up the last ten days of the Persian year, and was marked by making offerings to the dead. Adar is especially associated with the commemoration of the dead (Moses, Elijah and Miriam are all said to have died in this month, and Jewish graves are whitewashed at this time, a custom which can be traced back to Persia). Two of the Greek Additions to Esther (Additions A and F, see Chapter 9 ) certainly make history out of Persian mythology by using motifs centrally connected to the Persian New Year festival (Hutter). The festival is supposed to be a post-battle day of pleasure (9.19) and therefore perhaps mirrors seasonal rites such as conflict, which were part of the duality of ancient Iranian society. However, the dates of neither the Persian feast for the dead, nor of the New Year festival precisely coincide with those of Purim, and religions are notoriously conservative in such matters. (Moore,1977)

A further question arises as to whether the origins of Purim can be traced back behind the rise of the Persian Empire into the period of the Babylonian empire which preceded it. Geographically this is entirely plausible, as Susa and Babylon are both located in esastern Mesopotamia, and in view of the mythology that has come down to us from that vanished world the theory gains in plausibility, the main characters in the book of Esther can be equated with the gods and goddesses of ancient Babylon and Elam (a kingdom directly to the east of Babylon in the mountainous region now separating Iraq from Iran). The names of Mordecai and Esther, who are cousins, sound comparable to those of Mrduk, the Babylonian high god, and his companion Ishtar-the Babylonian Venus-who was his cousin. Hama was an Elamite solar deity and Vashti could be an Elamite goddess. Some of the symbolism applied to the characters in Esther and in Jewish interpretative tradition supports the hypothesis. Bearing in mind that Susa was on the boundary between ancient Babylon and Elam, it is possible that local tradition retained a memory of rivalry between these old deities, and of wars between their devotees.

The theory breaks down on the fact that there is no single myth or festival which runs parallel to the Esther story. There was a Babylonian puhru or assembly at which fates were determined for the coming year, and a feast was held, with an atmosphere of carnival misrule which the Jews as subject peoples could have enjoyed. But again the etymology is suspect and the feast is in the first two weeks of Nisan, which is the month after Adar. Furthermore, there is no role in it for an Esther. It is evident that, as Ringgren says, any borrowing that has taken place has been at best very indirect. (Clines,1984)

## When was Esther Written?

The implication of 9.20-32, which was taken up by Clement of Alexandria and may other ancient scholars, both Jewish and Christian, was that Mordecai wrote the book soon after the events it describes. At all events, it was assumed that the book was roughly contemporaneous with those events. But a careful reading shows that 9.20 does not even purport to refer to the whole book, and it is strange that Esther is nowhere referred to before the Christian era, not even in Sirach (where the great passage 'let us now praise famous men' in chs. 44-49 omits both Esther and Daniel). The day of Mordecai is mentioned in 2 Macc. 15.36, and 1 Macc. 7.49 which is earlier has a similar but incomplete reference; it is Josephus who first cites the Greek version of Esther in Apion 1.8. There is no firm evidence that Purim was observed by Palestinian Jews before the first century BC.

Furthermore, although the dating of biblical Hebrew is not an exact science, it has been thought throughout this century that the Hebrew of Esther is as late as any in the Old Testament, and that it contains many words not found elsewhere except in the Mishnah and other rabbinic writings. In addition, the intellectual standpoint of the book is late. (Moore,1977)

The question then is, how late? The argument put forward in the early part of this century that Esther dates from the Greek period and reflects in some way the struggles of the Maccabees has in the long run not found favour. Recently Horbury has published an instance of the use of the name 'Mardochaeus" (a Hellenized version of Mordecai) in a Jewish Egyptian tomb inscription of c. 150 BC and suggests that this is evidence that something like the Esther story was already known there before the time of the Maccabees. Indeed, as he also points out, the Maccabees relate to the founding of the festival of Hanukkah, which has a very different timing and rationale to Purim.

In favour of a setting in the Persian period, it has been suggested by Heltzer that the book was composed shortly after the suppression of a revolt in Judaea under Artaxerxes in 340 BC. Some Jewish scholars, following hints in rabbinic tradition, also argue that the conflict in Esther reflects tensions between repatriated Judeans and Samarians in the Achaemenid period. There was a Susian element among the elite of Samaria, and both parties lobbied the Persian overlords in the Samarian capital.

The colophon to the Greek version of Esther suggests that the book was brought to Egypt no later than 73 BC, and perhaps earlier in 114 BC. It had originated either in Jerusalem or in the eastern diaspora (which is indirectly referred to in 3.8) and was translated in Greek in Maccabean Jerusalem to make it accessible to the whole diaspora. The text itself may preserve a memory that each community was originally independent in its observance of the feast, the eastern diaspora celebrating on 15 Adar and the Palestinian on 14 Adar, but that it eventually became ecumenical and lasted two days (Est. 9.21). (Fox 2001)

## ESTHER

## THE TRADITION HISTORY

A special fueture of Esther studies is the existence of substantially different versions of the book in the Hebrew and the Greek languages, attested from ancient times. In this chapter we will examine the relationship between these versions, taking the Hebrew text as the standard of comparison.

### The Integrity of the Hebrew Text

There are very few textual variants in the standard Hebrew (or Masoretic) text of Esther: Paton's Esther lists twentynine, all of them trivial. This is unusual, and paradocically may be due to the fact that Esther was the subject of so much controversy in the second centry both within Judaism and (it can be conjectured) between Jews and Christians, that the need arose to have a fixed basis of discussion between rabbis, a basis that was then adhered to with great faithfulness.

What is not so clear is wheter the Hebrew text as we now have it was or was not an authorial unity. Source critics have long been suspicious of the authenticity of 9.20-10.3 fir several reasons: first, although the language of this secion is similar to that of the rest of the book it contains a different selection of key phrases; secondly, it often contradicts other parts of the book (for example 9.29-32 has Esther writing a letter which largely duplicates Mordecai's letter in 9.20-23, and both of these letters require the Jews to hold the anniversary of the failed pogrom as a festival, even though 9.19 has already said that this became customary); and thirdly, 10.2 actually suggests the existence of a separated source, 'the annals of the kings of Media and Persia'. Thus 9.20-32 and 10.13 are often regarded as separate additions. Clines in his commentary goes further and treats the whole of ch.9 regarding the vengeance of the Jews on their enemies as an addition which is not of a piece with the preceding chapters either linguistically or in terms of story line. The book would then have ended with the paradox of two mutually contradictory but unalterable royal decrees in existence, the one against the Jews and the other in their favour: 'the story thus reflected the irony of diaspora Judaism's position, both protected and threatened by the imperial power to which it was subject. (Clines,1984)

Yet it has to be admitted that the book would be incomplete for liturgical purposes without this material, which makes much more of the official institution of Purim than the rest of the book, and thus provides it with its major rationale. B.W. Jones would deny that the book lends itself to redaction criticism at all; and the rhetorical analysis of Berg makes a strong case in favour of the authenticity of 9.20-10.3

## The Septuagint and Additions

The most important Greek version of Esther is the one which is normally included in the Septuagint translation of the Old Testament (LXX) and for reasons which will appear later it is sometimes called the B-text. It is literarily stylish and faithful to the content rather than to the exact wording of the Hebrew- which it frequently condenses slightly-but overall it is 107 verses longer than the Hebrew version discussed above. The extra material occurs in six Additions customarily referred to by the letters A-F. The six Additions are customarily clustered together at the end of the book in Est. line, and their contents are (following clines, The Esther Scroll):

A. (11.2-12.6) A dream of Mordecai concerning the coming destruction, and his discovery of the chamberlains' conspiracy [A should be prefixed to 1.1].

B. (13.1-7) The contents of the edict against the Jews sent out by Ahasuerus at Haman's instigation [B follows 3.13].

C. (13.8-14.19) Prayers of Mordecai and Esther for deliverance [C follows 4.17].

D. (15.1-16) an account of Esther's appearance before the king in anxiety for her own safety (an alternative account to 5.1-20) [D follows C].

E. (16.1-24) The contents of the edict on behalf of the Jews sent out by Ahasuerus at Mordecai's instigation [E follows 8.12].

F. (10.4-11.1) The interpretation of Mordecai's dream as relating to the events of the narrative [F follows 10.3].

Because the long Greek B-text was familiar to Christians it was long regarded as canonical by the Church, even though Jerome in his Latin translation of the Bible, the Vulgate, gathered up the long Additions and placed them together at the end of Esther in deference to the fact that he knew that they were absent from the Hebrew. Only at the Reformation did Protestantism remove them to the Apocrypha altogether, on the ground that canonicity required a Hebrew or Aramaic original; subsequently the Roman Catholic Church decided at the Council of Trent (AD 1546) that although the Additions should still appear within the body of the Old Testament, after the basic text of Esther. This basic divergence between Protestant and Catholic-sponsored Bible translations still continues but is eased by the fact that some modern translations such as the nrsv offer both an mtbased Esther in the body of the Old Testament, and a Septuagint (B-text) based Esther in the Apocrypha. ( See appendix –A)

Both, the B-text as a whole and the Additions in particular are designed to add religiosity to the text (a quality conspicuously lacking from the Hebrew but particularly evident in Addition C); to buttress its authenticity (B and E); to satisfy the reader's curiosity for more details, particularly about Mordecai; and to meet the reader's possible objections to points of difficulty in the original, such as Esther's apparently happy acceptance of foreign concubinage. Addition D is pure drama, about Esther's entry into the king's presence, but has less emphasis on her courage than on God's providence. The name of God, previously absent, now appears over fifty times (not only in the Addtions but in the main text at 2.20; 4.8; and 6.1) Thus the B-text can be thought of as the first commentary on Esther. (See appendix –A)

Ironically, the material in the Additions which was designed to improve the book has been an important ground of complaint against it on the part of some Christian scholars who have noted that this material is, while unexpectedly sympathetic to Ahasuerus, still hostile to GHentiles in a generalized way-and in a way that the original story was not, making the Jew – Gentile controversy universal rather than particular. A separate commentary on the Addtions has been provided by C.A. Moore, who concludes that they were both a symptom and a result of Esther's questionable status, that is, they were invented to remedy the book's deficiencies, but such large-scale tampering was only admissible because the book's status was questionable. Moor's commentary is indispensable for work on the Additions but has been criticized for interleaving them not with the B-text but with the Masoretic text; his intension was to point up the contrasts between them, but it has been objected that the result is too much of a hybrid. (Moore,1977)

**The Greek Alpha Text**

The Greek text of Esther in contrast to the Hebrew has been extremely unstable. The very fact that the standard Greek text is known as the B-text immediately reveals that there is also an A or alpha text (sometimes called 'Lucianic', though scholars no longer believe that it is connected with Lucian, the Christian scholar and martyr). Moore, Clines and Fox among others envisage the A-text, which contains a relatively short and economical telling of the Esther story, as a failry close translation of a variant Hebrew tradition, either an ancestor or cousin of the Masoretic text, in which personal names, numbers, dates and repetitious elements include, for example, the assumption of the inalterability f Persian law, the authorization of a second day of fighting and celebration and Purim aetiology. No Jew is likely to have sacrificed these elements from the story once they were present in it, and this means that the Masoretic text which has become the standard Hebrew version cannot simply by assumed to be 'the' version that left the pen of the original author (against Bardtke)! Confusingly, however, the A-text has in course of time absorbed the six Additions which originated in the B-text tradition, plus a secondary ending corresponding approximately to MT 8.17-10.3, plus a few other verses, and is now longer than the mt. clines has helpfully supplied the only complete English translation of the A-text in his monograph The Esther Scroll (1984), which applies text criticism, source criticism, redaction criticism and literary criticism to establishing all the stages of growth (five are suggested) of the Esther tradition. (Clines,1984), ( See appendix – A)

**The Versions Compared**

The chronological relationship between the different versions of Esther is highly complex, but if it could be established, we would be able to observe the changes that the theology of the book underwent in the course of retelling. Useful summaries of the present state of ediscussion are provided in Fox, Character and Ideology (pp. 254-73), and Day, Three Faces of A Queen (pp. 226-32). (Fox 2001)

Very briefly, the hypothetical short Hebrew text which underlay the Greek A-text is probably as close as we can get to the fountainhead of the Esther tradition; it does not pre suppose the inalterability of Persian law but resolves the crisis brought about by Haman's plotting simply by allowing the edict arranging the pogrom to be annulled at Mordecai's request; Jewish influence at court is the safeguard against Jewish vulnerability; and the deliverance is celebrated once. Esther herself has a low profile. Second in line is the Masoretic text which introduces a coherent set of changes designed to resolve the crisis by way of a counterdecree and the battles of Adar, and an elaborate dialectical process institutionalizing the annual holiday of Purim. ( Wikipedia)

Events seem to have a momentum beyond the king's control, and the Jews depend to greater extent on communal effort to save themselves; the anniversary of their efforts is commemorated year by year as Purim is added to the Jewish calendar. In this story Esther has become stronger. Finally, in the (B-text) version the story has expanded again, and Clines has suggested that the effect of the Additions is 'to assimilate the book of Esther to a scriptural norm', especially as found in the Persian histories of Ezra, Nehemiah and Daniel. The intervention of God at critical moments, the use of dreams, prayers, the quoting of the decrees, are all features found in these histories. These are important new insights which have been accepted by Fox, for example. It is not, however, universally agreed that Clines's conclusions exhaust the significance of the Additions. Rather, Fox wishes to emphasize the impact of the introduction of religious themes which are at best only implicit in the Hebrew tradition: God is explicitly shown to be in control of history, and earthly reality will ultimately follow this 'hyper-reality'; man is able to obtain access to heavenly wisdom through dreams granted to the righteous (though dreams may give meaning to the past rather than predict the future) and as for woman, Esther is more stereotypically feminine than in the mt; finally, the people of Israel have an increased role in the playing out of the cosmic drama. Individual characters have become less important than cosmic generalities, and the festival of

Purim itself is de-emphasized. The story does not, of course, stabilize even at this point, for it continues to grow and be retold in every translation, Midrash and literary recreation. (Clines,1984), (See appendix –A)

Where did the versions originate? The texts themselves offer few direct clues. Although the end of Addition F (11.1) seems to refer to events of 114 bc or 73 bc, depending on one's interpretation of it, this may be an addition to the Addition; it could have been written in Egypt to commend Purim to Egyptian Jews by representing it as a festival endorsed by a Jerusalem pries. Charles Dorothy is one of the few people who have attempted to find a specific social context for each of the versions. He regards the B-text as relatively 'neutral', detaced from the events it observes, and intended for a Hellenized diaspora audience. The writer of the A-text by contrast was writing for fellow-Jews, feels closer to the story and is more a part of its actions. He is less Hellenized and more orthodox than the writer of the B-text, and possibly even wrote in Palestine. However, Dorothy has been challenged because his conclusions depend on the accuracy of his characterizations of the versions, which are open to question. Thus day and Fox believe that the A-text is really more tolerant of Gentiles than the B-text, and Day argues at some length that claims of more Jewishness and less Hellenism in the A-text is are 'inaccurate and incomplete'; in Day's own view the A-text is best treated as a Jewish-Persian amalgam, a model of diaspora Judaism, while the B-text in contrast gives Esther greater affinity with the religious community, and could therefore be Palestinian! The Masoretic text holds the middle ground in which Jewish-Persian relations are good but coolly professional and could come from anywhere. Further discussion of the literary differences between the three main versions will be found in Chapter 10. (Clines,1984), (See appendix –A)

By way of postscript to this discussion it should be mentioned that although no fragments of the canonical book of Esther have been found at Qumran (and significantly none of the liturgical calendars at Qumran include the festival of Purim), J.T. Milik has claimed to identify several fragments of an Aramaic proto-Esther [4Q pr Estar] in the materials reclaimed from Cave 4. Attempting to fit these in to the textual history of Esther, which he analyses at careful length, Milik concludes that the Masoretic text was itself translated form Greek-an originated shortly after the First Jewish War. Prior to this, Proto-Esther materials such as those represented in the Cave 4 fragments were circulating in Judaea and influenced the many variant traditions still extant. These proposals have yet to be fully absorbed into Esther studies. /Old Greek text and Alpha text see on the Appendix A.), (Clines,1984) ,(Fox 2001).

## 4.2. *Authorship and Date of the book:*

## 4.2.1 AUTHORSHIP

The Book of Esther offers no information regarding its author, reflecting a form of anonymity that is typical of Old Testament narrative literature. At no point does the author refer to himself, nor does he provide any direct or indirect indication of his identity as a historical individual. Nevertheless, because the narrative is narrowly focused on the circumstances and concerns of Jews living outside the land of Israel, authorship within the diaspora may be regarded as virtually certain. Moreover, the author's detailed and accurate familiarity with Persian society, administration, and court life strongly suggests that he belonged to the eastern Jewish diaspora.

Fox (140), following earlier scholars, proposes that the author's evident knowledge of the geography of Susa and his particular attention to the Susa-based date of the celebration of Purim (9:18–19) point to residence in that city itself. While this conclusion is highly plausible, Fox rightly notes that such familiarity with Persian affairs does not in itself require eastern origin. Contemporary works from roughly the same period—such as Herodotus' *Histories* and Berossus' *Babylonica*—demonstrate that extensive knowledge of the Persian world could be acquired without direct residence there (Fox 2001).

If the relational literary history of the book outlined above is accepted, the evidence suggests the involvement of two contributors: first, the author of the original narrative, likely close in form to what is commonly referred to as the Proto-Esther, and second, the author-redactor responsible for shaping the Masoretic Text. In my judgment, it is appropriate to describe this redactor as an "author" (on the issue of redactors as authors, see Fox, *Redaction*, 1–3, 142–43), given the extent to which his revisions fundamentally altered the nature of the earlier narrative. His additions—especially the concluding sections concerning the establishment of the festival of Purim in chapters 9–10—significantly reshaped both the genre and the purpose of the work.

Clines has offered particularly insightful analysis of both the theological and literary impact of the changes introduced by the Masoretic author-redactor, as well as of the narrative skill with which those changes were executed. Notable is his discussion of the implications of introducing the concept of the irrevocability of Persian law into the Proto-Esther narrative (*Esther Scroll*, 94–104). Authorship may rightly be attributed to a redactor who, while in one respect merely expanding a previously more concise storyline, in another introduced a striking and inventive dramatic development—namely, the necessity of a second royal decree—while at the same time preserving the stylistic qualities of the original composition (Clines 1984).

Despite these observations, the available evidence does not allow us to identify the author or authors of Esther as historical individuals in any concrete sense (Fox 2001).

## 4.2.2 DATE

Proposed dates for the composition of the Book of Esther have spanned a large portion of the Old Testament period. Nevertheless, the historical circumstances of the narrative itself establish clear boundaries within which its date must fall. It is evident that the book was written after the reign of Ahasuerus—identified with Xerxes I (486–465 B.C.)—and most likely a considerable time after his rule. Passages such as 1:1, 13–14; 4:11; 8:8; and 10:2 appear to presuppose a temporal distance of at least several generations, even though they do not suggest that the Persian Empire had faded into distant memory.

An important chronological marker is provided by the colophon attached to the Old Greek version of Esther, which likely establishes an earlier terminus for the book's composition. There is little reason to question the reliability of the information preserved there (cf. Moore, *Additions*, 251). The colophon states that "in the fourth year of the reign of Ptolemy and Cleopatra, Dositheus … and his son Ptolemy brought the book of Purim," presumably to Alexandria, although the destination is not explicitly named. This notice indicates that the Greek translation of Esther must have been completed prior to 114 B.C., the fourth regnal year of Ptolemy VIII, who is the most plausible candidate among the Ptolemies married to a Cleopatra and reigning longer than four years (see Moore, *Additions*, 250). Consequently, the Hebrew Vorlage must predate the first century B.C. by a sufficient interval to allow for circulation and recognition extensive enough to warrant translation into Greek (Moore 1977).

Within these chronological limits—roughly the fourth to second centuries B.C.—the available evidence does not allow for precise dating. Still, several considerations help narrow the range. First, contrary to the claims of some interpreters, the book does not portray the Persian government or most of the non-Jewish population as fundamentally hostile toward the Jews. While a segment of the population was prepared to act on Haman's decree, making the threat genuine, the enemies of the Jews are limited to those explicitly described as hoping to prevail over them, seeking to harm them, or hating them (9:1–5). These adversaries do not represent either the Persian administration or the empire's diverse population.

Although Ahasuerus bears serious moral responsibility for consenting to the destruction of the Jews, his decision does not arise from ethnic hostility. Rather, it reflects indifference; he is unaware of the identity of the people he condemns (see Explanation to 3:7–11). As the narrative's embodiment of the Persian world, the king reflects a political order marked by instability rather than inherent animosity toward Jews. This perspective is reinforced by passages such as 3:15d and 8:15b, as well as by the overall tone of the book.

Second, the converse is also true: Jewish hostility in the narrative is directed solely toward those who actively seek the community's destruction. As several scholars have noted, such a generally accommodating portrayal of relations between Jews and their surrounding society is more consistent with an author writing in the late Persian or early Hellenistic period—that is, the late fourth or early third centuries B.C. This makes it highly unlikely that the book reflects the conditions of the Maccabean era, as earlier scholars once proposed, when tensions between Jews and their rulers were particularly acute.

Linguistic evidence, while unable to provide more exact data, supports this historical assessment. In his comprehensive analysis of the language of Esther, Clines identifies fifty-eight features relevant to dating, seventeen of which do not appear in other Hebrew prose texts but do occur in Esther. To illustrate this evidence, thirteen of these features are discussed in detail in the Notes (see Notes on 1:8.a., 11.a., 15.b; 2:1.b; 3:8.b, 12.a; 4:11.b, 11.c; 6:6.a; 7:4.a; 8:5.b, 15.a; 9:26.b). Conversely, in eleven instances where Esther exhibits later linguistic forms, other prose texts preserve only earlier equivalents.

Taken together, this substantial evidence for the relatively late character of many of Esther's linguistic features leads to a cautious conclusion. Although a more definitive judgment regarding Esther's linguistic position among Hebrew prose texts awaits comprehensive diachronic and synchronic analysis, the book's language aligns more closely with the later phase of post-exilic prose rather than with its earlier stages. For this reason, a date earlier than the latter half of the fourth century B.C. is unlikely (Clines 1984).

These considerations point to the late Persian or early Hellenistic period—approximately the fourth century B.C.—as the most probable context for the redactional activity that produced the Masoretic Text of Esther, with the balance of evidence slightly favoring the latter portion of that period.

### *4.3. Canonical status and position of the book of Esther:*

## 4.3.1 CANONICAL STATUS

Determining the point at which the Book of Esther finally attained canonical status is especially difficult, since both the available evidence and the interpretation of that evidence remain uncertain and contested. As might be expected, the earliest testimony prior to the second century A.D. derives from Jewish sources, most notably the Essene community at Qumran (ca. 150 B.C.–A.D. 70) and the writings of Josephus (ca. A.D. 90). Unfortunately, the significance of this evidence is not easy to evaluate. In the case of Qumran, the problem is one of silence: Esther is the only book of the Old Testament not represented among the texts preserved by the Essenes. Although this absence could theoretically be explained by chance or the uneven survival of manuscripts, such an explanation seems unlikely. The contrast with the Cairo Genizah is striking, where fragments of Esther are more numerous than those of any biblical book outside the Pentateuch.

A more plausible explanation is that the Qumran community did not observe the festival of Purim and therefore had little reason to preserve the book associated with it. Some scholars further suggest that one of the dates prescribed by Esther for the celebration of Purim, the fourteenth of Adar, conflicted with the Qumran liturgical calendar, where that date fell on a Sabbath. If so, Esther may well have been accepted within the broader Jewish canon of the period but either rejected or ignored by the Qumran sect in particular. As a result, the absence of Esther at Qumran does not allow firm conclusions regarding its canonical status either within that community or within Judaism more generally (Moore 1977).

The earliest unequivocal evidence for the book's presence in the canon appears in *Midrash Esther Rabbah* 2.7, which preserves a brief quotation in Greek from Aquila's translation, produced around A.D. 128–129. This demonstrates that Esther formed part of the Hebrew text used by Aquila and thus enjoyed canonical standing by that time.

Alongside this positive evidence, however, there is equally clear testimony that Esther belonged to a group of five books whose scriptural status was debated in certain rabbinic circles, the others being Ezekiel, Proverbs, Ecclesiastes, and the Song of Songs. One major factor in these debates appears to have been the largely secular character of Esther, which constituted one of the principal reasons for questioning the canonical authority of all five books. The Greek translators of the Septuagint seem to have addressed this difficulty by introducing explicitly religious material into the narrative through the non-canonical Additions, particularly Additions A, C, and F. This suggests that the lack of overt religiosity in the Hebrew version was perceived as problematic and in need of correction. Whatever the intentions behind these additions, their effect was to reinforce the book's canonical legitimacy.

Further evidence of early resistance is reflected in traditions reporting objections raised when Mordecai and Esther sought to establish the observance of Purim. According to these accounts, opposition arose on the grounds that celebrating Purim might bring renewed trouble upon the Jews and that no new observances should be added to the Mosaic Law. Such statements imply that doubts about the book's authority existed from an early stage. In any case, several passages in the Babylonian Talmud make it clear that Esther's canonical status was under dispute by at least the early second century A.D. The earliest explicit reference appears in *b. Megillah* 7a, which records a rabbinic debate from the beginning of the second century concerning whether Purim constituted an illegitimate addition to the festivals prescribed in the Pentateuch.

Two later traditions, also preserved in *b. Megillah* 7a and dating to mid-second century A.D., record divergent rabbinic opinions regarding Esther's status. These discussions revolve around the technical criterion of whether a book "defiles the hands," a recognized marker of canonicity. In one text, it is stated that all agreed that Ruth, the Song of Songs, and Esther defile the hands—a declaration that itself presupposes earlier controversy. In another text, Esther is explicitly said not to defile the hands. Debate appears to have continued into the late third century, as evidenced by the opinion that the Esther scroll did not require a protective mantle, implying that it was not considered canonical (Clines 1984).

With respect to Christian sources, there is little unambiguous evidence for Esther's canonical acceptance prior to the end of the second century. A survey of the earlier evidence suggests that the book was probably regarded as canonical in the Western Church, though this cannot be established with certainty (cf. Moore, xxv–xxviii). The situation in the Eastern Church was markedly different. There, Esther was frequently denied canonical status. In the latter half of the second century, Melito, Bishop of Sardis—whose sources, though Palestinian in origin, were likely Christian rather than Jewish—omitted Esther from his list of canonical books. Numerous Eastern Church Fathers of the fourth century, including Athanasius, Gregory of Nazianzus, and Theodore of Mopsuestia, likewise rejected Esther's canonicity (Moore 1977).

The difficulty of interpreting this evidence is further intensified by the lack of consensus regarding the point at which the Jewish canon itself became fixed. Until relatively recently, scholarly opinion commonly held that the Pentateuch was closed by around 400 B.C., the Prophets by about 200 B.C., and that the Writings remained fluid until the so-called Council of Jamnia (Jabneh) around A.D. 90. This reconstruction has now been largely abandoned. It is widely recognized that the gathering of rabbis at Jabneh was not an authoritative council comparable to later Christian synods, and there is no record that it addressed the canonicity of any books other than the Song of Songs and Ecclesiastes—both of which continued to be debated for centuries thereafter. Moreover, the discovery and study of the Qumran texts and other Dead Sea materials have reopened discussion about how and when the boundaries of the canon were established.

Two main interpretations have emerged. One argues that the canon was effectively closed as early as the second century B.C., in which case later rabbinic debates reflect attempts to exclude books that were already canonical. The other contends that the canon took shape gradually under social and political pressures during the first two centuries A.D., meaning that rabbinic discussions of the five disputed books represent genuine deliberations over their canonical status.

In my judgment, the balance of the evidence favors the first view. According to this perspective, Esther would have achieved canonical recognition sometime in the second century B.C., possibly in connection with the collection of sacred writings attributed to Judas Maccabeus following the Antiochene persecution (2 Macc 2:14). If so, later debates concerned the possible removal of a book already accepted as Scripture. Support for this view lies in the fact that rabbinic objections appear as minority positions cited primarily in order to be rebutted. Nevertheless, if the alternative interpretation is correct—and the evidence for the earlier closure is far from conclusive—then Esther may not have attained full canonical status within Judaism until the conclusion of rabbinic debates in the third century A.D., and within Christianity more broadly until a century or more later (Clines 1984).

After the rabbinic controversies of the first four centuries A.D., Esther's canonical status within Judaism was rarely questioned. On the contrary, it became one of the most significant books of the Jewish canon outside the Pentateuch, largely because of its association with the festival of Purim, during which it is read annually and which became one of the most important celebrations of the Jewish liturgical year.

The situation in Christianity developed in the opposite direction. None of the Church Fathers composed a full commentary on Esther, and references to it in their writings are relatively rare. Where the book is mentioned, priority is typically given to the religiously expanded Additions of the Septuagint, which shapes the interpretive framework through which the rest of the narrative is understood. Not until the early Middle Ages did a commentary devoted to Esther appear, namely that of Rhabanus Maurus, Archbishop of Mainz, in the ninth century. Although Esther has been formally recognized as part of the Christian canon since the middle of the first millennium A.D., it has frequently been evaluated negatively, and its theological value and canonical standing have often been questioned. The absence of explicit reference to God, and the highly indirect manner in which divine activity is suggested, have naturally contributed to such concerns. Much of this negative assessment, however, arises from misunderstanding the purpose and theological intent of the book as a whole, as well as from misinterpretation of particular passages (see the discussion of Purim in the Theology section below).

With the advent of printing in the modern period, the Book of Esther came to occupy a fixed and largely uniform place within both the Jewish and Christian canons. By the tenth century A.D., during the era of the Tiberian Masoretes, all five Festal Scrolls—Song of Songs, Ruth, Lamentations, Ecclesiastes, and Esther—were regularly read at the five principal festivals of the Jewish liturgical year. As a result, these five writings were grouped together as a collection known as the *Megilloth* ("the Scrolls") and were normally positioned after Proverbs and before Daniel, Ezra–Nehemiah, and Chronicles at the conclusion of the Jewish canonical sequence. Within the Megilloth, Esther holds the final place, immediately preceding Daniel, both in historical and chronological arrangement.

When the Christian Church restructured the Jewish Scriptures according to its own canonical framework, Esther was classified among the "historical" books, which constitute the second of the four major divisions of the Christian canon. Because this section is ordered chronologically, Esther appears at its end, following Ezra–Nehemiah and directly before Job, which introduces the poetic and wisdom literature.

Before the modern era, however, the ordering of canonical books outside the Pentateuch was far from consistent. In Jewish canonical lists dating from before the formation of the Festal Scrolls collection, Esther is commonly placed near the end of the canon together with Daniel, Ezra–Nehemiah, and Chronicles. In fact, in three of the four earliest lists clearly derived from Jewish tradition—those attributed to Origen, Epiphanius, and Jerome—Esther is listed last among the Writings. This placement suggests that Esther may have been the final book incorporated into the canon. It is also possible that the sequence found in the earliest Jewish list—Daniel, Esther, Ezra–Nehemiah, Chronicles—represents an attempt to arrange the books chronologically, based on an inaccurate understanding of the historical period (Moore, c. 1977).

The textual foundation for this translation and commentary is the Codex Leningradensis as published in *Biblia Hebraica Stuttgartensia* (BHS). The Hebrew text of Esther has been preserved with exceptional care, which is especially fortunate given the limited usefulness of the ancient versions. Not only does the Old Greek Translation (OGT) contain several passages that are clearly secondary additions to the Hebrew narrative, but its rendering of the Masoretic Text is markedly loose and paraphrastic rather than literal. Moore, whose work represents the most recent comprehensive study of the Greek Esther, observes that "there is scarcely a verse in which the OGT does not omit a word, phrase, or clause of the MT" (*Additions*, 162). This assessment is readily confirmed by the frequent appearance of the siglum G* ("lacking in the OGT") in the critical apparatus of BHS.

The paraphrastic nature of the Greek translation led earlier scholars to question its value as a textual witness. B. Jacob judged it to be "more or less worthless" for reconstructing the original Hebrew text (ZAW

10 [1890] 270), and C. C. Torrey famously remarked that, unlike every other book of the Hebrew Bible, Esther lacks a faithful Greek translation of its canonical Hebrew form (both cited in Moore, *Additions*, 162). My own examination of the evidence confirms this judgment: the OGT is so free in its handling of the text that it can serve only a very limited role in recovering the original Hebrew. For this reason, I have not considered it necessary to address every Septuagintal addition or omission identified by F. Maass in the BHS apparatus (Moore, c. 1977).

In my view, among the many variant readings preserved in the versions and the conjectural emendations proposed in scholarly literature and recorded in BHS, only two should be preferred to the Masoretic Text. First, in Esther 3:7, the MT appears to have lost a clause through *homoeoteleuton*, which can be restored with reasonable confidence based on the OGT. Second, in 9:29 and 9:31—passages where the Greek translation is internally incoherent (cf. Fox, 286–87)—I have adopted three widely accepted conjectural emendations on grounds of internal consistency; these are discussed in the Additional Note on verses 29–32.

Finally, several additional variant readings may be suggested based on other Hebrew manuscripts or alternative Masoretic traditions. Four of these are of little significance, since they involve only grammatical variants or synonymous forms and do not affect the substance of the text (Moore, c. 1977).

## 4.4. *Theological Description of the book of Esther:*

## IS ESTHER THEOLOGICALLY VALUABLE?

The Book of Esther has long been regarded with a degree of unease by both Jews and Christians, though especially by Christians. The narrative it presents may be unfamiliar and can initially appear exaggerated or implausible. In brief, the story unfolds as follows. It is set in the Persian capital of Susa at the court of King Ahasuerus. The king is portrayed as fond of lavish banquets, and during one such drinking feast he orders his queen, Vashti, to present herself before his guests so that her beauty may be displayed. Vashti refuses. This refusal causes immediate alarm, as the king and his advisers imagine Persian women everywhere imitating her defiance. They therefore decide that Vashti must be deposed by an irrevocable royal decree, "written among the laws of the Persians and the Medes so that it may not be altered" (1:19), ensuring that "every man should be master in his own house" (1:22). A search for a new queen then begins, and it is determined that a beauty contest should be held, with the winner becoming Vashti's replacement.

At this stage Esther enters the narrative. She is a strikingly beautiful Jewish orphan who has been raised by her cousin Mordecai, a court official. Mordecai ensures that Esther is entered into the contest, advising her not to disclose her Jewish identity (2:10). In time, Esther is chosen as queen. Her position is strengthened when she reports to the king a plot against his life that Mordecai has overheard. The conspiracy proves genuine, the conspirators are executed, and Mordecai's loyalty is duly recorded in the royal annals.

The story then takes a darker turn. The king elevates Haman, an Agagite—identified with the Amalekites, traditional enemies of Israel (cf. 1 Sam 15:7–9)—to the position of chief minister. All officials are required to bow before him, but Mordecai refuses, provoking Haman's hatred. Haman's response is extreme: knowing that Mordecai is a Jew, he determines not merely to destroy Mordecai but to exterminate all Jews throughout the empire (3:6). A systematic plan is set in motion (Moore, c. 1977).

The preparations are carried out with chilling formality. Lots (*pur*) are cast to determine the date, and the chosen day is the thirteenth of Adar (3:7). Haman persuades the king to authorize the decree by claiming that the Jews are a people whose laws differ from those of all others and who fail to observe the king's laws, making them unworthy of tolerance (3:8). The king agrees, and an unalterable decree is issued ordering the destruction of all Jews and the confiscation of their property. Their sole hope lies in Esther's ability to intervene, yet this hope seems fragile: she has not been summoned to the king for thirty days, appears to have been forgotten, and approaching the king uninvited carries the death penalty (4:11).

The decisive turning point comes when Esther resolves to act nonetheless. With the support of a communal fast among the Jews of Susa, she gains an audience with the king and proceeds cautiously, inviting Ahasuerus and Haman to private banquets while withholding her true request. Haman interprets this as a sign of exceptional favor and becomes impatient to dispose of Mordecai before the appointed day of the pogrom. He therefore constructs enormous gallows, intending to secure the king's approval to execute Mordecai immediately (5:12–14).

That same night, however, the king is unable to sleep and has the royal chronicles read aloud. By apparent coincidence—or providence—he is reminded that Mordecai once saved his life and was never rewarded. The next day, the king asks Haman how best to honor "the man whom the king delights to honor" (6:8). Assuming that he himself is intended, Haman proposes a public triumph. His humiliation is complete when he discovers that Mordecai is the one to receive the honor.

This marks the beginning of Haman's downfall. Esther soon reveals to the king that she herself belongs to the people condemned by Haman's decree. Ahasuerus appears to have forgotten authorizing the order and reacts with fury. Haman seals his fate by throwing himself at Esther to plead for mercy while the king is briefly absent; when the king returns, Haman's posture appears compromising. He is promptly condemned and executed on the very gallows he had prepared for Mordecai, who is then appointed grand vizier in his place.

Although the original decree cannot be revoked, a second edict is issued granting the Jews the right to defend themselves. When the appointed day arrives, no Jews are killed; instead, five hundred of their enemies die in Susa and seventy-five thousand in the provinces.

At Esther's request, Haman's ten sons are also executed. Mordecai then instructs the Jews to commemorate the anniversary of the threatened destruction as a festival called Purim, named after the *pur*, the lot originally cast to determine the date.

It is not difficult to understand why the book has elicited such mixed reactions. On one hand, it addresses the historically grounded fear among Jews that they will be hated and persecuted because "their laws are different from those of every other people." Christians are ill-placed to object to a narrative in which Jews ultimately survive such a threat. On the other hand, the conclusion of the story appears to celebrate violence against Gentiles, and the central characters frequently act in morally or religiously questionable ways. Esther lives in circumstances incompatible with full observance of Jewish law; Mordecai risks catastrophe through his refusal to honor Haman; the king is portrayed as impulsive and easily manipulated; and similar concerns abound.

Compounding these difficulties is the fact that Esther is the only biblical book in which God is never mentioned by name, and in which no religious practice is highlighted apart from fasting. The cumulative effect can be to portray Judaism as purely ethnic rather than religious in character (Moore, c. 1977).

**Canonicity**

Esther appears to have been admitted into the Jewish canon no earlier than the period of the Council of Jamnia around A.D. 90, and possibly not until the academy at Usha convened around A.D. 140; some scholars even suggest that full acceptance may have occurred as late as A.D. 200. Its inclusion was not without controversy, and debates concerning its sacred status continued to surface in the Talmud, the codified form of oral law, well into the third century (b. Meg. 7a). These discussions focused on the claim that the Book of Esther did not "defile the hands." Although this terminology sounds strange in modern usage, in ancient Jewish thought holiness was conceived almost as a physical quality that could be transmitted through contact. Sacred objects such as scrolls were believed to convey holiness to the hands of those who touched them, rendering the hands "defiled." To say that Esther did not defile the hands therefore implied that it lacked sacred status.

Since similar objections were raised concerning at least two of the other five festival scrolls—collectively known as the *Megilloth*—this group of writings appears to represent a kind of boundary within the Old Testament canon (cf. Clines, *Esther*). Judgments about whether a scroll defiled the hands involved psychological and emotional responses as well as intellectual assessment, and they likely reflected recognition of the difficulties already noted. These included the relatively late date of Esther, making it one of the most recent books in the Old Testament, and concerns about its orthodoxy. A work was considered orthodox if it conformed to the teaching of the Torah, and in Esther's case the problem lay in its authorization of a festival not prescribed in the Pentateuch.

Nevertheless, none of these difficulties proved insurmountable. The narrative clearly affirms positive values, presupposes that the Jews are God's people, and implies divine sovereignty over historical events (4:14). The Mishnah suggests that the omission of God's name was intentional, so that it would not be accidentally profaned during the festive celebration that the book endorses. Moreover, Esther's close association with a widely beloved festival ultimately strengthened its standing rather than weakened it.

Taken as a whole, rabbinic tradition views Esther herself very favorably, identifying her as one of the seven female prophets of Israel, alongside Sarah, Miriam, Deborah, Hannah, Abigail, and Huldah. This claim is supported by appeal to Esther 5:1 ("she clothed herself in royalty"), which is interpreted to mean that she clothed herself with the Holy Spirit and received divine inspiration (Moore, c. 1977).

Clear evidence of the book's popularity is found in the abundance of surviving manuscripts. Esther appears in all complete private Bible codices, is appended to the Torah in most synagogue scrolls, and is included with other festival readings in liturgical collections. In addition, Jewish households sought to own a manuscript copy, since the Talmud prescribes that the scroll be read at Purim. As a result, countless manuscripts exist, many of them outstanding examples of Jewish calligraphic artistry. Esther is also unique among biblical books outside the Torah in having more than one Targum—

interpretive translations into Aramaic—and both the Jerusalem and Babylonian Talmuds provide extended commentary on it.

Indeed, the Talmud nearly traces the origins of Purim back to Moses by linking Exodus 17:14 ("I will utterly blot out the remembrance of Amalek from under heaven") with the description of Haman as an Agagite in Esther 3:1, identifying him as an Amalekite. Similarly, Deuteronomy 31:18 ("I will surely hide [*astir*] my face") is interpreted as an allusion to Esther's role in redeeming Israel at a time when God conceals his presence (b. Hul. 139b). The high esteem in which the book was held is further illustrated by the declaration of the medieval Jewish philosopher Maimonides (d. 1204) that although the Prophets and Writings would pass away in the messianic age, the Law and the Book of Esther would endure.

Within the Christian tradition, the reception of Esther was even more difficult. The book had no place in the Christian liturgical calendar, and Christians did not identify with the experience of being ethnically Jewish. One may wonder how differently the book might have been received had it spoken on behalf of "Israelites" rather than explicitly of "Jews." Instead, Christians often perceived themselves as representing the Gentiles against whom the narrative seemed directed and consequently objected to what they viewed as its ethic of retribution. Esther was accepted into the Western Church at the Council of Carthage in A.D. 397, but only together with the apocryphal Additions—six passages introduced by Alexandrian Jews in the Greek translation to compensate for the absence of explicit religious elements in the Hebrew text. In the Eastern Church, Esther was not received until the eighth century.

In contrast to its strong reception in Jewish tradition, Esther attracted little attention in Christianity from the New Testament period through the Reformation. Martin Luther famously expressed deep hostility toward the book, declaring that he wished it did not exist because it "Judaizes too much" and contains excessive pagan elements, and asserting that it should never have been included in the Old Testament canon (Moore, c. 1977).

A further shift occurred during the Reformation in the Western Church, when Luther initiated the removal of the apocryphal Additions to Esther as part of a broader effort to restore Scripture to its original form. Since that time, Protestant and Anglican Bibles have included only the Hebrew version of Esther within the Old Testament, relegating the Greek Additions to the Apocrypha, which contains material present in the Septuagint but absent from the Hebrew canon. It is often overlooked that this represents a relatively recent modification of the Old Testament canon, albeit one limited to churches shaped by the Reformation (Moore, c. 1977).

### Modern Reactions to Esther

In this century, both Jews and Christians have reassessed their reactions to Esther, with the result that an unexpected rapprochement may be taking place. On both sides, more attention has been paid to the literary genre of work, which is no longer thought to be a piece of pure history (see Chapter 8 ).

On the Jewsish side, Greenstein has mounted a spirited defence of Esther by explaining how it functions in the Jewish liturgical year, implicityly disapproving its abstraction from that context. It should be judged on its positive qualities, not on its negative characteristics which become more apparent outside of the context.

A more subtle approach is taken by Goldman, who has pounted out that although Jewish and Christian readers have disagreed as to whether Esther is ethical or not, neither side has paid much attention to the author's possible use of irony – a question which has importan implications for the interpreter. Certainly, Esther is full of 'rhetorical irony', such at the plot reversal wherby Haman is hanged on the gallows he had built for Mordecai, but Goldman argues that it also generates an ironical attitude in the reader ('generative irony'), prompting him or her to question the attitudes and assumptions that are being portrayed. For example, the fact that the Jews are given permission to massacre their enemies (8.11) has long troubled commentators, who have tried to argue either that the Jews only attack those who attack them (Gordis; but the Jews still kill over 75,000 men, according to 9.5); or that this is poetic justice required by the story-line. Goldman, presuming a Jewish readership, sees the significance of 8.11 in quite different terms: it shows Jews and Persians behaving alike, and this, he says, is highly ironical and leads to 'a bold questioning of the Jewish self-image' which is a highly ethical act. What is not so clear is whether the original author intended such irony (Goldman calls such an intention 'intuitive irony'); it is possible that he did not, but one cannot prove it, though there are other scholars who have called Esther a sapiential satire. In any case, it is a well-established principle of lieteray criticism; whether biblical or secular, that the author's intensions cannot entirely circumscribe the meaning of the text and that the reader makes a crucial contribution to determining its meaning. At the extreme, however, some Jewish voices have been raised against Esther. In 1938, Shalom BenChorin urged the abandonment of the festival of Purim and the banishment of Esther from the canon, as 'unworthy of a sacrificial people'. (Clines, 1984)

It is paradoxical that simultaneously some Christian scholars are becoming more appreciative of Esther. It is true that critical voices continue to be raised, both on old grounds and on new ones. Thus Mosala, a black South African scholar, objects that the book does not question the Persian feudal system but aspires only to survival' or at best to some degree of influence within that system, and that it entirely subsumes gender struggle to this nationalist and survivalist programme: 'South African women cannot consent to the claim that such a biblical text supports them in their struggle'. Similarly, the sociologist points out that even the statements that the Jews undertook 'no looting' (9.10, 15, 16) supports a feudal ideology in which property assumes greater importance than people, and the choice of a female character to achieve such ends could be objectionable to women.

These interpreters are raising objections which can be raised to a greater or lesser extent against any biblical text, given the changes in sociological assumptions that have occurred in the two thousand years and more sicne these texts were written. The authority of a sacred text that does not reflect one's life experience to a sufficient degree is going to become questionable. But is it true that a text produced in a hierarchical, patriarchal society need be rejected automatically as 'unredeemable words of subjugation'? Fewell, herself a feminist scholar, would argue to the contrary, noting, for example, how in the case of Esther the author mocks the fragility of male sovereignty in the Vashtiepisode that opens the book. The text may stand for values which are timeless, such as the honoring of Esther's decision to plead for her people at the possible cost of their life, and in google, what is Scripture? Has recently pointed out that in former ages of biblical interpretation it would have been assumed that the highest and best possible interpretation of the text was the right one, since any lesser interpretation would have been dishonouring to God who was the presumed inspiration of the text. (Its added, pointedly, that if this had not been the case biblical studies would not enjoy either the standing or the funding that they do enjoy in modern universities). (Clines, 1984).

Interestingly, however, Esther is also gaining support from Christians who are beginning to appreciate and identify with its championship of the oppressed. Christians, in other words, are both beginning to show imaginative sympathy for the plight of the Jews, and to feel similarly stigmatized them selves. Put bluntly, Esther deals with fear and anxiety in the audience and by allowing them to see that fear played out on an objective stage it has therapeutic value: even if the fear remains, it has been 'named'. The comment of Ps. 37.12, 'The wicked plot against the righteous', now looks less isolated within Christian tradition. In the (OT short Story) acknowledges that this story of threat and anxiety is intended to help the audience cope with their own fear and anxiety, so the modern Christian can recongnize 'analogies of context.

Christians cannot simply read Esther as if they were Jews, however, because Esther raises the profoundest question, viz. the meaning of the election of Israel – the scandal of particularity. It is not good to see the savage retribution pictured in Esther as the long-term solution (or even as an interim solution) to the tensions caused by this particularity. Rather, some scholars' suggestes that instead of entering the situation Esther describes we should try to stand back from it and see, retrospectively, that God has kept Israel alive for his salvific purposes regardless of her merits or demerits, as an action of undeserved grace. This holds true whether one conceives of Israel as the Jewish community, the Christian community, or both. 'Christ both unites inseparably and draws the sharpest cleavage between the old and new covenants.

This some what detached view is not, however, representative of more recent scholarship on Esther, particularly within the liberation theology movement, which emerged in the 1960s in Latin America (and has attracted the interest and support of both Jews and

Christians). Craghan discussed the place of Esther liberates herself by liberating others. (It is interesting that the two biblical books named after women, namely Ruth and Esther, plus the apocryphal book of Judith, have all been claimed as liberation texts, though each offers a slightly different paradigm of liberation. Craghan compares them all. (Clines, 1984)

It is a fundamental conviction of liberation theology not only that ths starting point for theological reflection is the liberation of the poor, but also that Orthodoxy must be accompanied by orthopraxis. Orthodoxy (correct doctrine) is seen to be important but without orthopraxis (right action) there may be little one can say about sound doctrine. Form this point of view, it matters very little that God is not specifically mentioned in Esther, if he is made known-as He is –in and through the events it describes. From the point of view of Hispanic Americans (Lating Americans who live as a minority in north America) Esther id deeply meaningful for three reasons (Costas) first, she remembered her roots and did not become wholly assimilated to Persian society, even though she offered it her loyal support. The book offers hope and support for the, many minoritieis who wish to live this way in modern pluralistic societies. Secondly, she remembered her true vocation. It is easy for the Christian vocation to become deformed by conforming too much to the dominant system, so that the Church does not speak out against injustice or oppression or makes feeble protests from the sidelines and remains practically in active. Thirdly, Esther remembered God: this is seen as the well-spring of all her positive actions, and as the guarantee of her long-term prosperity (Jer. 22.15-16) Secular humanism may be less of a threat to faith than a lack of radical obedience among Christians to the declared will of God in the case in the face of social or political opposition.

Costs acknowledges that Christians have been uneasy about the ethnic particularity and indeed about the incipient feminism in Esther, but argues in contrast to Anderson that all victims can identify with the Jews in the story – and conversely that Jewish oppressors (visiting injustice on the Palestinians and Lebanese) cannot rightly claim this story as their own, citing the names of Jewish soldiers who have faced prison sentences for refusing to fight on these fronts, he concludes that the memory of Esther (and Mordecai) 'can only be claimed in faithfulness to the cause of justice, in solidarity with the victims of injustice, and in daring obedience to the God who stands on the side of the poor, the powerless and the oppressed'. There is value in the modern 'hermeneutic of suspicion', but it must be complemented by a 'hermeneutic of hope'.

In fact, it has recently been noticed that although the story overtly satirizes Persian law it also implicitly condemns a way of thinking about law which has from time to time characterized both Judaism and Christianity, namely that it is something that can never be changed – even when changed circumstances make its contents obviously problematic. As Fewell syas, Esther elbows into the fixed provisions of the Torah to make room for the new holiday of Purim, and in so doing keeps the canon from stagnating and becoming as problematic as the laws of Medes and Persians. (Clines, 1984)

## THEOLOGY

Blessed are you, LORD our God, sovereign of all creation, who has set us apart through his commandments and instructed us to read the sacred scroll.

Blessed are you, LORD our God, sovereign of all creation, who performed mighty acts for our ancestors in former times, at this very season.

Blessed are you, LORD our God, sovereign of all creation, who has preserved our lives, sustained us, and enabled us to reach this holy occasion.

*(Blessings recited before the reading of the Scroll of Esther in the Purim evening service; cf. Esth. 9:3)*

From the preceding examination of the genres, themes, and aims of the Book of Esther emerge its central theological emphases, however indirectly these are conveyed through its literary form. Because the book's final shape exhibits a duality of genre and theme, its theological focus is likewise twofold. On the one hand, it arises from the book's conclusion (9:6–32), which centers on the establishment and character of the festival of Purim; on the other hand, it grows out of the problem-driven narrative (1:1–9:5; 10:1–3), recounting deliverance from Haman's decree through the faithfulness of Mordecai, the courage and resourcefulness of Esther, and the providential ordering of events by God (see Theme and Purpose above).

## A. The theological emphases of the "denouement" (9:6–32)

The dominant concern of this section is the response to the horrific threat posed by Haman's edict of annihilation, and it is this crisis that establishes the book's primary theological orientation. The significance of Purim must be derived from the form the festival takes within the narrative itself. Although it is evident that some version of the festival existed prior to the book's final composition, the author deliberately leaves its earlier origins embedded in tradition rather than making them explicit (see Explanation to 9:20–32). Over time, various theories have been proposed regarding a possible non-Jewish origin for the festival, such as Lewy's suggestion of a connection to Persian New Year celebrations. While some proposals appear more plausible than others, they rest on no firm evidence within the text and contribute little to an understanding of Purim as portrayed in the book; they will therefore not be pursued here.

Several defining features of the festival deserve emphasis. First, the authority by which Purim is established is twofold. (a) Mordecai, acting as leader of the diaspora community, writes to bind the Jews to its observance. He does not legislate in the strict sense or issue commands; rather, he "requires" observance (see Comment on 9:21 and Explanation to 9:20–22), grounding this obligation in the collective memory of the crisis summarized in his retrospective account (9:24–25). (b) At the same time, the Jewish community itself actively assumes this responsibility (see Explanation to 9:23–28). Authority thus resides not only in communal leadership but also in the community's own initiative—first in celebrating deliverance and then in formally committing to its perpetual observance.

Second, the narrative clearly assigns Purim cultic significance. Its observance is mandatory (note the force of "to require" or "to impose"; see comment on 9:21), and its enduring and universal character is repeatedly underscored. It is to be observed every year (v. 21), across all generations, families, provinces, and cities; it is never to be abolished, nor is its observance ever to lapse among the Jewish people or their descendants.

Third, Mordecai defines the festival as a commemoration of the rest and rejoicing that followed the crisis. In doing so, the character of Purim is substantially reshaped from its earlier form (cf. Clines, *Esther Scroll*, 160–62). The celebration is not focused on military triumph or the destruction of enemies. Although fighting did occur in Susa on the fourteenth of Adar, the contrast drawn in 9:17–18 shows that this detail serves only to explain the difference in dates of celebration. In the provinces, that day was marked not by combat but by joy and festivity. Accordingly, Purim does not commemorate victory in battle, nor does it sanction malicious delight in the death of adversaries. Instead, it celebrates the experience of relief from persecution, that is, the joy of deliverance from an existential threat.

This emphasis is especially clear in the brief retrospective of events in 9:21–25, which leads the Jewish community to commit solemnly to the annual observance (vv. 26b, 23a). Notably, this summary makes no reference at all to battles or military success (Clines, *Esther Scroll*, 164); its sole focus is deliverance from Haman's plot. The same theological orientation is reinforced by the very name of the festival, Purim, which the text explicitly connects to the *pur*, the lot cast by Haman in 3:7 to determine the date of Jewish destruction (9:26a; cf. Clines, *Esther Scroll*, 164). Both the narrative that motivates the festival and the name by which it is known direct attention away from warfare and bloodshed and toward the thwarting of evil and the experience of salvation from impending disaster.

Equally significant is Esther's instruction that Purim is to be observed in continuity with practices the Jewish community had already accepted within its religious life—namely, fasting and mourning (9:31). This further underscores that Purim is not intended as a celebration of military achievement, but rather as a commemoration of rescue from danger and catastrophe. The joy of the festival is therefore deliberately shaped by the memory of suffering that preceded it. Purim marks a month that was transformed "from sorrow to gladness and from mourning to festivity" (v. 22). As such, it establishes a framework for joy that is reflective and purposeful: joy is not merely an uninhibited release of emotion, but a conscious participation in the reversal of grief and the experience of deliverance from mourning.

As demonstrated in the earlier discussion of genre, the criteria for establishing Purim in verses 26–28 presuppose the retelling of the story itself. Commemorating the experience of past generations requires recounting that experience anew. Hearing the narrative of crisis and rescue is essential to re-entering the joy that the festival remembers. In this sense, the Book of Esther functions liturgically as a festival reading—a lection whose purpose is to shape and sustain communal memory.

From this examination of Purim's character, it becomes clear that the festival summons Jews of the diaspora to celebrate deliverance even when confronted with extreme and unimaginable evil. Despite the troubling nature of such a call—particularly in light of Jewish historical experience—the Jewish community has embraced it eagerly and wholeheartedly. The observance of Purim must have begun very shortly after the book's appearance, as evidenced by the reference to the "day of Mordecai" in 2 Maccabees 15:36, indicating that the festival was already established by the first half of the first century B.C. Its early observance is also confirmed by Josephus' first-century A.D. testimony that Jews continued to celebrate these days under the name Purim, as well as by the Mishnah tractate *Megillah* (dating from the first two centuries A.D.), which is devoted entirely to regulations concerning Purim—its dates, the public reading of the scroll, and interpretive traditions surrounding the text.

Purim remains one of the most prominent and beloved festivals in the Jewish liturgical calendar. The Book of Esther itself is unique among Old Testament writings outside the Torah in having a second Targum dedicated to its interpretation, and the volume of midrashic and exegetical literature devoted to it surpasses that of any other non-Pentateuchal biblical book. Its high esteem within Judaism is often illustrated by the statement attributed to Maimonides that, when the Messiah comes and the Prophets and Writings pass away, only the Torah and Esther will remain. The book's significance is further reflected in the fact that, although medieval Jewish interpretation of the Second Commandment prohibited depictions of the human figure, this restriction was not applied to the decoration of Esther scrolls. The richly illustrated manuscripts produced over the centuries testify to the deep affection with which the book has been regarded and preserve some of the finest achievements of medieval Jewish art (Gordis, *Megillat Esther*, 15). So overwhelming has been Esther's acceptance that Christian scholars, when addressing difficulties associated with the book, often appeal to the exceedingly rare instances in which Jewish authorities questioned its canonical status.

The emphasis on joyful deliverance that the book assigns to Purim is vividly reflected in Jewish practice. The festival is marked by exuberance, humor, and high spirits. That this character developed early is attested by the famous saying of the Babylonian teacher Raba (m. Meg. 7b), who maintained that one should drink on Purim until unable to distinguish between "Blessed be Mordecai" and "Cursed be Haman." A festive meal is traditionally held on the evening of the fourteenth of Adar and may continue late into the night. Gifts of food are exchanged—most famously *hamantaschen*, triangular pastries known as "Haman's pockets" or "Haman's ears"—and charity is given to the poor. During the public reading of the scroll, children shake noisemakers or hiss whenever Haman's name is spoken, while the so-called "verses of redemption" (2:5; 8:15–16; 10:3) are read aloud with special emphasis.

Disguises and masquerades, often involving dramatic reversals of social roles, are another hallmark of Purim. In modern Israel, this spirit is expressed through the annual *Adloyada* parade in Tel Aviv—named after Raba's dictum "until one does not know"—which draws thousands of participants. From the Middle Ages until the Holocaust, European Jewish communities also developed the tradition of *Purim-shpils*, satirical monologues and group performances staged during the festive meal. Over time, these evolved into elaborate theatrical productions on biblical themes, reflecting contemporary European dramatic styles. In the Talmudic academies of Eastern Europe, students even selected a "Purim Rabbi" who was permitted to parody teachers and playfully manipulate sacred texts (Gordis, *Megillat Esther*, 16).

Throughout all these practices, normal expectations of restraint and decorum are temporarily suspended, allowing satire, humor, and playful inversion to flourish—an atmosphere that closely mirrors the ironic and subversive spirit of the Book of Esther itself.

Asking why the Book of Esther and the festival of Purim it generated have so deeply shaped the Jewish consciousness may seem self-evident, yet in a post-Holocaust context the question bears repeating. First, as noted earlier, Esther is the only book in the Old Testament devoted entirely to the concerns of Jews living in the diaspora. Since the Roman destruction of Jewish life in Judea during the first and second revolts, Jewish existence has been overwhelmingly diasporic—at least until the modern establishment of the State of Israel. Second, one of the book's central themes is the account of how the leadership of Mordecai and Esther, together with the providence of God, delivered a dispersed Jewish community from the gravest danger imaginable: the threat of total annihilation.

Across their history—and especially during the past century in the Western world—Jews have repeatedly encountered the destructive potential inherent in diaspora societies, ranging from subtle and overt discrimination to persecution, dispossession, and mass violence. Despite the joy, satire, and carnival atmosphere that characterize Purim celebrations, Jewish tradition preserves a sober awareness of the festival's meaning through the practice of instituting "Special Purims." These are commemorations modeled on Purim that mark specific escapes from destruction. They often include festive meals, charitable giving, and the synagogue reading of a scroll recounting the deliverance, accompanied by prayers of thanksgiving. Such observances were established by individual families or communities and are therefore known as "the Purim of …" followed by a place or family name. Lists of these commemorations—stretching from the twelfth through the twentieth century—make sobering reading. For the Jewish community, the story of Esther is not abstract history; it is lived experience.

For those outside the Jewish community of faith, it is difficult to grasp how unsettling the call of Purim—to celebrate deliverance in the face of catastrophic evil—can be. Jewish history has too often unfolded in ways that contradict the book's outcome. In countless instances, pogroms succeeded rather than failed. This tragic pattern reached its horrific climax in the Holocaust, when Hitler and the Nazi regime—spiritual heirs of Haman—succeeded where Haman did not, annihilating six million of Europe's seven million Jews and nearly erasing European Jewish culture. In those circumstances there was no Mordecai, no Esther, and no deliverance. Faith itself struggles to maintain confidence in divine providence under such conditions. Yet, without minimizing this horror, one might cautiously hope that the message of Esther and Purim remains vital—indeed, increasingly urgent—in a post-Holocaust world, precisely because it summons the community to sustain faith and hope in the face of the irrational and diabolical forces that the story so powerfully embodies in Haman and his scheme. Purim proclaims that even the Holocaust, for all its devastation, did not bring about the end of Judaism or the Jewish people.

In this light, what Esther and the celebratory joy of Purim mean to Jewish life is best articulated by Jews themselves:

*Purim is playing time in Jewish tradition. It fulfills a crucial function. As Nietzsche observed, "I know of no other way of coping with great tasks than play." Purim*

These playful and artistic expressions of Purim reveal a remarkable resilience within the Jewish spirit. The narrative of Esther addresses a deadly serious subject—an attempted genocide that, fortunately, was thwarted. Yet Haman's plot was not an isolated incident. Versions of it recurred throughout Jewish history, culminating in the near-successful genocidal campaign of Hitler. Jews were rarely able to treat Esther as distant history; it was almost always painfully contemporary. Life lived under the constant threat of catastrophe endangered not only physical survival but psychological endurance. To awaken daily in the shadow of death was nearly as destructive as death itself. Survival—and sanity—depended in part on an extraordinary capacity: the ability to mock and laugh at oppressors.

Among the principal sources of this capacity for play and subversive humor stand the Book of Esther and the festival of Purim that emerged from it.

It is neither surprising nor troubling that when the Jewish Scriptures—the *Tanakh* (Torah, Prophets, and Writings)—were received by the Christian Church as the Old Testament, the Church did not adopt Purim as a celebration of deliverance from evil. Christian faith expresses redemption and deliverance in other ways, reshaped by belief in the Messiah. Yet while the Church accepted the Book of Esther along with the rest of the Jewish canon, it often did so without enthusiasm. Martin Luther's well-known hostility to Esther—

wishing it did not exist because it "Judaizes too much"—is representative, as is Eissfeldt's view that Luther's judgment should be decisive. Purim itself fared no better; Ironside dismissed it as a festival that had degenerated into irreverent festivity and patriotic excess. Much of this negative appraisal, especially before World War II, was shaped—often unconsciously—by the latent antisemitism that has deeply influenced Western thought. Cornill could claim that Esther displayed Judaism's least appealing traits without disguise, while Herrmann's survey of Esther interpretation catalogs a troubling history of antisemitic readings.

Yet many of these critiques rest on serious misreadings of the text. The Jewish response in 9:1–5 has frequently been portrayed as a slaughter of defenseless Gentiles, and the book is accused of promoting aggressive nationalism and hostility toward non-Jews. Critics describe it as vindictive, fanatical, and ethically deficient, and some even advise Christian preachers to avoid it entirely. However, sustained close readings such as that presented throughout this commentary—demonstrates that these interpretations are misguided. The violence described is fundamentally defensive (see the comments on 9:1–5), and the book's genre as a diaspora narrative centered on deliverance from existential threat precludes reading it as nationalist propaganda. Mordecai and Esther, though imperfect, are no more morally compromised than many biblical figures, Old or New Testament alike. Far from endorsing radical nationalism, Esther calls the faith community to remember and celebrate rescue from evil and destruction.

Encouragingly, more recent Christian scholarship—represented by Baldwin, Bardtke, Gerleman, Meinhold, Moore, Roberts, and especially Clines—has offered more nuanced and sympathetic readings.

Rather than fueling suspicion, Esther should trouble the Christian conscience, particularly after the Holocaust. The book declares that hostility toward Jews is incompatible with God's will. Given that much of the suffering inflicted upon Jews over the past two millennia—including the Holocaust—occurred in societies that identified as Christian and was often met with silence from the Church, Esther should move Christians toward repentance, humility, and a renewed resolve that the future must not repeat the failures of the past.

Finally, because Esther functions as a festival reading—shaping the meaning and spirit of Purim—it speaks not only to the Old Testament community but also to the New Testament Church. Christians, too, have lived as minorities in hostile environments, whether in the Roman Empire, under modern totalitarian regimes, or within today's increasingly secular societies. The story of Esther offers hope that "relief and deliverance" can arise through the interplay of human responsibility and divine providence. Purim calls every community of faith to celebrate deliverance—even when confronting evil that appears overwhelming and incomprehensible.

## . Theological Focus of the "Problem-Based Plot" (1:1-9:5; 10:1-3)

The narrative of Esther highlights the synergy between divine providence and human initiative in the deliverance of the Jewish people. The loyalty of Mordecai, the courage and resourcefulness of Esther, and God's providence combine to bring about this salvation. While in the Book of Ruth, God's presence is subtle yet discernible—His actions are often more implied than directly stated—Esther takes this subtlety to another level. The author never mentions God explicitly nor attributes any events directly to divine causality. Yet, God's providence is undeniably present, conveyed through unexpected coincidences and dramatic reversals that propel the plot forward. In contrast to the Book of Ruth, where God's role is more pronounced, Esther offers a more implicit portrayal of divine action. Nevertheless, the presence of divine providence in the story is clear.

The salvation of the Jewish people in Esther depends equally on divine intervention and human action. Mordecai's loyalty and Esther's courage and strategic thinking are as crucial to the outcome as the remarkable twists of fate that signal divine involvement. The book suggests that human effort and divine providence work together. "Without the wisdom and bravery of the Jewish characters, the divine coincidences would have come to nothing; and without those coincidences, no amount of human cleverness would have saved them." This dynamic—the interplay between human agency and divine intervention—contrasts with the more explicit portrayals of God's direct involvement in other parts of the Old Testament. In those stories, God often acts in ways that override natural laws, leaving little room for human input. Esther, on the other hand, underscores the complementary relationship between divine and human action.

Theologically, the goal of both divine providence and human effort in Esther is the deliverance of the Jewish people. An ironic yet significant statement is placed in the mouth of Haman's wife, Zeresh (6:13), which reveals the author's belief in the invincibility of the Jewish people. This is not a form of "manifest destiny" but rather a conviction rooted in the faith traditions of the Old Testament. The book's narrative aligns with the broader biblical themes of divine deliverance, as seen in stories like those of Joseph and the Exodus. The overarching theme of God's covenant with Israel is foundational: God's promise to Abraham that his descendants will bless all the families of the earth (Gen. 12:3). Therefore, the deliverance of the Jewish people holds significance beyond their own survival.

From a Jewish perspective, this idea is succinctly captured by Gordis, who writes:

> "The preservation of the Jewish people is a religious duty of utmost importance. This is because Israel has carried the responsibility of God's mission throughout history, beginning with the Covenant at Sinai. At Sinai, Israel learned that it cannot live solely for itself but is 'a kingdom of priests and a holy nation' (Exod. 19:6). Israel's eternal role is to 'open the eyes of the blind, free the prisoners, and bring those in darkness to light'

(Isa. 42:6). As Israel lives, it preserves the hope of the Messianic age, when 'there will be no evil and no destruction on God's holy mountain, and the earth will be filled with the knowledge of the Lord as the waters cover the sea' (Isa. 11:9)."

In this way, the deliverance of the Jewish people is not just about their survival—it is about fulfilling a divine purpose that extends beyond their borders, pointing toward universal redemption.

# Chapter 5. Textual Analysis of the book of Esther:

## *5.1. Literary Genere of the book*:

**ESTHER AS LITERATURE**

In the Intrduction, we discussed the books of Esther as examples of the short story genre, finding common ground perhaps in their joint comparison with the Joseph story in Genesis. Joseph and Esther are alike as exemplars of the same genre (together with Dan. 1-6 and Judith), the diaspora short story. But genres are never pure. To what extent does Esther partake of other genres? Can both Esther and Joseph be described as 'historicized wisdom tales?' Has the Joseph story influenced the precise content of Esther?

**The Genre of Esther**

**Esther as Festival Lection**

The present function of Esther is clearly as a festival lection. The primary requirement of the rabbinic Purim observance is to hear the reading of the scroll so that the community remembers its ancestors' experience. What is not so clear is whether the story was written as a 'festival aetiology'. That is, as a narrative that explains the origin of the festival. Ringgren and Gerleman have argued that this is the case, but Meinhold argues that while this is the book's purpose, it is not its genre. Fox, however, argues that this purpose is intrinsic to the MT of Esther.

## Esther Modelled on Exodus?

Another suggestive hypothesis which we owe to Gerleman has it that Esther was patterned after Exodus 1-12 and contains all its essential features: the setting at a foreign court, the mortal danger to the Jews, acts of deliverance and revenge, the triumph of the Jews over their foes, and the establishment of a festival (Passover). As with the Joseph story, it is possible to find more detailed comparisons than that: Esther and Moses are both adopted (Exod. 2.9; Est. 2.7) and keep their origins secret (Exod. 2.10, 20) Each narrative provides the hero with a spokesman (Esther for Mordecai, Est. 2.20; 4.8; 9.20-23; and Aaron for Moses, Exod. 4.15-16), and each portrays the Amalekites as the arch-enemies of Israel (Exod. 17.8-16). Both Esther and Moses have to appear repeatedly before the monarch to intercede for their people (Exod. 7.14-12.28; Est. 5.2; 7.2; 8.3). And the destruction of Israel's enemies in Est. 9.1-6 parallels the destruction of the Egyptians in the Exodus. Therefore, it may be that Esther has adapted a centr4al tradition of salvation history and adapted a central tradition of salvation history and adapted it to the diaspora situation by making it less overtly religious.

As with the Joseph comparison, closer inspection shows that Gerleman's proposal, intriguing though it is, can be pushed too far (Berg). For example, the comparison of Esther with Moses is surely in tension with the comparison also made of Esther with Aaron in her capacity as spokesperson for Mordecai. More generally, the two stories do not share the same attitude to the foreign court, nor do they deal with the same problems –a point that can be clearly seen by considering how different are the festivals, Passover and Purim, which are connected to these stories. Recent work by Nina Collins has shown that the elements in the Esther story to which Gerleman particularly appeals are not present in the Greek A-text which, as we have seen, is possibley an older version of the story than that in the Masoretic text, so that the Exodus comparison, so far as it goes, is a secondary overlay on the Esther story. Exodus, like Joseph, has exercised some influence on the book of Esther, but it is 'neither controlling nor pervasive' (Berg). One can at least agree with Clines that whether the author intended us to read Esther as a commentary on Exodus 1-12, the presence of both in the same canon now invites us to do so.

**Esther a Historicized Wisdom Tale?**

The book is classified both Joseph and Esther as 'historical wisdom tales', appealing to (a) their shard concept of a rather remote deity, and corresponding anthropocentrism; (b) lack of interest in Jewish history or community; (c) use of static typological characters; and (d) the use of wisdom motifs such as that of the wicked man meeting a bad end (prov. 26.27), or of a principal character being adopted by a wise man (not found in Joseph but arguably true of Esther and also featuring in Ahiqar). In this, Talmon built upon the insight of von Rad that the Joseph story 'illustrates the realization of wisdom precepts in practical life'. In addition, the motif to the 'wise courtier' may be a significant link (Humphreys), although it is not clearly present in Esther, where wise behavior is split between both Esther and Mordecai (who foolishly refuses to bow to Haman, a not inconsiderable figure in his own right.) But we have already seen that there are difficulties in regarding Esther as historical, and again it canm be objected that once Talmon plundered Esther for his purposes he has impoverished it and left it lacking any connection with Purim, which is arguably anticipated from the beginning of the book. There are important non-wisdom elements in Esther which have not been considered, and as ever there are problems in pinning down any literary theme or technique as peculiar to the wisdom tradition, even if it could appropriately be used there. (Fox 2001)

Fox undercuts this line of thought still further by insisiting that strictly there are very few examples of the 'historicized wisdom tale' apart from the preamble to the Aramaic Ahiqar and the Egyptian (Demotic) Onchsheschonqy, and that most of the wisdom features Talmon claims to find in Esther are in fact more characteristic of didactic wisdom (i.e Proverb-type literature). Even then, some of the features claimed are false: Proberbs mentions God repeatedly; Esther finds Jewish national history of central concern. What really unites stories like Joseph, Esther and indeed Daniel 1-6 is not so much wisdom as a 'palace intrigue's background. (Fox 2001)

The comparison with the Joseph story was first made by Rosental (1895) and has since been accepted by Gerleman, Talmon, Humphreys and Bardtke. It is based not only on a general similarity in setting and events, whereby a Jew can rise from lowly status in a foreign country and use his or her position to save others (despite initially being a passive character, and despite being forgotten at a crucial moment), but also on the use of shared motifs such as two eunuchs who act against the king (Gen. 40.1-3; Est. 2.21-23), the king having troubled nithts (Gen. 41.9-45; Est. 6.1-11), the banqueting scenses, the reversals of fortune, the hangings- and there are even some instances of parallel phrsing such as Gen. 41.42-43//Est. 6.11; Gen. 39.10//Est. 3.4; Gen. 44.34//Est. 8.6.

It can, however, be objected (e.g Berg, Fox) that the similarities of phrasing are rather ordinary so that their force depends on valid comparisons of other kinds being made between the two texts, and that in fact the amount of weight given to the comparable themes and motifs varies greatly from story to story. Fox raises the serious objection that Joseph deals with voluntary exile in hard times-hardly something that the book of Esther wishes to advocate.

One further scholar should be mentioned in this connection. Mentioned has described the connection between Joseph and Esther as being due primarily to a shared structure, which, however, Esther puts to the service of a more secularized intellectual attitude stemming from its transmission in a different (i.e disaspra) community. The difficulty with this thesis is that the structural units Meinhold identifies in Joseph are sometimes overlapping and non-successive, and it looks as though he has in practice imposed the structure of Esther on Joseph's story, which is the opposite move to the one he seeks to demonstrate (so Berg). Interestingly, the Joseph story, like the book of Esther, is not referred to elsewhere in the Bible. Perhaps, therefore, both are late, with Joseph being written between 650 and 425 BC, although this view would be controversial.

To sum up, it appears that Esther may be in some sense a reinterpretation of the Joseph story, but that the reasons are not clear and the divergences between the two are as important as the similarities. There is insufficient ground for describing either as historicized wisdom tale.

**Relation to Other Contemporaneous Literature**

Linda Day and others have noted that Esther bears certain likenesses to Hellenistic novels or 'romances' in its structure, its interest in luxury, its satiric quality, its erotic concern with the Persian king's love-life and its portrayal of the heroine as a young, attractive victim, somewhat alone and at the mercy of impersonal controlling forces. Of course it is the Additons that move most to ward these Greek norms, but even with the Additons the Esther story remains distinctively different from the 'romance' genre in that eroticism and adventure are not the dominant concerns in any of the versions.

Esther can also bear partial comparison with other Jewish literature of the same period, such as the books of Judith and Susamma, which are alike in tending to expand the rolds of female characters; or Daniel 1-6, a comparison that Fox finds interesting because the two are though close in date still different enough not to have been produced by imitation or borrowing, so that one can deduce that both were shaped by something external to either-the attitudes and goals of their time.

**Esther as Folklore**

Finally, it should be mentioned that Niditch cuts a way through the multifarious comparisons of Esther with other tales by suggesting that they are caused by the shared use of 'traditional style composition' which inhabits 'the gray are where idion meets formula', and is typical of folklore. Folktales are also often made of combinations of plots, and this too is a feature of Esther in which some scholars have claimed to identify more than one 'source' story, while others have insisted that the work is a untiy. The book is keenly interested in peremmially popular topics such as the exercise of authority, and the behavior of women and foreigners, and it champions the trickster and underdog as it promotes an ironic form of justics. The characteristics which made Talmon allocate Esther to the wisdom tradition could very well locate it in the folk tradion instead. Readers who wish to pursue the comparison will find that many of the motifs used in Esther (the banished wife, the foolish king) feature in Thompson's Motif Index of folklore. It will be noticed that the more one inclines to see Esther as folklore, the less probable it appears that the book is history. Scholarships need not doom themselves, says Brenner, to look for this 'mirror kingdom.

## Internal Structure and Literary Techniques

In a phase of scholarly criticism now ending, the study of any biblical text as literature was in fact done with an eye to historical matters. And a prior assumption was made that the text could be analysed into portions stemming from different hands (identifiable on grounds of internal consistency) and /or segments of oral tradition (which can be recognized because they take on arrange of characteristic forms), the whole being put together by a redactor – or perhaps a sequence of redactors. In this way, the pre-history of the received text could be reconstructed and each element allocated to this most likely historical setting. This type of scholarship, which has been dominant for at least a century, is losing its hegemony for two main reasons, on positive and the other negative. The negative reason is that its favored tools (source criticism, form criticism and redaction criticism) are now seen to be methodologically flawed: partly incompatible and by no means 'objective' in that scholars of equal integrity and competence could and did apply the methods and reach widely divergent conclusions the positive reason is that insofar as historical criticism does produce results which command a wide degree of acceptance its task is largely complete. Scholarships can move on to apply new tools to its task-principally tools which study how texts function as wholes in their present form, tools which can produce refreshing insights that cut across the findings of historical criticism but are of course no more 'objective'. Modern scholarship has made the fundamental discovery that 'objectivity' is something of a chimera.

This change is readily apparent in Esther scholarship. Historical criticism had already by the beginning of this century cast doubt on the historicity of the tale, but the analytical and excavative method can of course equally be applied to the illumination of the pre-history of a text which is not historical. Indeed, the quest to uncover the stages by which the Esther tradition grew is, as explained in Chapter 9 above, very much a live area of study, dominated by Clines and more recently widened by Milik, Day and others. This discussion is unusual in that it is as much or more interested in stages of the Esther tradition which post-date the Masoretic text as it is in the stages that predate it. But here is the possibility of applying source and redaction criticism to the Masoretic text that will first concern us.

Two significant scholars in this field are Cazelles and Bardtke. Cazelles, nothing that a prominent feature of Esther is its 'twoness' (two lists of the king's servants [1.10, 14]; two references to assembling the women [2.8, 19]; two consultations between Haman and his wife and friends [5.14; 6.13]; two unsummoned appearances by Esther before the king [5.2; 8.3]; two accounts of the deaths of Haman's sons [9.6-10, 13-14]; two fasts [4.1-3, 16]; two feasts hosted by Ahasuerus in ch. 1 and two by Esther in 5.5 and 7.1; all leading up to two days for the festival of Purim!) suggested that Esther is a conflation of two stories. One could be a 'liturgical' text drawing upon a bacchanalian Persian new year festival and centring round Esther and the people of the Persian provinces, while the other could be more 'historical', centring on Mordecai and on intrigues at court having to do with a persecution of the Jews of Susa.

A variant of this theory, suggested by Bardtke, is essentially that there were three stories, two being much as described by Cazelles and the third being the brief story of Vashti the deposed Persian queen, which perhaps began as an apocryphal harem tale. Bardtke suggested that the author of Esther had all these stories at this dispoal in some lost Jewish midrashic collection and innocently combined them by identifying Esther with Mordecai's niece (named as 'Hadassah, that is Esther' in 2.7).

The evidence of 'two ness' is undeniable, and it is odd that the book has one bad character but two good ones. Nevertheless, it is fair to object as Berg does that the 'seams' in Esther are not all that visible; even the Vashti story which at first sight se3ems easily detachable from the rest, is essential to the whole story because it explains how Esther, a lowly Jewess, came to be queen at all, and gives some indication of how dangerous it will be for her ever to disobey Ahasuerus. The other supposedly separate stories are even more difficult to separate or reconstruct, and it is noteworthy that even Clines, who of course does doubt that the MT of Esther is an authorial unity confines his suspicions to the marial in chs. 9 and 10

Another proponent of historical criticism who should be specially mentioned Dommershausen, who has done the most careful form –critical work on Esther, lableling all the components in turn (e.g ESt. 1 'narration', 2.1-4 'servant speech'; 2.5-7 'biographical note' and so on) and examining the precise ways in which the literary techniques used vary from the Esther norm and thus magnify the effect of key scenes in the story. Dommershausen's work is a good illustration of the fact that historical criticism at its best does pay faithful attention to the literary feature of the text under study and indeed is founded on them. But he has also been criticized (Berg) for displaying the weakness of historical criticism, namely that he has failed to see how each of his 'forms' is influenced by its context and thus appreciates fully how the book pulls together as a whole, as a complete short story.

The most schematic understanding of the structure of Esther is that of Radday (1973) who suggested a chiastic scheme, but this is overshimplified.

How does the story function as a whole? Alter describes biblical narrative as containing elaborately integrated systems in a scale ascending from the leitwort to the motif to the theme (an idea which is part of the value system of the narrative), and finally to the sequence of action; the last three of these are 'significant structuring principles in Esther.

On the broadest level, Esther is a classic linear tale with a beginning (1.1-2.23), middle (3.1-9.19) End (9.20-10.3), separated not only by distinctive subject matter but also by chronological gaps. The first phase is leisurely, taking some six years, the second more stressful taking place within a year (and much of the key action within eitghteen days,), and the third has broadened out into the continuing time in which the festival of Purim I celebrated regularly. As to its theme, Esther has been described as a 'politico-philosophical guide to life and survival' (so Brenner in the Companion to Esther), dealing particularly with how the poerless can achieve their goals, and with the inversion of fate; it can also be seen as meditating on the nature of law.

On the next level, there are several important structuring devices. One is the recurrence of the motif of feasting: Esther has twenty of the forty-six occurrences of misteb in the Hebrew Bible, and feasting is the dominant motif of Purim itself. Feasts, of which there are ten in all (and the subsidiary motif of fasts) are important occasions for bringing out the irony of the tale, as characters gain and lose power. They may also emphasize the honour and wealth of the main protagonists, not only Ahasuerus at the beginning, but also by implication the Jewish community feasting at Purim at the end. With Mordecai arguably presiding as king, on the basis that the feasting motif appears in the very first chapter, in the tow fold form that will be reflected in the two-day observance of Purim at the end of the book, Berg argues that the whole book does lead up to the institution of Purim, a connection some have denied, although she admits that it is not clear that the original narrator knew the festival by that name.

Reversal is also a major structuring device, espeiecially in the secion from Esther 3-8 inclusive. Fox and Berg have independently argued for a series of 'theses' and 'antitheses' which mirror each other in the book, and Berg believes that the turning point comes with the end of the 'theses' in 4.13-14 (between the two fasts, the two royal edicts, and the main pairs of banquets) and the start of the 'antitheses', although Fox locates it at 6.10 between Esther's tow banquets, the point at which the actions begin to make good the reversals hinted at in the unfolding of the story. The author has made highly effective use of peripety, defined by Aristotle in his Poetics as an action or situation producing the opposite of the intended result. Brenner (Companion to Esther) has not only explored the way in which symmetries and repetitions mirror the 'inversion of fate's theme but also categorizes. A set of eleven duplication and multiplication techniques used in Esther. None of these is unique to Esther but their cumulative weight is 'quite exceptional' and surely forms part of the message of the book, as well as its medium. (Moore, c.1977)

Kingship is a dominant motif. The *mlk* root which stands behind the words for 'king' 'queen' and 'rule' occurs over 250 times in 167 verses. (Repetiton is Esther's most characteristic literary weakness, which is why the Greek translator found it possible to 'fillet' the book.) Berg speculates that the Purim feasts were hosted by royalty and that this was part of their nationalistic attraction.

Related to the kingship motif is that of obedience and disobedience. It is noticeable that only the Jews are rewarded for the latter. Unlike Vashti, Esther appears before the king when she wishes to (5.1), and even makes the king appear at her banquets, twice! The obedience/disobedience motif hints at an important function of the Esther story in a community living in circumstances never envisaged by the Torah. (Dat, the word used for law in Esther, is only otherwise found in Deut. 33.2 and Ezra 8.36) Not even the Law, it seems, takes precedence over the community's welafare. Jewish identity may be dangerous to the holder and may demand self sacrifice of them, so that mutual loyalty-which does not exclude loyalty to the foreign power –is of paramount importance. The author is convinced that loyalty to both the temporal ruler and to Judaism is possible in an alien state and indeed essential in that the future of Judaism is largely bound up with the future of diaspora Jews.

It is even possible that the way in which the many coincidences that are a feature of Esther occur in connection with peripety is intended to convey the subliminal message that the Jews are meant by God to inviolable. This is a controversial point for two reasons First, one message of the book is probably that humans have to make a 'correct' response to history, it history despite its expected course is to 'radically realign itself in a favorable direction'. It contains the danger of a false 'divine right' theology – or more properly an ideology. These are both reasons that could explain why the author has been so reluctant to mention God (even when it is difficult to avoid doing so, as in 4.14 and the fasting scenes). From the standpoint of Judaism, this does not mean that the book beleves in blind fate rather than the providence of God, but it does mean that God's providence is veiled in everyday life; the book stops short, however, of caliming overtly that the Jews have a special place in the divine purpose. Its partial secularity is deliberate.

It remains to consider the role of characterization in forming the theology of Esther. A new departure here has been made by Fox who devotes much of the second half of his commentary volume to studies of Vashti, Xerxes, Haman, Mordecai, Esther, the Jews collectively, God despite his never being mentioned) and the World. This is a direct counter position to that of Moore, who stated that the major characters in Esther are 'so superficially drawn that it is difficult to identify very long or intensively with either the book's villains or heroes.

It is, however, very instructive to see how Fox's surveys of previous responses to these supposedly cardboard characters reveal a great range of responses, as readers project their own thouthts into the silences. Paradocically, the flattest character emerges as that of Mordecai, whose behavior is always direct, shows no development, but is ultimately opaque. The others, though sketchily drawn, function as effectively and suggestively as the characters in fairy-tale.

Work on the relative literary characteristics of the versions is also well under way. The complexity of this task, already hinted at in the discussion in Chapter 9 above on the identification of social contexts for each of the versions, is under lined by the fact that two case studies by Kristin de Troyer on Est. 2.8-18 and Timothuy Beal on Esther 1 (both in the companion to  Esther), reach opposite conclusions as to the 'gender' of the A and B texts, finding that the Masoretic text and the A-text are covertly male, but that the B-text softens the bias; finding the Masoretic text's sympathy for Vashti to have trace effects over the whole book. This difference of opinion no doubt reflects the difficulty of attempting to 'gender' texts, that is, to ascertain whether they relfct or promote characteristically male of female concerns, at all.

However, Day's comparative study of the characterization of Esther in all three of the major versions raises different concerns, offering both a suggested methodology for the assessment of character (Three Faces of a Queen, pp.24-25) in literature, and some observations on the implications of the three very different Esthers that emerge. Day wishes to argue that it is the Esther story in essence that is or should be canonical, not a particular version, so that all the Estheres should be equally valid concerns for feminist criticism. The versions should be viewed as extensions of the well-known inner-biblical phenomenon of providing doublets or other multiples of its material (culminating in the provision of four Gospels). Each had different insights to offer, and those which do not happen to be in the Bible may sometimes prove to contain 'more orginal' or otherwise preferable' material. It will be evident that this raises very large questions which protestant and Catholic traditions happen to have favored different version) than in the case of other books. But it is a question that may spread into the interpretation of the other biblical books in the next phase of biblical study, reflecting the modern view what the Bible is not so much an authoritative source as an invaluable resource.

### 5.2. Theme, Purpose of the book:

**THEME AND PURPOSE**

It is widely recognized that in narrative genres, resolution and denouement play a crucial role in determining the theme and purpose of the work. This is because the relationship between events in a narrative often follows a cause-effect pattern (whether stimulus-response or occasion-outcome), and the effects, naturally, are emphasized more than the causes. As such, these discourse elements—resolution and denouement—are key to understanding the central and dominant idea of the plot.

This concept directly informs the theme and purpose of Esther, which has a dual nature. This duality is evident in the contrast between the "problem-resolution" elements and the "denouement" that follows. The denouement does not merely describe the outcomes of the problem-resolution sequence; rather, it outlines the dates, significance, and character of the Purim festival, while also aiming to establish its permanent observance within the Jewish community. Despite this apparent incongruity with the problem-based plot, the denouement draws from the story to explain the origins of the festival. Thus, understanding the theme and purpose of the story itself is essential before we turn to the theme and purpose of the denouement.

## A. The Theme and Purpose of the "Problem-Based Plot" of Esther 1:1-9:5; 10:1-3

### 1. General Considerations

The theme of Esther's narrative can be seen in the portrayal of the dangerous and unpredictable nature of life for Jews in the diaspora. This element plays a significant role in shaping the plot throughout the book.

### a. The Role of Non-Speech Narration

One notable feature of Esther is the use of non-speech narration, which serves as the primary method of plot development and characterization. This approach contrasts with the narrative style of the Book of Ruth, where the plot is advanced mainly through dialogue, which reveals the character of the protagonists. In contrast, Esther uses narration to move the plot forward, which gives the plot structure and development an equal, if not greater, role in determining the story's theme and purpose.

## b. The "Domain" of the Narrative

An important aspect of the story is the domain in which it unfolds. Almost all of the events in Esther, except for two brief scenes in Haman's home (5:9-14; 6:12-14) and the brief description of the final Jewish victory (9:1-5), occur within the royal court of Persia. Some of these scenes even take place in the throne room and the king's private quarters. Three of the main characters—King Ahasuerus, Queen Esther, and the Grand Vizier Haman—are central figures in the court, with Mordecai eventually replacing Haman. The story is deeply invested in the themes of power and wealth, as shown by the fact that Radday notes that, of the 3,270 words in the book, 439 words relate to concepts such as staff, etiquette, and wealth. Therefore, the narrative is firmly set in the heart of the royal power that governs its world.

## 2.The "World" of the Story: The Jewish Diaspora

Within the larger domain of the Persian court, the narrower world of the story is that of the Jewish diaspora. Two key elements in the narrative establish this context clearly:

## a. The Significance of Mordecai's Title, "The Jew"

Mordecai's designation as "the Jew" when he is introduced in the story is a crucial aspect of his identity throughout the book (Esther 2:5; 5:13; 6:10; 8:7; 9:31; 10:3). This epithet is not just a simple identification but serves to highlight his role in the story. It is notable because, in the entire Old Testament, this is the only instance where a native member of Israel is identified by a gentilic rather than a patronymic. For example, foreigners who lived in Israel were often identified by their country of origin, such as "Uriah the Hittite" or "Ittai the Gittite." However, Mordecai is always referred to as "Mordecai the Jew" to emphasize his status as a diaspora Jew. This signifies that "Jewishness" in the context of Esther is closely tied to diaspora existence.

## b. The Narrative's "Diaspora Agenda"

Another important feature of Esther is its focus on the Jewish diaspora. The book provides an example of God's salvation in the diaspora, contrasting with other post-exilic literature such as the books of Isaiah, Haggai, Zechariah, Obadiah, Ezra-Nehemiah, and Daniel, which primarily focus on the return of exiled Jews to Israel. While these other works emphasize the rebuilding of Jerusalem and the temple as the ultimate form of divine redemption, Esther portrays God's deliverance occurring within the diaspora itself. This marks a shift in the traditional view of the exile, which was generally seen in negative terms— as a period that was valuable only in preparation for the return. In contrast, Esther offers a positive view of Jewish life in exile, showing that salvation is possible even when the Jewish people are outside their homeland.

 The key term here is "remained." Humphreys has argued that Jeremiah's message to the exiles (Jer 29:4-7) introduces a unique approach to life in exile, where the exiles are encouraged to engage with the foreign culture they find themselves in. However, Jeremiah's intention was not to establish a permanent diaspora lifestyle. Instead, he emphasizes the reality of the exile, which was expected to last for around seventy years, serving as a form of judgment (as seen in verses 8-14), rather than setting the groundwork for a sustainable and permanent existence outside of Israel. While this tradition might have been preserved within Jewish diaspora communities and could have influenced the way they rebuilt their lives and theological perspectives, the idea of a permanent diaspora existence was not given meaningful attention in post-exilic literature.

The contrast between the concerns of the Judeans in the diaspora and the focus of post-exilic literature in Palestine is sharply evident in the book of Esther, especially when considering three significant examples from Persian to Hellenistic times:

(i) Nehemiah, like Mordecai, holds an important position in the Persian court in Susa. However, his entire focus is on the restoration of Jerusalem (Neh 1-2), to which he returns (2:5). When introduced in Susa, Nehemiah is referred to as "Nehemiah son of Hacaliah" (1:1), and in Jerusalem, his title is "Nehemiah the governor" (8:9; 10:1; 12:26). Therefore, Nehemiah's life and actions cannot be seen, as

Humphreys suggests, as evidence of a lifestyle for the diaspora. Nehemiah's heart is firmly set on Zion, and this is equally true for the narrator of the book of Nehemiah.

(ii) Daniel also serves in the Persian court, but the focus of the Book of Daniel is on the future of the Judean community in Palestine. Daniel prays facing Jerusalem (Dan 6:10-11), expresses anguish over the seventy years of devastation prophesied for Jerusalem, and receives a vision about its future (Dan 9).

(iii) Zerubbabel, Darius' personal bodyguard, requests the rebuilding of Jerusalem and the temple when promised anything he desires. His focus is on restoring the temple vessels and rebuilding the holy city.

In stark contrast, the Book of Esther follows a very different agenda. Neither Esther nor Mordecai expresses any concern about Jerusalem, the temple, or its religious practices. Even after the threat of Haman's decree is removed and the enemies of the Jews are defeated, Esther and Mordecai do not show any particular interest in Palestine. Their singular focus is on establishing the festival that commemorates the deliverance in the diaspora (see Mordecai's decree in 9:20-22 and Esther's in 9:29-32). In the praise of Mordecai, "the Jew," it is specifically "among the Jews" (i.e., the diaspora) that he is honored, and it is their welfare, and that of their descendants, that he constantly seeks (10:3).

Unlike the broader post-exilic literature of Israel, which is concerned with the restoration of the land and the temple, the Book of Esther focuses specifically on the concerns of the Jewish diaspora. It paints a picture of the diaspora world as a perilous and uncertain place for the Jewish people.

1, The Narrator's Characterization of the Protagonists: As mentioned in the Genre section above, one of the clearest ways the narrator reveals the quality of the situation is through the characterization of the protagonists. This is evident in the portrayal of each of the main characters.

**a. The characterization of the king and his realm**:

The story's theme, which highlights the dangers and uncertainties of life for Jews in the diaspora, is primarily seen through the depiction of the environment in which the story unfolds. This is first established in the exposition of the book, primarily in the first two chapters. In most Old Testament narratives, the exposition (what Alter refers to as "expository information") consists of brief statements, offering background details that aren't tied to a specific time but rather lay the groundwork for the story. The Book of Esther, however, diverges from this typical structure. While it introduces us to the major characters—Ahasuerus, Esther, and Mordecai—the events of the exposition go beyond being a mere prelude. Instead of concise recounting, the narrator expands these facts into a more detailed and embellished narrative, achieving much more than just telling a story. Through satire and parody, the narrator sets the stage for the world in which the events of the story will unfold.

This is especially clear in the opening scenes of chapters 1:1-22. Here, we encounter an orderly, yet unstable world ruled by an unyielding law. However, this law provides little assurance of stability or justice for those under its control. The law is irrevocable (1:19), but its foundation lies in the whims of an all-powerful king (1:1), portrayed in the first section of the story as spending his time hosting extravagant banquets. The first banquet is humorously exaggerated, lasting an unbelievable six months, showcasing the king's wealth and grandeur (1:4). The lavish setting of the second banquet, marked by excessive wine flowing freely, further illustrates the opulence of the king and his court (vv. 5-8).

In the second episode (1:10-22), the king is portrayed humorously as losing a battle of wills with his wife, Vashti, when he demands she appear before him, adorned with her crown, for display in front of the drunken guests. Vashti, however, shows the only sense of dignity and respect in this extravagant world by refusing to comply. Unable to solve the situation on his own, the king turns to his council, whose comically inflated titles and ridiculous legal advice serve as a mockery of their wisdom. The sages, described as "those who understand the times" and "who know law and legal process" (1:13), ultimately issue an absurd and irrevocable decree that all women, regardless of status, must honor their husbands, and every man should be ruler in his own household (1:20, 1:22). This scene establishes the king as a vain and pompous ruler, obsessed with honor and prone to impulsive actions. His reliance on his council for even the most personal matters highlights his ineffectiveness as a leader. In stark contrast to the king's behavior, Vashti's refusal to be paraded like a common object before the drunken crowd adds a layer of critique, as the narrator mocks the opulence and excesses of the world in which the story takes place.

The opening scene of the story does provide some essential details needed for the narrative, but the narrator uses these facts satirically to depict the world in which the story unfolds. This type of humor is "tendentious," as it serves not only to mock but also to reveal the conditions that diaspora Jews must endure, providing both ridicule and a lesson.

This tone of satire continues in the second act (2:1-18). While recounting Esther's rise to queenship, the narrative also mocks the indulgent and hedonistic nature of this world (see Explanation). For example, when the king regrets banishing Vashti, his young servants advise him not to form a political alliance through marriage with one of the powerful families in the empire, which could have strengthened his rule. Instead, they suggest that he gather beautiful young women from across the empire and select the one who pleases him most to replace Vashti as queen (2:4). The first requirement for pleasing the king is described in an exaggerated and mocking manner: the women undergo beauty treatments for a full year (2:12). The second criterion, while phrased more delicately, is equally transparent. "In the evening, she would go in, and in the morning she would return to the harem, but now under the custody of Shaashgazz, the king's eunuch in charge of the concubines. She would not return to the king unless he took pleasure in her and summoned her by name" (2:14). By subtly implying that the king's and his courtiers' only criteria for selecting a queen are a woman's physical beauty and sexual appeal, the narrator casts a sarcastic light on the Persian monarch and his court. After exposing the king's extravagant display of wealth and the absurdity of his court in the earlier chapters, where laws are created to uphold their dominance, the narrative now reveals them as shallow men who view the woman fit to rule beside the king based solely on her appearance and sexual performance.

The portrayal of the king as a man indulgent in excess, driven by impulse, obsessed with his own honor (see Fox, 171-177), and incapable of making decisions independently, aligns with how he is depicted throughout the narrative. For instance, in a later scene, when Haman presents his outrageous plan to exterminate an unnamed group within the empire for trivial reasons, and offers a large bribe, it is the king's self-absorbed preoccupation with his own pleasures that leads him to grant Haman full authority without question. He dismisses the matter with the casual remark, "Do with the people and the money as you please" (3:11) (see also discussions in the Explanations to 5:7-8; 6:1-11; 7:8c-10; 8:3-8).

Thus, the narrator's characterization of the king and the Persian court continues to emphasize the absurdity and instability of the world they rule. The satire, while mocking, also serves a critical purpose. It exposes a world governed by a self-indulgent ruler, who is not inherently evil but is impulsive, easily swayed by those around him, including his nobles (1:10-22), his servants (2:1-4), his grand vizier (3:7-11), and even his queen (5:1-8; 7:1-10). The king's world, while not malicious by design, is clearly dangerous. It is a world where the law holds no guarantee of justice or security (Fox, 249). Instead, it is easily manipulated by those with fragile egos who can bend the state's authority to their personal gain.

Nevertheless, this unstable world, while perilous, is not inherently hostile to the Jews. The reaction of the people in Susa to Haman's decree (3:15d), in contrast to the detached indifference of the king and Haman, reveals that the only real enemies of the Jews are those few who "hoped to triumph over them" and those who "sought to do them harm" (9:1-2).

The opening satire thus sets the stage for a world fraught with uncertainty, where Jews must navigate a dangerous existence in the diaspora. As Fox (249) points out, "Such a world is not inherently evil, but it provides fertile ground for terrifying dangers." The scope of these dangers is evident in the magnitude of the crisis that follows. While the Jewish community had experienced the devastation of their capital and temple in Babylonian exile and would face similar tragedies under Antiochus Epiphanes, the threat posed by Haman's decree is far more chilling. Though the narrative subtly reassures the reader that the threat will not be executed, the nature of the danger underscores the precariousness of life for Jews in the diaspora, constantly vulnerable to annihilation, even within a seemingly ordered society.

## b. The characterization of Haman.

The gravity of the crisis is not only conveyed by the nature of the situation but also by the relentless depiction of Haman, the one responsible for it. Like Mordecai, Haman is portrayed as the ultimate adversary of the Jews, which is emphasized through his epithet, reiterated at key moments in the narrative (see 3:10; 8:1; cf. also 9:10, 24; see especially the Explanation to 3:1-6). However, Haman is not defined merely by his title or even by his actions, as is Mordecai (see below). His true character is revealed through the narrator's direct observations, especially regarding his internal thoughts. Haman's emotions, motivations, and actions are laid bare by the narrator, who provides direct access to his feelings and internal monologues. His inner turmoil is made transparent to the audience, and the narrator leaves no room for mystery. Apart from some references to the king's actions and emotions (his anger in 1:12; 7:7; his pleasure in 1:21; 2:4; his affection for Esther in 2:17), it is Haman's feelings that the narrator continually exposes. For example, Haman's anger is evident in 3:5 and 5:9, his joy in 5:9, his shame and grief in 6:12, and his fear in 7:6. The narrator also reveals Haman's thoughts (6:6), deliberations (3:6), and perceptions (7:7). In contrast, Mordecai and Esther's personalities are mainly shown through their actions and speech. For instance, Mordecai's grief is communicated solely through his actions (4:1), whereas Haman's grief and shame are directly stated (6:12).

This characterization suggests that Haman's anti-Semitism is not merely a result of racial or religious animosity (cf. Fox, 181), even though the author subtly hints at such underlying enmity by playing on Haman's and Mordecai's backgrounds. Instead, Haman's evil stems from his immense pride and fragile ego. His deep-seated sense of inferiority is what drives him, as revealed in the first three scenes in which he appears. In 3:1-6, his wounded pride cannot be healed by the mere destruction of his enemy. It is only through the complete annihilation of the Jewish people that he believes his anger will be assuaged. In 5:9-14, Haman admits to his wife and friends that everything else in his life feels meaningless due to the existence of one man, Mordecai (see Explanation). And in 6:1-11, when the king speaks of "the man whom the king desires to honor," Haman's inflated ego leads him to assume that the king is referring to him, prompting him to propose the honor of Mordecai instead. Thus, Haman is depicted as the embodiment of irrational evil.

The fact that such unhinged evil can so easily manipulate the power structures of Persia makes the world of the diaspora all the more dangerous and uncertain. However, this is not the central theme of the story. The narrative is not merely about human courage or cleverness (contrary to Humphreys' view, which suggests that the story presents "a style of life for the diaspora Jew that affirms that the Jew can remain loyal to his heritage and God and yet live a creative, rewarding, and fulfilled life within a foreign setting"). The theme must encompass the resolution of the story, which is brought about by the actions of Mordecai and Esther (for the role of resolution in determining theme, see the discussion in the Theme and Purpose section of the Introduction to *Ruth*). Therefore, we now turn to the narrator's depiction of the roles played by Mordecai, Esther, and the Jewish people.

## b. The characterization of Mordecai.

The enormity of the threat posed by Haman's edict is chillingly portrayed, but the core message of the story is not merely the reversal of this decree—it is how the reversal unfolds. The salvation of the Jewish people is not solely due to divine intervention but also hinges on the access to power that Mordecai and Esther possess.

Though Mordecai is the key figure in the narrative (see Fox, 185, and the discussion of the denouement [9:6-32] and Purim below), he does not take the lead in reversing the edict. That honor belongs to Esther (see below). However, Mordecai plays a pivotal role in initiating the reversal and is introduced first as one of the book's central characters. His importance to the story's theme is indicated early on, notably in 2:5, where he is identified with the epithet "a Jewish man." This label is significant not only for his role in the plot but also for his character development (see Fox's insightful study of Mordecai, 185-95). The use of this epithet in 2:5 is especially notable because, strictly speaking, it is not necessary. His patronymic and family lineage could have been enough to identify him. Additionally, Mordecai is consistently referred to as "Mordecai the Jew" throughout the story, particularly when the identification is essential to the plot. For instance, Haman refers to him as the one whose existence renders his world meaningless (5:13); the king uses the same epithet to identify him when he honors Mordecai (6:13); and the narrator highlights his role in countering Haman's decree (8:7). This identification establishes Mordecai not just as a character but as the quintessential Jew. Mordecai's status at the story's conclusion—where he is robed in royalty (8:15) and gains power both in Susa and throughout the empire—further reinforces his symbolic role as a representative of Jewish survival and triumph. In the final encomium (10:3), Mordecai is described as second in rank only to the king himself, a powerful figure among his people.

Mordecai's actions throughout the story underscore his loyalty, especially to Esther, whom he raised (2:7, 10-11), and to the king (2:21-23). Most importantly, he is unwaveringly loyal to the Jewish people. Every action he takes is motivated by the desire to protect and save the Jews (for instance, his public lamentation in 4:1-3 is aimed at drawing Esther's attention to Haman's decree). It is through Mordecai's urging that Esther eventually risks appealing to the king. Furthermore, Mordecai devises the clever solution to counter the irrevocable edict, issuing a new decree that nullifies Haman's (see Explanation to 8:9-14). His unwavering commitment to his people is epitomized in 10:3, where he is praised for his constant pursuit of their welfare.

Despite the deep loyalty that defines Mordecai's character, the narrator never explicitly describes his emotions or thoughts. In stark contrast to Haman, whose feelings are often laid bare (see above), Mordecai's internal world remains largely mysterious. His words are quoted only once, when he convinces Esther to approach the king

(4:13-14). Remarkably, even when Mordecai communicates with Esther in earlier passages, the narrator often opts for indirect discourse, which keeps his true motivations ambiguous (see the structure and Explanation to 4:4-17). This leaves us to wonder about Mordecai's personal motivations, especially regarding his refusal to bow to Haman. The only suggestion offered is the long-standing tribal enmity between Mordecai and Haman (see Explanation to 3:1-6), but this only deepens the mystery of his character.

Thus, Mordecai's character is primarily defined by his single-minded loyalty to the Jewish people. He embodies the archetype of the ideal diaspora Jew, representing what the community should aspire to in terms of loyalty, integrity, and action. However, his characterization as a "flat" or "type" character suggests that his role is less about personal depth and more about embodying the ideal of diaspora Jewish resilience.

**d. The characterization of Esther.**

While Mordecai is the first hero introduced in the story and the instigator of the reversal of Haman's edict; it is Esther who plays the most crucial role in effecting this reversal. As such, she becomes the focal point of the narrative, and her character is central to the unfolding plot. Unlike the other characters, who are largely defined by a single characteristic (the king's impulsive self-indulgence, Haman's pride, and Mordecai's loyalty), Esther is depicted with complexity and depth, as her character undergoes significant development over the course of the story. This complexity is achieved largely through her actions and speech, rather than through direct statements about her feelings or motivations, as is the case with Haman.

Esther's introduction is subtle and indirect. Initially, she is presented as Mordecai's ward, a role that remains significant even after she becomes queen (as seen in 2:10, 20, where she continues to obey Mordecai). The narrator conveys Esther's arrival in the king's harem as an unavoidable fate, expressed through passive verbs ("the king's edict was proclaimed … many young women were gathered … Esther too was taken," 2:8). However, as the story progresses, the portrayal of Esther shifts. Though her beauty and favor with Hegai (the king's eunuch) are emphasized, suggesting an almost passive participation in the events, there is a growing indication that she is not merely an object to be acted upon. Her role becomes more active as the story advances.

Esther's transformation is most striking in the exchange between her and Mordecai in 4:4-17. This is a turning point in her development, as she shifts from being a passive participant to an active leader. When Mordecai urges her to approach the king on behalf of the Jews, Esther initially hesitates, citing the risk to her life as she has not been summoned by the king for thirty days (4:11). Mordecai counters this by reminding her that her own survival is at stake and suggesting that perhaps she has become queen for such a time as this (4:14). Esther's response is not one of resignation but of determination—she agrees to take action, and her resolve is evident as she orders a three-day fast in preparation for her appeal to the king (4:15-16). Her final words, "If I perish, I perish," are a courageous expression of her willingness to risk everything for her people.

This marks a decisive shift in Esther's character. Before this moment, she had been under Mordecai's guidance and authority; now she takes charge, issuing orders and setting the conditions for her appeal to the king. In the narrator's summary in 4:17, a striking contrast is drawn between Mordecai's previous directive to Esther and the new authority she exerts, as Mordecai now obeys her orders.

Esther's transformation continues in the events of chapters 5 and 7, where she fully assumes control. Her approach to the king is strategic and courageous, using her position and her appeal to his affection to gain leverage. The banquet strategy she employs is entirely her own, and she executes it with skill and shrewdness, eventually getting the king to commit himself to granting her request before she even reveals it (5:7-8). Her second banquet is a masterstroke of diplomacy, where she tactfully and subtly places the blame on Haman while maintaining the king's favor (7:1-6a).

In the final chapters, Esther secures a victory for the Jews, first by ensuring that Haman's wealth and power are transferred to Mordecai (8:1-2) and then by using her charm and wit to convince the king to revoke Haman's edict and allow the Jews to defend themselves (8:3-8). Esther's role in the reversal of the edict is both heroic and central to the Jews' deliverance.

Esther's character arc represents a profound transformation. She begins as a passive and objectified figure, valued only for her beauty, but she becomes the central agent in the salvation of her people. Her courage, resourcefulness, and diplomacy make her the primary force behind the Jews' deliverance. Unlike the other characters, whose motivations are largely consistent throughout the story, Esther's growth reflects the complexities of living in a foreign, patriarchal world where women were often devalued. Yet, through her actions, Esther proves herself a model of resilience, courage, and leadership.

Her development as a leader, despite the constraints of her environment, makes Esther a dynamic and complex character. Her transformation from a passive figure into a force to be reckoned with stands as a testament to her personal strength and the crucial role that women can play even in oppressive circumstances. Esther, therefore, becomes not just an ideal figure in the narrative, but one whose character and actions resonate with the resilience and agency of Jewish people, particularly within the context of the diaspora.

Her story challenges the conventions of her time and provides a model for leadership, courage, and sacrifice that has reverberated throughout history.

**e. The characterization of the Jews.**

The Jewish people are an ever-present force throughout the Book of Esther, but they are not given an explicit introduction in the exposition (chapters 1-2). The mention of Mordecai as "a Jewish man" hints at the existence of the Jewish people, yet they are not described directly in the narrative. Instead, their presence is most notably felt through the perspective of their enemies, particularly Haman, the Agagite. Haman's portrayal of the Jews is significant: they are described as "scattered," "unassimilated," and as having "laws different from those of every other people" (3:7-11). These attributes emphasize the Jews' distinctiveness and their separation from the wider Persian world, suggesting they live as outsiders within the empire.

The narrative never directly characterizes the Jews as a collective group, nor do they speak directly in the first part of the story. Instead, the Jews are portrayed passively, as a group acting only in response to events. The first time they act is when they mourn and fast after hearing of Haman's edict (4:3). They then celebrate and feast after Mordecai's counter-edict, marking a dramatic reversal (8:17). Throughout these events, the Jews remain passive actors, with their actions presented using impersonal, passive constructions. Their role, until the resolution, is largely passive waiting for events to unfold as others shape their fate.

However, this passivity changes in the final resolution of the crisis. After Mordecai's counter-edict is issued, the Jews take active measures to protect themselves (9:1-5). Here, they are portrayed as acting independently, in accordance with the law, and their actions signal a crucial shift in the plot. While their actions are described in brief and summary fashion, this shift marks a significant moment in the narrative. The Jewish people, once passive, are now acting decisively in their own defense. Additionally, they establish the festival of Purim, further demonstrating their active participation in their own delivery (9:23-28).

Importantly, the Jews are not depicted as hostile toward the Persian court or the Persian world at large. There is no evidence in the text to suggest that the Jews harbor any inherent animosity toward the empire. Their only adversaries are those who actively seek to harm them. The story portrays no conflict between the Jewish people and the Persian society they live within, and the narrative shows that they are accepted by the Persian court, as evidenced by their ability to gain royal favor and support.

Despite this, there are moral complexities in the narrative, particularly with the actions of Mordecai and Esther. First, Mordecai's refusal to bow to Haman is presented as a form of ethnic pride, subtly conveyed using patronymics in the narrative (3:1-6). While Mordecai's motives are not explicitly discussed, his pride and loyalty to his heritage are taken as intrinsic virtues by the narrator, and his refusal to bow is treated as an acceptable act of defiance, even though it ultimately escalates the conflict.

Second, Mordecai's edict, like Haman's, allows for the destruction of not just the men but also the women and children of those who seek to harm the Jews (8:11). The inclusion of women and children in the decree reflects the language of Haman's original edict, emphasizing the total reversal of the threat. Third, Esther's request for a second day of slaughter in Susa (9:13-15) further complicates the moral landscape of the story. These actions, though part of the narrative's plot development, raise ethical questions about the level of violence involved in the resolution.

The moral failures of the characters, particularly Mordecai and Esther, lie more with the narrative choices than with the characters themselves. The narrator uses these actions for literary functions, such as highlighting the reversal of Haman's decree and explaining the two days of celebration. While these actions are morally ambiguous, they do not render the characters bloodthirsty or driven by hatred. Instead, the emphasis remains on the survival and deliverance of the Jewish people in a world fraught with danger and uncertainty.

Thus, the Jewish people are presented not as aggressors, but as survivors navigating a perilous world. They face immense challenges but ultimately take action to secure their survival, marking their transformation from passive victims to active agents in their own deliverance. The portrayal of the Jews in the narrative emphasizes their resilience, loyalty to their heritage, and commitment to preserving their identity, even in the face of overwhelming adversity.

4. The role of God in the story, as was the case in the book of Ruth, God is not one of the characters in the narrative, and it is not possible to speak in any way of a "characterization" of him. Yet, in my opinion God (or at least his providence) is present in the story in (a) the series of unlikely circumstances and extraordinary

coincidences with which the book abounds and (b) the remarkable series of reversals the characterize plot.

**a. The unlikely circumstances and extraordinary coincidences.**

The deliverance of the Jews from Haman's edict is just as much a consequence of these factors as it is a result of the loyalty of Mordecai and the sagacity and cunning of Esther. On the one hand, they involve, the overall shape of the plot, whether it is the vacancy for a queen at the Persian court, the accession of a Jewish queen, Mordecai's discovery of the plot, Esther's favorable reception by the king, the king's insomnia, Haman's early arrival at the palace of even his reckless plea for mercy at Esther's feet, the chance occurrences have a cumulative effect. "Each of these incidents regarded by itself might well appear to be the result of chance, and to have no bearing whatever upon the success or otherwise of the great plot. But taken together, the element of chance disappears; they all converge upon one point; one supplements the other." The whole course of events is shaped by "the guiding hand of the Great unnamed."

On the other hand, these factors also extend to the critical details of the plot itself. This can be most clearly seen if constitutes the decisive turning point in the course of Haman's confident plans to exterminate the Jews, his decision to ask the king to have Mordecai hanged (act 5, 5:9-6:14). There, five coincidences occur of such an extraordinary nature that they can hardly be anything but the narrator's cipher for "divinely arranged" (see Explanation to 6:1-11).

## b. The remarkable series of reversals.

Equally striking is the remarkable series of reversals that characterize the plot. This principle is explicitly articulated by the author when he observes that, "on the day in which the Jews' enemies hoped to triumph over them, that was overturned, in that the Jews triumphed over those who hated them" (9:1; see Comment and Explanation). Fox helpfully terms this "Peripety" ("structure," 296, drawing on terminology from Aristotle), i.e., the principle that an action or event intended or expected to produce a certain result produces its direct opposite. These "reversals" are remarkable not just for their number. The careful reader cannot help but note that the narrator in several instances consciously draws attention to the reversals by using identical, or nearly identical, phraseology in both the event and its opposite (cf. Berg, *Book of Esther*, 106).

This is most fully and consciously employed in the high point of the resolution, in which the report of the drafting, promulgation, and wording of Mordecai's counter-edict in 8:9-16 repeats in detail the language of the report of the drafting, promulgation, and wording of Haman's edict in 3:12-15 (see the chart in the structure/setting and the discussion in the explanation sections). The identity of language is also striking in several of the other cases as well. This deliberate mirroring of phrases between the two opposing edicts emphasizes the complete reversal of fortunes for the Jews and their enemies. The act of repetition underlines the significance of the change in power and

serves as a literary device to enhance the thematic reversal of fate.
Extent Action

3:1-2 King Ahasuerus promoted Haman son of Hammedatha, the Agagite. He advanced him in rank and gave him precedence over all his other nobles. And all the king's officials at court bowed down and did obeisance to Haman, for so the king had commanded.

3:10 Then the king took his signet ring form his hand and gave it to Haman son of Hammedatha, the enemy of the Jews.

4:1 Mordecai … tore his clothes, put on sackcloth and ashes, went out into the city, and raised a loud and bitter cry.

4:3 And in every single province to which the command and edict of the king came, there was great mourining among the Jews, with fasting weeping, and lamentation, while many made their beds on sackcloth and ashes.

5:14 And his wife Zeresh and all his friends said to him, "Have gallows erected, fifty cubits high and in the morning speak to the king and have Mordecai hanged upon it. Then go with the king ot the banquet full of joy."

5:14 And his wife Zeresh and all his friends said to him, "Have gallows erected, fifty cubits high, and in the morning speak to the king and have Mordecai hanged upon it."

6:6-9 Haman thought, "Now, whom would the king desire to honor more than me?" so he said," … let royal robes be brought which the king has worn and a horse which the king has ridden, with a royal diadem upon its head. Let the robes and the horse be given to a noble and let him robe the man whom the king desires to honor and lead him through the city square and proclaim before him, : "This what is done for the man the king desires to honor."

**Reversal**

9:3-4 [Mordecai] had come to occupy a position of great power in the palace, while his fame was spreading through all the provinces, Mordecai was growing increasingly powerful.

8:2a Then the king took off his signet ring which he had taken from Haman and gave it to Mordecai.

8:15a Then Mordecai went out from the king clad in a royal robe of violet and white, wearing a large gold turban and a purple cloak of fine linen.

8:17a And in every single province and every single city to which the command and edict of the king came, there was joy and gladness among the Jews, with feasting and celebration, while many of the peoples of the land professed to be Jews.

6:13b-14 Then his advisers and Zeresh his wife said to him, "Since Mordecai, who has already begun to defeat you, belongs to the Jewish race, you will not get the better of him, but will most certainly fall before him." While they were still talking with Haman, the king's eunuchs arrived and brought him in haste to the banquet.

7:9-10 Then Harbonah … Said, "Look, the gallows which Haman erected for Mordecai, whose report benefited the king, is standing at Haman's house, fifty cubits high," "Hang him on it!" said the king. So, they hung Haman on the gallows he had prepared for Mordecai.

6:11-12 So Haman got the robes and the horse. He robed Mordecai and led him through the city square mounted on the horse, and he proclaimed before him, "This is what is done for the man whom the king desires to honor!" and Haman hurried home mourning and is shame.

In this respect, the book of Esther differs from the book of Ruth. Since the author of Ruth primarily portrays the quality of his characters rather than that of a situation, the providence of God primarily acts through the quality of life of the characters; God acts in the acts of *hesed*, "kindness, graciousness, and loyalty," of Ruth and Boaz. But here the narrator is portraying the quality of a situation, and hence the providence of God acts through the coincidences and the remarkable reversals that advance the plot.

However, remarkable coincidences and dramatic reversals do not in and of themselves demonstrate that God is behind them. Forsaking the position he took in his article on structure (see Structure), argues that the evidence of the book implies that God is totally veiled. Hence, the author intends to convey total uncertainty about the presence of God.

"By refusing to exclude possiblility, the author conveys his belief that there can be no definitive knowledge of the working of God's hand in history" (247). Fox does not equate this view witgh skepticism. Rather, "the willingness to face history with openness to the possibility of providence is a stance of profound faith. (Fox, 2001)

However, I do not believe the context permits us to read the author this way; the meaning of a discourse at all levels, up to and including genre, just like the meanings of its words, depends upon context. The context in this book is decidedly in favor of reading all of these elements as a statement about divine providence. First, the author himself hints in two places that his context is indeed the OT's world of faith. In 4:3 he depicts the Jews as fasting at the news of Haman's edict, and in 4:15-17 Esther orders (and Mordecai carries out) a three-day, twenty-four-hour fast "for me," i.e., in preparation for her entry to the king. Even though the name of God is not mentioned, "what purpose do these acts serve if not to affect God's will? Likewise, in the context of the strong statement that Mordecai has just made of Esther in 4:14 that there is noother source besides her who can affect deliverance for the Jews. The hope that she occupies the queenship for just such a time as this (see Comment) is surely a statement that is intended to affirm divine providence, not one that denies it. Second, the theme of periphery, in which God acts to affect the reversal on behalf of his people, is a dominant one in the OT. In this context the function of peripety has more than aesthetic value. It "points to divine direction of human events" and so "mirrors the author's worldview and at the same time communicates that view to the reader. Third, that the book echoes in its conceptions and in some cases its language both the Joseph and the Exodus narratives (see the discussion in Unity and Redaction above) and hence draws consciously on one of the central themes of the OT, the deliverance of Israel, further indicates that the author writes in a religious rather than a secular context, and specifically he evokes a context of OT faith. This background is surely also made clear in a subtle but unmistakable manner by the way in which the three-day, twenty-four-hour fast that Esther requires of the Jews of Susa, 4:15-17 (which is a continuation of the fast already begun by the Jewish community in general, 4:3). Commencing as it did on the thirteenth day of the first month (3:12; see Comment on 4:16), would have canceled the celebration of Passover. (Clines, 1984)

Indeed, in such a context the storyteller is no theological sophisticate promoting a religionless Judaism, but an Old Believer whose ultimate act of faith is to make the protective providence of God for granted" (Clines, Esther Scroll, 155-56). Finally, I agree with Clines (296), Contra Berg (Book of Esther, 178), that "there is nothing hidden or veiled about the causality of the events of the Esther story: it is indeed unexpressed, but it is unmistakable, given the context within which the story is set. (Clines, 1984)

5. *Conclusion: The theme of Esther* 1:1-9:5; 10:1-3. On the grounds of this study of the characterization of the plot and its characters, the theme of the story can be stated as follows. In the dangerous world of the diaspora with its opulence, excess,

uncertainty, and evil, the loyalty of Mordecai to the Jewish people and the king, the courage, shrewdness, and sagacity of Esther, both of whom willingly accepted roles of leadership in that world, and he reliable providence of God delivered the diaspora Jewish community from the terrible threat of annihilation, demonstrating that a viable life for diaspora Jews is possible even in the face of such propensity for evil.

A. *The theme and purpose of denouement*, Esther 9:6-32. The theme of the denouement is immediately clear from the fact that it does not simply portray the consequences of the problem-based plot that preceedes. Its purpose, rather, is to obligate the Jewish community to institute an annual celebration whose purpose is to memorialize the days of celebration and joy that occurred after the dramatic deliverance on 13 Adar (see the discussion in the *Explanation* to this pericope and in the *Genre* section above).

Thus, the contents of the first scene, vv 6-19, are primarily devoted to accounting for the two different dates on which different parts of the Jewish community celebrate the festival. In so accounting for these dates, the narrator introduces the new theme of the days of rest and celebration that took place on the days following the victory in battle (see the discussion in *Explanation*). In the original circumstances, these festivities could only have been a spontaneous celebration of the victory that took place on the preceding day, and it seems highly probable that the continuing celebration described in v 19 would have had largely the same character. This theme of celebration is picked up in the directives of Esther and Mordecai set forth in the following scene, but the character of the celebration is transformed in a most significant way.

In the second scene of the denouement, vv 20-32, Mordecai writes to obligate the Jewish community to turn this spontaneous celebration into a perpetual, annual festival (see Explanation and esp. the Theology section below). He sets its character by establishing the festival not as a commemoration of the days of military victors but as a commemoration of the days of rest and joyful feasting that followed the days of fighting and bloodshed: "the days in which they had rest from their enemies and the month which was transformed for them from sadness to joy and from mourning to a holiday" (v 22). Hence, he establishes its dates as 14 and 15 Adar, the days immediately following the battles. The author then relates that the Jewish community corroborated what Mordecai had written by obligating themselves to both the dates and the character of the festival. Finally, Esther also wrote, adding her authority as queen to the establishment of Purim.

The theme of the book of Esther must combine the themes of both its redactional sections. The theme of the whole then is: The festival of Purim, to be held on 14 and 15 Adar and established by the joint leadership and action of Mordecai, Esther, and the Jewish community itself, is to consist of joyful days of feasting and the sending of presents of food to one another and gifts to the poor as a perpetual, annual commemoration of the transformation from sadness to joy and from mourning to a holiday that marked the days following their deliverance from the terrible edict with which Haman sought to annihilate them. This deliverance from the threat of annihilation in the dangerous world of the diaspora, with its uncertainty and propensity for evil, was effected by the loyalty of Mordecai to both the Jewish people and the king, the courage, shrewdness, and sagacity of Esther, both of whom willingly accepted roles of leadership in that world, and the reliable providence of God, demonstrating that a viable life for diaspora Jews is possible even in the face of such propensity for evil. (Moore C. D. 1997)

### *5.3. Structure/, Setting of the book:*

**<u>Outline</u>**

**Act 1. Introduction and Settings: Esther Becomes Queen of Persia (1:1-2:23)**

Scene 1.  The departure of Queen Vashti (1:1-22)

Episode 1. The banquets of king Ahasuerus: Persian pomp and circumstance (1:1-9)

Episode 2. Queen Vashti is deposed: Persian folly and foolishness (1:10-22)

Scene 2.  Esther becomes queen (2:1-18)

Episode 1. Ahasuerus decides to seek a new queen (2:1-4)

Episode 2. Esther is taken to the royal harem (2:5-11)

Episode 3. Esther is chosen as queen (2:12-18)

Scene 3.  Mordecai uncovers a plot (2:19-23)

**Act 2. The Crisis: Haman's Plot to Destroy the Jews (3:1-15)**

Scene 1. Haman decides to annihilate the Jews (3:1-6)

Scene 2. Haman sets in motion a plot to annihilate the Jews (3:7-15)

Episode 1. Haman obtains the king's permission to annihilate the Jews (3:7-11)

Episode 2. Haman orders the annihilation of the Jews (3:12-15)

## Act 3. Mordecai's Stratagem: Esther Must Consent to Appeal to the king

**(4:1-17)**

Scene 1. Mordecai and all the Jews lament over Haman's edict (4:1-3)

Scene 2. At Mordecai's comman Esther consents to appeal to the king (4:4-17)

Episode 1. Mordecai refuses the clothing Esther sends him (4:4)

Episode 2. Mordecai orders Esther to appeal to the king (4:5-9)

Episode 3. Esther consents to appeal to the king

## Act 4. Esther Begins Her Appeal: She Invites the King and Haman to a

**Banquet (5:1-8)**

Scene 1. Esther invites the king and Haman to a banquet (5:1-5a)

Episode 1. Esther gains an audience with the king (5:1-2)

Episode 2. Esther invites the king and Haman to a banquet (5:3-5a)

2. Esther again invites the king and Haman to a banquet (5:5b-8)

## Act 5. Haman's Stratagem Backfires: He is Humiliated and Mordecai Honored (5:9-6:14)

Scene 1. Haman's hubris: his wife and his friends persuade him to ask the king to hang Mordecai (5:9-14)

Scene 2. Haman's humiliation: the king commands him to honor Mordecai (6-1-11)

Episode 1. The king discovers the failure to reward Mordecai (6:1-3)

Episode 2. Haman advises the king how to reward the man he wishes to honor (6:410)

Episode 3. Haman so honors Mordecai (6:11)

Scene 3. Haman's end: his wife and his friends predict his downfall (6:12-14)

## Act 6. Esther Makes Her Appeal: The Fall of Haman (7:1-10)

Episode 1. Esther pleads with the king for her life. (7:1-6a)

Episode 2. Haman attempts to plead with Esther for his life (7:6b-8b)

Episode 3. Haman loses his life (7:8c-10)

**Act 7. Esther Appeals Again to the King: She and Mordecai Counter**

> **Haman's Plot (8:1-17)**

Scene 1. Esther and Mordecai acquire authority to issue a counter decree (8:1-8)

Episode 1. Mordecai is admitted into the king's presence (8:1-2)

Episode 2. The king grants Esther and Mordecai authority to write an edict on behalf of the Jews (8:3-8)

Scene 2. Mordecai issues the counter decree (8:9-17)

Episode 1. The counter decree is written and promulgated (8:9-14)

Episode 2. Mordecai leaves the king's presence with honor and the Jews rejoice (8:15-17)

**Act 8. The Jews Are Victorious: They Put All Enemies to the Sword (9:1-5)**

**Act 9. The Festival of Purim Is Instiued: Mordecai, Esther, and theJewsih**

> **Community Set Its Dates and Establish Its Character (9:6-32)**

Scene1. The events that occasion the celebration of Purim over two days (9:6-19)

Episode 1. How the fighting in Susa took Place on 13 and 14 Adar (9:6-15)

Episode 2. Why the Jews in Susa and the Jews elsewhere celebrate on two different days (9:16-19)

Scene 2. Mordecai, Esther, and the Jewish community set the dates of Purim and commit themselves to its perpetual celebration (9:20-32)

Episode 1. Mordecai writes to the Jews to require them to celebrate annually 14 or 15 Adar as days of joyful festivity (9:20-22)

Episode 2. The Jews commit themselves, their descendants, and all who join them to the perpetual annual observance of the two-day festival of Purim (9:23-28)

Episode 3. Esther writes to confirm the observance of Purim (9:29-32)

**Act 10. Epilogue: An Encomium on Mordecai (10:1-3)**

*5.4. Explanation and Analysis:*

*5.4.1. Esther Becomes Queen (1:1-2:23)*

**Explanation:**

**Episode 1: The Banquets of King Ahasuerus: Persian Grandeur and Ceremonial Splendor (1:1-9)**

In this introductory episode, the storyteller lays the groundwork for the narrative by outlining the events that serve as its backdrop. The essential facts are straightforward and can be summarized briefly: Who? King Ahasuerus. When? During the third year of his reign. Where? In the fortified city of Susa. What occurred? Two banquets were held. The first was for the prominent nobles and officials of his court, lasting 180 days. The second was a 7-day feast for the men of Susa. Meanwhile, Queen Vashti hosted a separate banquet for the women. The structure of this episode clearly highlights these fundamental events, which are summarized into three main points, each detailing the hosting of a banquet.

The narrator goes far beyond merely presenting the basic facts. Throughout the rest of the content, which consists of additional descriptive and modifying clauses, the narrator subtly begins to set the tone for the story. For example, the first temporal clause (v. 1) attached to the main statement not only introduces one of the key characters, Ahasuerus, but also defines his character by adding a lengthy appositional clause that highlights the vastness of his empire: "One hundred and twenty-seven provinces from India to Ethiopia"— essentially, the entire known world. This description implies absolute and boundless power. This portrayal aligns with the way the narrator satirically presents the opulence and excessive nature of the Persian court in the rest of the scene's descriptive clauses. We don't have to wait long to see this characterization unfold. The following circumstantial clause (v. 4a-b) explicitly highlights the grandiosity and excessive display of the Persian king's power: "Displaying the wealth and glory of his empire, and the grandeur and magnificence of his majesty" (v. 4a). Then, the temporal phrase at the end of this clause (v. 4b), which describes the length of the festivities, introduces an extravagant exaggeration—the banquet lasted for 180 days! Since lunar months are typically 29 or 30 days long, this equates to nearly six months. As Bardtke (279) points out, in the context of the preceding clause, this serves as another over-the-top showcase of royal wealth and splendor.

The portrayal of the Persian royal court's opulence and excess is most vividly depicted in the detailed noun clauses (vv. 6-8) that follow the description of the second banquet (v. 5b). The brief, exclamatory phrases in v. 6, with their poetic tone, powerfully convey the awe and astonishment the narrator wants us to experience in response to such luxury and grandeur (see Fox, 16-17). Fox captures the sentiment well: "The exclamatory listing creates a flood of images that overwhelm the senses, evoking both a hedonistic enjoyment of wealth and a recognition of its excess." Verses 7 and 8 further emphasize the lavishness of the banquet, highlighting the extravagance of the serving vessels, the abundance of wine, and the guests' freedom to drink as much as they desired. The third independent statement (v. 9) stands out as significantly different from the first two. It is concise and direct, without the addition of circumstantial clauses, suggesting a distinct shift in tone and mood. Unlike the previous statements, there is no mention of extravagance or luxury, no descriptions of grandeur, ornate decorations, or lavish adornments. There is no depiction of royal wine being freely consumed in abundance. While the nature of a women's banquet in ancient Persia is left to speculation, the narrator clearly aims to draw a stark and deliberate contrast between the opulent and excessive banquets of the king and his male guests, and the more restrained gathering of Queen Vashti and her female companions (see especially Fox, 167-69). The second episode will highlight this contrast even more sharply, using satire to underscore the disparity. The narrator casts a mocking eye upon the royal court he depicts: A king who rules the entire known world spends his time hosting extravagant banquets! The first banquet, lasting six months, is held for the king's highest-ranking nobles and courtiers, with the sole purpose of showcasing the wealth and grandeur of his empire. The second banquet, hosted for the citizens of the capital, is set in an environment overflowing with wealth—from the opulent canopy above to the intricate mosaic floor of the king's private garden, from the golden couches where guests recline to the numerous golden vessels from which wine flows freely. The episode ends with a simple, unembellished statement about Queen Vashti hosting her own banquet for the women. This stark contrast between the king's and the queen's celebrations serves as a subtle and ironic setup for the comedic events that are about to unfold.

**Episode 2: The Removal of Queen Vashti: Persian Foolishness and Folly (1:10-22)**

In the second episode, the narrator continues to outline the events and circumstances that serve as the backdrop for the crisis that will drive the plot forward. Like the first episode, the actual events that set the stage for this crisis are few and could easily be summarized: Due to Queen Vashti's defiance, the king issued a decree removing her from her position and ordered that a more suitable woman be chosen to replace her. These are the essential facts needed to set up the story of how Esther would eventually rise to a position where she could influence the unfolding events.

Vashti's refusal to be paraded like a mere concubine (cf. Fox, 168) before the drunken masses in the Citadel of Susa reflects her sense of dignity and self-respect, setting her apart from the mockery that the narrator directs at the rest of the royal court. This response is portrayed positively, creating a sharp contrast that intensifies the narrator's scorn for the royal and courtly world in which the story unfolds (cf. Fox, 167-69).

To cover his inability to resolve the situation, the king resorts to standard court procedure (v. 13b). He seeks advice from his most trusted counselors, elevating a domestic conflict to a political issue. These advisors, presented in exaggerated detail (v. 14), fail to be the "sages" who "understand the times" (v. 13a). Instead, they lose all sense of reason and decorum, hysterically assuming that Vashti's defiance will lead to widespread disrespect in marriage (v. 17) and rebellion in their own homes (v. 18). Their solution is ironically fitting they impose upon Vashti what she has already chosen herself—she "shall not come again into the presence of King Ahasuerus" (v. 19). By issuing an empire-wide decree demanding respect from their wives, they inadvertently spread the very issue they sought to prevent.

(2) The narrator's extended treatment emphasizes that the Persian Empire is ruled rigidly by law. However, this law offers little assurance of stability or fairness for those subjected to its rule. On one hand, it is unchangeable (v. 19), but on the other, it originates from

the capricious will of a weak, unstable ruler whose primary concerns seem to be his own pride and pleasure.

Thus, the opening scene of the story sets a satirical tone, preparing the reader for more of the same:

The first chapter establishes a tone that remains unforgettable, conditioning the reader to view the king, his princes, and their laws with skepticism, and to be alert for the underlying ironies that will unfold throughout the story. Without the obvious satire of the opening chapter, we might question the appropriateness of reading irony into the rest of the book. Chapter 1 creates a foundation for critical interpretation.

However, mockery also reveals a darker side. It exposes a society fraught with peril, governed by the arrogance and vanity of fools, whose fragile egos can manipulate the state's legal and administrative powers to serve selfish and trivial purposes. In such a society, it will not be surprising to see this same state apparatus used to carry out the destruction of one of its minority groups, or to find that the king can casually approve and even take pleasure in such actions.

**Explanation:**

In this second scene, the story continues to unfold by describing the events and circumstances that lead to Esther replacing Vashti as the queen of Persia, a pivotal development for her role in thwarting Haman's plot to annihilate the Jews. As in the first scene, the narrator elaborates on the key facts, which could have been briefly stated, but by doing so, he achieves two objectives. First, he maintains the tone and mood set in the initial scene (as discussed earlier). Second, he begins to develop the new characters introduced in this scene, particularly Esther. The scene is structured into three distinct episodes.

**Episode 1: Ahasuerus Decides to Find a New Queen (2:1-4)**

The first episode outlines the events that lead to the king's decision to replace Vashti and the steps he would take to do so. It begins with a reflection on Ahasuerus' thoughts (v. 1), where he recalls, "he remembered Vashti and what she had done, and the actions taken against her." This suggests that he might have regretted the situation, particularly the hasty decision made at the time. Furthermore, the passive construction used in reference to her banishment implies that he did not take much personal accountability for the decision (as pointed out by Fox, 26). This adds to the portrayal of the Persian king and his world, continuing the theme established in the previous scene.

Although Ahasuerus rules over a vast empire, he remains constrained by his own laws, and notably, he refuses to accept responsibility for the consequences of those laws.

**Episode 2: Esther is Taken to the Royal Harem (2:5-11)**

This episode describes the circumstances surrounding Esther's arrival at the king's palace along with the other young women who are being considered to replace Vashti. The narrator pauses his narrative to introduce Esther (vv. 5-7), and in doing so, also introduces Mordecai, as he plays a crucial role in Esther's life, especially in the harem (v. 10). Their relationship is pivotal to the unfolding story, so the narrator gives them a much more detailed introduction than typically given to characters in biblical narratives (cf. the introduction of Boaz in Ruth 2:1). This also serves to begin their characterization.

Mordecai's identification as "a Jewish man" is key to establishing the story's setting in the Diaspora (see the Theme and Purpose section in the Introduction to Esther). He also shares Mordecai's patronymic, revealing the significance of his ancestral background, which will be crucial to understanding the antagonism that arises between Mordecai and Haman later in the story (see below). In a detailed clause, the narrator notes that Mordecai's family (or possibly Mordecai himself) was exiled with Jehoiachin, likely indicating that they belonged to the noble or upper classes of Judahite society.

The relationship between Mordecai and Esther is also clarified; though she is his cousin, he adopted her as his daughter, which is important for the narrative that follows, as she remains under his authority even after becoming queen (v. 10, especially v. 20 below).

Esther is introduced as "a very beautiful young woman," fitting the description of those selected as candidates to replace Vashti. The narrator's emphasis on her beauty goes beyond the basic requirement for the candidates, who are simply described as "young women, lovely of appearance" (vv. 2-3). Esther is not only described as "beautiful of figure," but also "lovely of appearance," making it clear that her exceptional beauty will make her an obvious choice to be swept into the king's selection process.

The narrative of Esther being taken to the palace (v. 8) is presented concisely, with minimal detail. However, both the choice of language and the structure used make it clear that the key figures involved had no control over what happened. By referencing the unchangeable royal decree (see 1:19) in v. 8a, the narrator emphasizes that Esther's entry into the king's harem is a fate beyond her control, one that neither she nor the king can avoid. Additionally, their lack of agency is highlighted using three passive verbs in v. 8: "…was proclaimed… were gathered… was taken." This sequence of actions depicts an unstoppable chain of events. Thus, contrary to the interpretations of some commentators, the narrator effectively precludes any criticism of Mordecai's role in this situation. Within v. 9, as the narrator describes Hegai, the king's eunuch in charge, and his reaction to Esther, he begins to portray her as someone actively involved in the unfolding events. First, the statement that "the young woman was pleasing in the eyes of" Hegai suggests that Esther could very well be the one to fulfill the king's attendants' suggestion that "the young woman who is pleasing in the eyes of the king" should become queen in place of Vashti (v. 4). The repeated use of this expression subtly reinforces this idea, and the ensuing events continue with this implication. The phrase the narrator uses to describe the impression Esther makes on Hegai carries an active sense of "winning or earning favor" (see comment), suggesting that Esther plays a role in earning this attention. Hegai's quick actions—giving her cosmetics, food, and the "especially chosen maids" along with the "best part of the harem" (v. 9d)—indicate that Esther has captured his special interest. In this way, Esther succeeds even before Ahasuerus sees her.

The episode continues with further development of Mordecai's character. The narrator reveals that the relationship between Mordecai and Esther remains one of guardian and ward, as Esther follows Mordecai's directive to conceal her Jewish heritage (v. 10a). However, the narrator offers no explanation for why Mordecai would have given this instruction. While it might seem reasonable to assume that Mordecai feared Esther would face the same kind of prejudice in the king's palace that he anticipated from Haman, there is no evidence of such prejudice so far in the story. Instead, the lack of explanation for Mordecai's command creates a sense of unease, suggesting that revealing Esther's background could be exceedingly dangerous, thus foreshadowing the challenges to come. The episode concludes by showing Mordecai's deep concern for Esther's well-being: he paced in front of the harem daily to check on her, anxious to know "how she was and what was happening to her" (v. 11).

**Episode 3: Esther is Chosen Queen (2:12-18)**

The beginning of episode 3 consists of a lengthy and intricate temporal clause (v. 12). The main temporal phrase, "when each young woman's turn came" (v. 12a), is followed by a second temporal clause that provides the timing for each woman's turn (v. 12b). Here, the narrator uses excessive exaggeration: the beauty treatments for the candidates last an entire year! He emphasizes this point by inserting an extended aside that adds further hyperbole: "six months in oil of myrrh and six months in perfumes and other cosmetics used by women" (v. 12c). Clearly, the narrator does not intend to take this literally. Instead, through this almost absurd exaggeration, he continues his sharp satire of the Persian court's ridiculous artificiality and wasteful excess.

In the first subsection of episode 3, vv. 12-14, the narrator provides a brief account of the events involving each of the young women vying for the position of queen. This segment continues the narrator's satirical portrayal of the king and his court, as the description is filled with sensual overtones. Two clear criteria emerge by which the king will choose the woman who will replace Vashti as queen: (1) her beauty and (2) her ability to sexually please him. The first criterion is openly stated and underscored by the recurring motif of "cosmetics," which reaches its peak in the exaggerated description of the year-long "beauty treatment" (see above). The second criterion, while more implicit, is equally apparent. After spending the evening with the king, each woman would return to the harem in the morning, only to be kept under the care of Shaashgaz, the eunuch in charge of the king's concubines, and she would not be called again unless the king "took pleasure in her" and specifically "summoned her by name" (v. 14). The exact reasons for the king's pleasure are left unstated. As LaSor notes, the story is "told with exquisite reserve—yet devoid of sensual details." Though the narrative is indeed restrained and free of explicit sensual content, it is undeniably laden with sensuality.

This sensual undertone is also reflected in the choice of language. In this context, the phrase "to go to" (used four times) carries a double meaning, alluding to sexual intercourse (see comment). Fox points out that the detailed description of the harem, the beauty treatments, the women's visits to the king, and their subsequent return to the harem—where they would wait for another possible summons—is not strictly necessary for the plot. However, the focus on sensuality here serves not for its own sake but as a critique of the excessive indulgence in sensual and sexual matters in the story's world. It mocks the self-indulgent nature of the ruler and his court, where the only qualifications for the new queen are her beauty (enhanced through a lengthy cosmetic regimen) and her sexual appeal. This stands in stark contrast to the criteria laid out by Herodotus, who states that the king could only marry a woman from one of the seven noble families of Persia, implying that political considerations and the balance of power were key in those decisions, as both history and common sense suggest.

Only after providing a brief account of what transpired when each young woman visited the king does the narrator shift to focus on Esther (vv. 15-18). By splitting the narrative into these two sections, the narrator avoids including the sensual details (however subtly they were presented) associated with the other candidates, thereby softening, or even avoiding, any negative implications about Esther. In fact, the narrator offers a positive portrayal of Esther by contrasting her actions with those of the other women. The opening sentences of the two sections, vv. 12-13 and v. 15, are structurally similar but differ in content. Unlike the other women, who demanded "everything" they wanted to take with them to the king's chambers (highlighted by its position at the start of the sentence, v. 13b), Esther "requested nothing but what Hegai advised" (v. 15). This contrast suggests that while the other women were extravagant in their dress and adornment, Esther was modest and sensible, choosing to dress according to Hegai's expert advice, who, after all, understood the king's preferences better than anyone. Furthermore, despite the compromises required by her role—such as potentially breaking Jewish dietary laws—Esther's actions here demonstrate a refusal of excessive luxury, aligning her with other figures in the diaspora who maintained their integrity, such as Daniel (cf. Dan 1:8-15).

The narrative's subtle hints at Esther's superiority and future success set the stage for the king's admiration: "the king loved Esther more than all the women" (v. 17a). The king's reaction is emphasized further with the recurring motif of "winning favor," which is heightened in this episode. There are two key mentions of this motif (vv. 15c, 17b), and the second instance combines two previous phrases, "she won his favor" (v. 9b) and "she won their approval" (v. 15c), into the powerful statement: "she won the king's favor and approval more than all the girls" (v. 17b). With the declaration "he made her queen in place of Vashti," the narrative comes full circle, mirroring the earlier event when the king sought a new queen (see v. 4).

Lastly, the phrases "he placed a royal crown upon her head" (v. 17c) and "he gave a great banquet in Esther's honor for all his nobles and courtiers" (v. 18a) tie together the first two episodes and bring closure to the story. Esther now wears the royal crown that Vashti refused (v. 11), and the "great banquet" in her honor mirrors the first banquet Ahasuerus hosted "for all his nobles and his courtiers" (1:3), while also providing a contrast to the banquet Vashti held (1:9).

**Explanation:**

This scene brings the exposition to a close, establishing the setting and circumstances for the story. It does so by recounting the unrecognized service that Mordecai provided to the king, which becomes crucial for the events of 6:1-13. After this, the narrator will swiftly move to the crisis that propels the plot forward.

The scene begins with a temporal clause, indicating that these events occur after those previously described, and subtly referencing the king's earlier portrayal as indulgent. It then emphasizes that Mordecai held a position in the palace (described as "sat in the king's gate"; see comment). The narrator offers no clue as to whether this position has always been his or if it resulted from Esther's new status as queen, presumably achieved without revealing their relationship (see below). The clear purpose of mentioning this position is to show how Mordecai came to be in a position to overhear the plot against the king and communicate it to Esther.

The narrator also reiterates (cf. v. 10) that Esther has continued to hide her relationship with Mordecai and her Jewish identity. This repetition highlights its significance. It helps us understand two key points in the upcoming narrative. First, it clarifies why the king remains completely unaware of Esther's nationality when Haman proposes his plan to destroy the Jews (3:8-11) and, more importantly, when Esther reveals Haman as the instigator of this plot (7:3-5). Second, the reversed order of "parentage" and "nationality" here, compared to 2:10, explains why Mordecai, despite being Esther's adoptive father, continues to hold a minor position in the palace administration. This position will play a significant role in the brewing conflict between Mordecai and Haman.

The narrator also notes that Esther continued to obey Mordecai as she had when she was under his care (v. 20b). This explicit mention, especially in a scene otherwise marked by brevity, signals that the Jews had an established access to the Persian court, an access that could be used to address Jewish issues. This access will be crucial when the story's central crisis is revealed (see Explanation above).

The events in this scene are presented as briefly as possible. We learn nothing about what motivated the plot against the king or how Mordecai discovered it. However, it makes sense that Mordecai would inform the king through his adopted daughter, now the queen, and that she would relay the information "giving credit to Mordecai" (lit. "in the name of Mordecai") is crucial for the unfolding events in 6:1-13, for which this scene serves as a setup. Also vital to these upcoming events is the fact that the incident was recorded in "the daily court record before the king." The fact that it was recorded in the king's presence suggests that he was fully aware of it, regardless of the phrase's exact meaning. As some commentators have noted, Herodotus describes Persian kings as particularly attentive in rewarding such acts, even keeping a list of "king's benefactors." From this perspective, Ahasuerus's failure to reward Mordecai at the time is a significant oversight on his part, though the narrator does not point this out directly. This omission sets the stage for the king's decision to correct the mistake in 6:1-3, a dramatic turn that will propel the plot forward in chapter 6. Finally, Mordecai's unacknowledged deed contrasts sharply with Haman's unexplained rise to power in the next verse.

With this brief scene, the narrator concludes the exposition, setting up the story's circumstances. He has introduced three of the four main characters and begun to shape their roles, and he has established the crucial event that will enable the resolution of the crisis: Esther's rise to queen. With the necessary details in place and the tone set, the narrator immediately transitions to the crisis that will ignite the plot.

### 5.4.2. The Crisis Haman's Plot to Destroy Jews (3:1-15) ...

**Explanation:**

The second act introduces the crisis that will propel the story forward—Haman's plan and decree to wipe out all the Jews across the entire empire of Ahasuerus. After taking considerable time in the exposition to establish the tone and mood of the story, the narrator adopts a much more concise and restrained approach here. In fact, the narrative is so minimal and reserved that readers are often left to infer details from what is not explicitly stated.

## SCENE 1: HAMAN DECIDES TO ANNIHILATE THE JEWS (3:1-6)

This first scene of two (see Form/Structure/Setting above) explains the cause of Haman's plot: the longstanding animosity between Haman the Agagite and Mordecai the Jew, particularly the deep hatred Haman harbors for Mordecai. The narrator introduces the fourth and final key character in the story, Haman, son of Hammedatha the Agagite. The narrative is succinct, revealing that the king promoted Haman by elevating his rank and giving him precedence over all other nobles (v. 1). However, the narrator provides no explanation for this promotion, as his focus is on the fact that the king ordered all the court officials to bow down and show honor to Haman (v. 2a). In introducing Haman, the narrator provides his patronymic and ethnic identity in a manner similar to how Mordecai was introduced earlier. This type of identification is not provided for Esther or King Ahasuerus because such details are not essential to their characterization. The term *Agagite* used here carries significant ethnic weight (cf. Clines, *Esther Scroll*, 14). Agag was the king of the Amalekites who was defeated by Saul and executed by Samuel (1 Sam 15), and the Old Testament consistently emphasizes the deep, unrelenting hostility between the Amalekites and the

Israelites. Amalek is portrayed as the ultimate enemy of Israel. The conclusion of the story about the Amalekites' attack on Israel in the wilderness (Exod 17:8-16) notes, "Yahweh will have war with Amalek from generation to generation," and the book of Deuteronomy declares, "…you shall blot out the memory of Amalek from under heaven: you must not forget" (cf. also 1 Sam 15:2-3). Additionally, Agag himself is presented as a symbol of Israel's ancient enemies in Num 24:7.

Haman's ethnic identity as an Agagite is likely intended to be linked with Mordecai's lineage. Mordecai's patronymic (see comment on 2:5) traces his descent from Kish, a Benjaminite, and Saul, a descendant of Kish, defeated Agag, the Amalekite king. Thus, the patronymics of these two characters subtly highlight that both are heirs to a long-standing history of ethnic conflict and enmity. The narrator's identification of Haman signals that he is the primary adversary of the Jews, a point made clear through this carefully chosen sequence of details.

3:10 Haman son of Hammedatha, the Agagite, the enemy of the Jews

8:1     Haman, the enemy of the Jews

8:3     Haman, the Agagite

8:5     Haman son of Hammedatha, the Agagite

9:10    Haman son of Hammedatha, the the enemy of all Jews

There is a chiastic structure in the use of Haman's two titles. The most complete identification, which includes both titles, forms an inclusion with a climax, heightened by the addition of the word "all." Between these two complete identifications, there are shortened forms that omit one of the titles, arranged in a chiastic pattern. For example, in 8:1 and 9:10, Haman is referred to as "the enemy of the Jews," while in 8:3 and 8:5, he is simply called "the Agagite." This alternating use of terms clearly equates "Agagite" with "the enemy of the Jews." This connection is further supported by ancient interpretations, such as Josephus referring to Haman as "the Amalekite," and the Targumim adding the phrase "descendant of Amalek" to "Agagite." The Septuagint (LXX) replaces "Agagite" with "bougaion" in 3:1 (a term with an uncertain meaning), and "Macedonian" in 9:24, both of which can be interpreted as derogatory terms in the Greek context. In this way, the Greek translators "updated" the text, using terms familiar to their Greek-speaking Jewish audience to signify a "hated enemy" of the time (Moore, 36).After establishing Haman's high status and his entitlement to be honored by all the king's officials, the narrator quickly gets to the main issue: Mordecai's refusal to bow and show respect as commanded by the king (v. 2b). The narrator is subtle and indirect here, much like he was with the use of patronymics, providing no explicit reason for Mordecai's refusal. Since a good narrator must offer enough information for the audience to understand the story, it seems clear that the narrator assumed no explanation was necessary, at least for the original audience. He likely believed they would immediately recognize that Mordecai's refusal was due to his Jewish identity. The narrator only mentions Mordecai's Jewishness in two ways: first, to explain why his fellow officials reported his actions to Haman (v. 4b), and second, to show why Haman felt it was beneath him to punish only Mordecai (v. 6b), rather than tying it directly to Mordecai's refusal to bow. But why would Mordecai's Jewish identity be sufficient reason for either his refusal or Haman's extreme pride? Clearly, it's not due to Mordecai's religion or temperament (see comment). Instead, the narrator points out that Haman's pride is driven by ethnic hatred, as revealed by the fact that "they had told him who Mordecai's people were."

The underlying cause for both reactions lies in the ancient enmity between Jews and Amalekites. Mordecai's refusal can be understood as a statement of ethnic pride; he would not bow before a descendant of the Amalekites (cf. Deut 25:17-19). Haman's response, on the other hand, is unmistakably rooted in racial hatred, a hatred that is both callous and senseless. In comparison, Mordecai's pride seems less significant. The narrator leaves Mordecai's deeper motivations concealed, offering only a "sense of ambiguous depths of character" (see Theme and Purpose in the Introduction to Esther).

In his excessive arrogance, Haman failed to notice Mordecai's refusal to show him respect (v. 5a), but Mordecai's fellow officials were not so oblivious. They repeatedly confronted him, asking why he defied the king's command (vv. 3-5a). Ultimately, driven by a desire to test whether Mordecai's reasoning would hold up (v. 4b) and likely frustrated by his violation of the king's law and his ethnic pride (see comment), they reported his actions to Haman.

Had Haman witnessed Mordecai's refusal in private, his reaction might have been different. However, now that the matter was public, his response was predictable: he was furious (v. 5). Mordecai's refusal to bow to Haman represented both civil disobedience and a personal insult. But Haman's anger stemmed solely from the personal affront, as the narrator explicitly states, "since they had told him who Mordecai's people were" (v. 6a). His hatred was fueled by tribal and ethnic animosity, but the intensity of his reaction goes beyond mere enmity. Haman believed it was beneath him to deal with Mordecai alone (v. 6b). He could have either forced Mordecai's compliance or punished him for defying the king's order, but doing so would have shown that Mordecai's actions had affected him deeply. This highlights Haman's immense pride and vanity, qualities that the narrator will emphasize in his later portrayal (cf. especially 5:11-13). Instead of confronting Mordecai directly, Haman pretends indifference, delaying his response to Mordecai's blatant defiance until much later (cf. 5:9). Instead of a personal retaliation, he decides to destroy the entire Jewish people. The narrator's blunt, almost indifferent tone in presenting this decision (v. 6b) suggests that it was made without hesitation or any moral qualms. Eventually, Haman will feel compelled to personally eliminate Mordecai (5:9-14), but for now, he opts for genocide as a means of eliminating his enemy. Thus,

Haman is driven solely by power, devoid of mercy or compassion. He embodies the ultimate in callous, unfeeling, and irrational evil.

## SCENE 2: HAMAN SETS IN MOTION A PLOT TO ANNIHILATE THE JEWS (3:7-15)

### Episode 1: Haman Obtains the King's Permission to Destroy the Jews (3:7-11)

Having briefly told us about Haman's decision to target his enemy by exterminating his entire ethnic group, the narrator moves on with a remarkably concise account. He provides no details about how Haman arrived at this decision, instead relating to the key events in a simple manner. He mentions the choice of the day (v. 7) and how Haman gained the king's approval for his plan (vv. 8-11), without any reference to the difficulty of obtaining the king's audience—a matter that will later prove to have serious consequences (4:11). The narrator maintains a subtle, reserved style throughout, withholding much information until later. Not until the second episode does the narrator elaborate on how Haman plans to carry out this horrific deed, and even then, it is revealed only indirectly as the decree is spread throughout the empire (vv. 12-14).

The narrator starts by recounting how Haman cast lots to determine the most opportune day for the annihilation of the Jews (v. 7). The day chosen seems maliciously ironic: the number 13 was considered unlucky by both the Persians and Babylonians, and the thirteenth day of the first month (the day the decree was dispatched in v. 12) is the day before Passover, the Jewish holiday commemorating their deliverance from Egypt.

Once the date was selected, the narrator swiftly transitions to Haman's proposal to the king. Haman reveals himself to be a manipulative and malicious slanderer. He begins by downplaying the identity of the targeted people, referring to them as "one person," suggesting that they are unimportant (see comment). He goes on to say they are "scattered and unassimilated" throughout the empire, accusing them of being socially and religiously distinct. This description casts them as a pervasive, suspicious presence in the empire.

From this subtle insinuation, Haman escalates to outright, though false, accusations (vv. 8c-d). The translation issues here arise because Haman uses the Persian term *dat* in both clauses, which can mean "custom, regulation" (as in Esth 2:12) or "law" (as in Esth 3:14, 4:11). Haman shifts from claiming that the Jews' customs are different from those of the empire to accusing them of defying the king's laws. The first part is true, but it applies to all peoples within the empire, which the Persians prided themselves on as a diverse society. The second part, however, is a blatant lie, as the Jews in the book are consistently law-abiding (cf. Fox, 215). By using the same term, Haman implies that their different customs justify the accusation that they defy royal law.

Haman then appeals to the king's sense of racial superiority and fear, arguing that allowing these people to continue existing would not be in the king's best interest, insinuating that their very presence threatens the king's honor. Haman's use of innuendos, half-truths, and lies paints the Jews as a dangerous and lawless group that threatens the king's welfare. Finally, before the king can even consider the validity of these accusations, Haman offers a massive bribe: if the king approves the decree to annihilate the Jews, Haman will pay ten thousand talents to the royal treasury. This staggering sum, clearly exaggerated, serves as satirical hyperbole, emphasizing the lengths to which Haman is willing to go to secure his plan.

Ahasuerus responds to Haman's outrageous proposal with no questions or objections but simply hands him his signet ring— granting him the full power to act on his behalf. Accompanied by the casual, almost dismissive statement, "do with the people and the money as you please," the king reveals his complete lack of interest in the situation. This response not only underscores his minimal involvement in the matter but also reflects his utter disregard for the lives and welfare of those affected. The issue is so trivial to him that it does not warrant any serious thought or concern. While Haman embodies pure evil, the king exemplifies dangerous indifference.

**Episode 2: Haman Orders the Annihilation of the Jews (3:12-15)**

After receiving the king's approval to exterminate the Jews, Haman wastes no time in putting his genocidal plan into action. The narrative is conveyed using the passive voice: "It was written" (vv. 12a, b), "it was sealed" (v. 12c), "dispatches were sent" (v. 12), and "a copy of the order is to be promulgated … being publicly displayed" (v. 14).

This choice of language emphasizes the cold, impersonal, and mechanical nature of the process. Additionally, the scope of the dispatches is vast: the edict, written in the king's name and sealed with his signet (therefore carrying his direct authority), is sent to the heads of the three main divisions of the empire's administration (v. 12).

The decree calls for the destruction, slaughter, and total annihilation of all Jews—men, women, and children—along with the plundering of their belongings, to take place on the thirteenth day of the twelfth month (v. 13). However, the execution of this mass extermination is only hinted at, as the edict is to be "promulgated as law in every province and publicly displayed to all peoples, so that they might be ready for this day" (v. 14). It is here that the full scale of Haman's horrific scheme becomes clear. His plan will exploit deep-rooted tribal and racial animosities, pushing him to the extreme of wiping out an entire population, driven by baseless suspicion and fueled by unchecked greed.

The genocide is set to take place eleven months from now. This delay serves a dual purpose: it prolongs the suffering of the Jews, who have no escape from the far-reaching power of the Persian Empire, which encompasses the known world, and it allows ample time for antisemitic sentiments to escalate, increasing the likelihood of retaliation (v. 14c).

The act concludes with four brief but impactful scenes. The first two describe the swift dissemination of the decree as couriers rush to carry out the king's orders. The edict is issued from the citadel of Susa, meaning it is directed to the court and surrounding areas, which is why Mordecai is immediately aware of it (4:1). The next two scenes illustrate the effect of the decree: while the king and Haman calmly sit down at a banquet, the city of Susa (referring to the inhabitants, not just the palace) is thrown into confusion and unrest. This stark contrast between the calm of the king and Haman and the turmoil of the city serves to emphasize their detached indifference. The king and Haman are unperturbed, while the citizens of Susa are in a state of anxious disorder.

The "problem" that drives the rest of the narrative is clear: Haman, the Agagite and enemy of the Jews, has secured a decree under Persian law that all the empire's people are to destroy, kill, and exterminate all Jews, including women and children, and to seize their possessions on a single day, the thirteenth of the twelfth month, Adar. Public violence, murder, and plundering are sanctioned to avenge Haman's bruised pride. Given the power Haman holds and the irreversible nature of Persian law, the fate of the Jews appears sealed.

Or does it? A crucial character has yet to appear in this grim act, though it is obvious to the audience: one member of the Jewish community, unknown to both Haman and the king, sits in the royal palace as the Queen of Persia. What can one lone figure, even one so highly placed, do against such overwhelming odds? Perhaps not much, but the narrator has not left us without hope. Esther, as depicted earlier, is actively involved in the unfolding events (see

Explanation to 2:5-11), and it is emphasized repeatedly (2:10, 20) that she continues to follow Mordecai's guidance (see Explanation to 2:19-23). Thus, the Jewish community has a potential connection to the Persian court, one that may not be as insignificant as it seems. The narrator will soon reveal how this connection could play a pivotal role (see 4:1-3).

In the meantime, a severe three-day fast is decreed, highlighting the gravity of the situation. Fasting typically lasted from morning until evening (cf. Judg 20:26; 2 Sam 1:12), and the focus here is on deep intercession with God and the seriousness of the crisis. The phrase "night and day" likely holds no special significance, as the biblical day traditionally began in the evening (cf. Gen 1). Notably, the decree to annihilate the Jews was issued the day before Passover (see Explanation to 3:7-11), and this timing would not have been lost on Jewish readers. The three-day fast Esther initiates would have started on the eve of Passover, effectively canceling the celebration, despite the directive in Exod 12.

### 5.4.3. Mordecai's Plan (4:1-17)

**Explanation:**

The grave threat facing the Jews of Persia was introduced in act 2 (see Explanation there), without any hint or suggestion of Esther's involvement. However, the position Esther holds, albeit hidden, within the Persian court (act 1) and the way she is characterized (act 2) naturally lead us to hope—albeit briefly—that she might play a pivotal role in rescuing the Jews from Haman. After giving us reason to place our hopes in Esther, the narrator moves forward without exploring alternative options. This next act directly addresses the first step toward resolving the crisis—the potential destruction of the Jews. It details how, at Mordecai's urging, Esther agrees to approach the king on behalf of her people.

## SCENE 1: MORDECAI AND THE JEWS LAMENT OVER HAMAN'S DECREE (4:1-3)

This short scene depicts the deep sorrow and mourning of Mordecai and the Jewish people in response to the king's decree. Their grief is expressed through traditional cultural rituals of lamentation and intercession. It sets the stage for the following interaction between Mordecai and Esther, as Mordecai does not express his anguish privately or quietly. Instead, he openly mourns, venting his sorrow in the city streets, approaching even the entrance of the royal court. While he likely would have entered the court and cried aloud "back and forth in front of the court of the harem" (2:11), he is forbidden from doing so while dressed in sackcloth (v. 2). The king's realm of lavish pleasure must remain undisturbed by such displays of mourning (see act 1 above). Mordecai's public lamentation is clearly intended to bring the crisis to the queen's attention in the most forceful way possible, which is exactly what happens (v. 4).

## SCENE 2: ESTHER AGREES TO APPEAL TO THE KING (4:4-17)

The second scene focuses on the dialogue between Esther and Mordecai. In this conversation, Mordecai informs Esther about the situation and persuades her to risk her life by appealing to the king on behalf of the Jews. This scene unfolds in three well-crafted episodes, each intensifying the communication between Esther and Mordecai, becoming more direct and detailed as the dialogue progresses.

**Episode 1: Mordecai Refuses the Clothing Esther Sends Him (4:4)**

In the first episode, Esther, deeply troubled upon hearing about Mordecai's condition from her maids and eunuchs, sends him clothes to remove his sackcloth, presumably so that he can enter the royal court and explain the situation. His refusal prompts her to inquire further.

**Episode 2: Mordecai Commands Esther to Appeal to the King (4:5-9)**

Episodes 2 and 3, in contrast to the first, describe the dialogue between Esther and Mordecai through an intermediary, Hathach, because Mordecai must remain outside the royal court. The second episode slows the narrative as it details Hathach's role as the messenger. In this dialogue, Esther asks what has happened and why (vv. 5-6), and Mordecai responds (vv. 7-8). Mordecai provides Hathach with all the details of the events, including the bribe Haman offered the king to allow the destruction of the Jews (v. 7; cf. 3:21-22). He also sends a copy of the royal edict for Esther to see and understand the gravity of the situation. Mordecai doesn't merely request Esther to intervene, as might be expected from someone of lower rank addressing the queen; he commands her to act, clearly asserting his authority as her guardian. This authority, which she respects, has been highlighted by the narrator throughout (2:10, 20; see Explanation to 2:19-23). The episode concludes with Hathach delivering Mordecai's message to Esther (v. 9).

**Episode 3: Esther Consents to Appeal to the King (4:10-17)**

In this third episode, the narrator shifts his approach, using direct speech to report the actual conversation between Esther and Mordecai. This change in style signals that this is the pivotal moment in the scene. The exchange is composed of three parts: (1) Esther's objection to Mordecai's command (v. 11), (2) Mordecai's response to her objection (vv. 13-14), and (3) Esther's eventual agreement to appeal to the king (v. 16).

Esther objects to Mordecai's command, stating that going to the king without being summoned would risk her life. The narrator leaves us to infer the reason for her hesitation (beyond the obvious danger to her life). Esther's reluctance may not be a sign of fear, but rather a sign of her uncertainty about her influence on the king. She has not been called into the king's presence for thirty days, a fact that Mordecai likely does not know (Clines, 301). Her hesitancy reflects not only the risk of her life but also her doubt about the effectiveness of her appeal, given that her favor with Ahasuerus seems to have waned.

Mordecai's response is direct and to the point. He stresses that Esther will not be safe in the palace any more than the other Jews (v. 13), which is not a reproach but a statement of fact. He makes it clear that if she remains silent, help will not come from any other source, and both she and her family will perish (v. 14). Then, as the climax of his appeal, he suggests that perhaps Esther has become queen for just such a moment as this, implying a divine purpose behind her position.

Esther, without further objection, shows no hesitation in her decision. She immediately orders that all the Jews in Susa, along with her maids, participate in a three-day, twenty-four-hour fast (v. 16). Mordecai's suggestion of divine providence has clearly resonated with her. The fast is intercessory ("on my behalf"), meant to seek divine favor in the face of the danger she is about to face. It is an especially strict fast, not only lasting twenty-four hours, but also coinciding with the time of Passover, meaning the Jewish community will forgo their most important festival to focus on intercession. This highlights the sharp contrast between the indulgent feasting of the Persians (as the narrator has previously sarcastically emphasized, cf. 1:4) and the intense fasting of the Jews.

Esther's response shows firm resolve. Her words, "If I perish, I perish," are not an expression of resignation but a statement of courageous determination. Responsibility for the resolution of the crisis now rests on her shoulders.

Hope for the Jews' deliverance has emerged, though it is fragile. It lies in the hands of a queen who is currently out of favor and who has previously been focused on beauty treatments and royal duties (Fox, 67). However, the narrator has subtly introduced the possibility of divine providence, both through Esther's command for the Jewish community to fast and Mordecai's suggestion that her position as queen may serve a divine purpose (v. 14d). Furthermore, Esther is portrayed not as a passive participant in the events but as someone actively involved in the unfolding situation (see Explanation to 2:5-11). Could she be the one to rise to the challenge?

Esther's delay is intentional and not merely a narrative device to build suspense or allow for Haman's humiliation. In understanding Esther's purpose, the decisions she makes make perfect sense in light of her context. She is taking the initiative and steering the events that follow, which underscores her pivotal role in the unfolding story (see Explanation).

### 5.4.4. Esther Begins Her Appeals (5:1-8)

**Explanation:**

## SCENE 1: ESTHER INVITES THE KING AND HAMAN TO A BANQUET (5:1-5A)

**Episode 1: Esther Gains an Audience with the King (5:1-2)**

Esther's resolve, which was firmly expressed in the previous act when she ordered a three-day fast for herself (4:16), remains strong and unshaken. On the third day of the fast, while it is presumably still ongoing, she puts on her royal attire and gathers the courage to approach the king, determined to act with the boldness of her earlier declaration, "If I perish, I perish!" (4:16). The narrator skillfully delays revealing the outcome of this pivotal moment. He provides detailed descriptions of both Esther's position and the king's, ensuring that we understand she is indeed visible to the king: "she stood in the inner court of the palace in front of the king's residence, while the king sat on his royal throne in the royal residence, in front of the entrance to the building" (v. 1). This builds tension as we anticipate the outcome of her daring action, with the potential consequences still fresh in our minds from her plea to Mordecai (4:11).

The narrator heightens the significance of this moment by almost restarting the act. In v. 2, he introduces the result of Esther's bold move using a second temporal clause, starting with the same syntactic structure as in v. 1. Just as she had gained the favor of both Hegai (2:9) and the king himself (2:17), Esther finds favor in the king's eyes and is granted access to his presence.

**Episode 2: Esther Invites the King and Haman to a Banquet (5:3-5a)**

Esther's decision to risk her life by appearing unbidden before the king signifies the gravity of her request. Upon seeing her, the king immediately inquires about her request (v. 3a), offering an extravagant promise, "Even if it's for half my empire, it shall be granted." While this is clearly an exaggerated, stereotypical expression, it emphasizes the king's tendency toward excess and his mercurial nature. Previously, in a similarly casual manner, he had condemned an entire people to death (3:11), yet now, without knowing Esther's intentions, he offers her whatever she desires. Esther does not immediately take advantage of this offer, which contradicts her earlier fears (4:16). Instead, adhering to protocol and etiquette, she invites the king and Haman to a banquet (v. 4), and the king promptly agrees to Haman's attendance.

## Episode 3: Esther Again Invites the King and Haman to a Banquet (5:5b-8)

During the wine course at the banquet, the king once again asks Esther about her request, reiterating his promise of generous compliance. Esther responds by inviting the king and Haman to another banquet the following day. This delay in Esther's request is not due to narrative clumsiness, but part of a carefully planned strategy. She doesn't immediately reveal her request, instead first asking, "My request and my petition?" (v. 7), before pausing and rephrasing it (v. 8). This partial revelation not only emphasizes the gravity of her request but also heightens the king's curiosity.

Esther becomes even more diplomatic in her speech than before, using the highly polite phrase "If I have found favor with the king and if it pleases the king." More importantly, she modifies the second conditional clause, shifting the focus to the potential fulfillment of her request, saying, "If granting what I ask and fulfilling my request pleases the king, let him … come to the banquet." With this phrasing, Esther subtly secures the king's commitment, making it nearly impossible for him to refuse her request.

This strategic maneuver demonstrates that Esther is not acting blindly or without thought, nor is the narrator clumsily introducing unnecessary events. Esther is shrewdly executing a well-considered plan, forcing the king to commit himself before she even reveals her request.

Moreover, since the king has previously relied on his advisors' counsel, Esther knows that the time for her to unmask Haman must leave him no opportunity to change the king's mind. By ensuring that Haman is present at the banquet, Esther also ensures the king will act swiftly once her request is made.

The act concludes with Esther's confirmation that on the following day, she will make her request known, doing "as the king has said." This phrasing subtly shifts the power dynamic, framing her action as one of complying with the king's request, rather than making a bold demand. As Clines points out, the dialogue from vv. 3-7 is a delicate negotiation where Esther achieves her objective without revealing her full intention. The narrative is rich and layered, showcasing the narrator's masterful craftsmanship in developing this suspenseful and strategic moment.

With Esther's promise at the end of v. 8 that she will reveal her request at the upcoming banquet, we expect the narrator to quickly resolve our curiosity about what will happen next, especially after the tension built up for both the protagonists and the readers. However, the narrator does not immediately fulfill this expectation. Instead, he interrupts the plot and shifts focus, taking the story in a new direction that revolves once again around the relationship between Haman and Mordecai.

In terms of meaning, it's clearer in English to interpret the passage as such. It seems unlikely that Haman's wife and friends genuinely held the opinions they express here, especially considering that just the previous evening, they had advised him to build a gallows and ask the king to have Mordecai executed on it. As several commentators have pointed out (e.g., *Esther Scroll*, 43; Moore, 66), it's more probable that these advisers reflect the sentiments of the narrator and the audience. The Old Testament frequently references the deep hostility between Israel and Amalek (Exod 17:14-16; 1 Sam 15:2-8; 2 Sam 1:8-16), and it strongly suggests the ultimate triumph of Israel (Num 24:7, 20). For the narrator and the readers, it is an inevitable conclusion that the house of Saul—Mordecai's ancestral line, as indicated by his patronymic (see 2:5-6)—will prevail over the house of Agag, the Amalekite lineage, to which Haman is connected through his patronymic (see 3:1 and Explanation there).

### 5.4.5. Harman's Stratagem (5:9-6:14)

**Explanation:**

As we saw at the end of the previous act, the stage seemed set for the narrator to immediately reveal the events of the upcoming banquet and Esther's request to the king. However, there is a surprising shift in the very first verse of this fifth act, where we are not immediately taken to the banquet, Esther, or her request, but instead brought back to the present day and a renewed focus on Haman and Mordecai. The narrator builds suspense by keeping us on edge about the outcome of Esther's appeal and shifts the focus to continue exploring the dynamic between Haman and Mordecai.

Although the scene revisits the relationship between Haman and Mordecai, and while it does show how Mordecai is eventually rewarded for saving the king's life, these details are secondary to the central focus of the scene, which is Haman. Mordecai plays a brief role, primarily serving as a foil to highlight Haman's eventual and total downfall. In the first scene, the narrator uses Haman's exaggerated obsession with his own status, power, and privilege to showcase his extreme overreaction to Mordecai's refusal to show him the difference he believes he deserves.

In the second scene, Mordecai's failure to honor Haman sets the stage for the dramatic reversal in which Haman, intending to ask the king to have Mordecai executed, instead finds himself publicly forced to honor Mordecai with the very recognition and respect he had hoped for. In the third scene, Mordecai again acts as a foil in the complete turnaround of the advice given by Haman's wife and friends. Initially, they confidently suggested a plan for Mordecai's demise, but their advice shifts to a grim realization that Haman's public humiliation at the hands of Mordecai signals the beginning of his downfall.

## SCENE 1: HAMAN'S RAGE – HE DECIDES TO ASK THE KING TO HANG MORDECAI (5:9-14)

Haman leaves the banquet with the king and Esther feeling elated and triumphant (5:9), his pride bolstered by being invited to another banquet with just the king and queen. However, his joy is short-lived when he encounters Mordecai on his way home. Mordecai, who apparently cannot avoid crossing Haman's path, again refuses to show him any respect. This time, his behavior is even more insulting: not only does he not bow, but he also does not raise or show any fear in Haman's presence. The narrator emphasizes this as an even more blatant affront to Haman's dignity.

Haman's response, as before, is driven by his excessive pride and vanity. Rather than admitting that Mordecai's actions have affected him, he pretends indifference, telling himself he is "keeping himself under control" and heading home (5:10a). Previously, the narrator showed us Haman's pride through his inner thoughts, revealing that he thought it was beneath him to deal with Mordecai alone (3:6). Now, however, in the privacy of his own home with his wife and friends, Haman openly expresses the depth of his frustration. Despite his wealth, status, royal favor, and the queen's personal invitations to banquets, he says, "all of this means nothing to me every time I see Mordecai the Jew at the king's court" (5:13). Haman's bitterness is not just because Mordecai refuses to bow, but because he cannot tolerate Mordecai's very existence. Haman becomes a vivid example of excessive pride masking a fragile ego.

Consumed by his obsession with Mordecai, Haman is clearly uncertain about what to do next. It is his wife, Zeresh, and his friends (though Zeresh is the main spokesperson, as per the Hebrew order in 5:14) who suggest a course of action. The irony here is subtle: Haman, the grand vizier, is portrayed as powerless and emasculated, a sharp contrast to the male dominance enacted by the king and his council in the previous act (1:20-22).

Recognizing that Haman's spite will not be satisfied by Mordecai's death alone, Zeresh and the others propose a more public form of humiliation: Mordecai must be hanged on massive gallows, 80 feet high, visible to all of Susa (5:14a). Haman, delighted by the suggestion, orders the construction of the gallows immediately (5:14d). He fully expects that the next day, he will gain the king's approval for Mordecai's execution and, as his wife and friends confidently predict, he will attend the banquet "full of joy" (5:14c).

## SCENE 2: HAMAN'S HUMILIATION – THE KING COMMANDS HIM TO HONOR MORDECAI (6:1-11)

At the end of the previous scene, Haman appeared to be on top of the world. His decree, backed by the king's authority, was set to annihilate the Jews, including Mordecai, his personal enemy. If the king could easily approve the extermination of an entire people, surely securing his consent to eliminate just one man would be simple. But Haman's plans are about to collide head-on with divine intervention.

The king, unable to sleep (coincidence 1), orders the reading of the daily court record, where he discovers that Mordecai had previously uncovered a plot to assassinate him (coincidence 2) and realizes that Mordecai had received no reward for this act (coincidence 3). Determining that this oversight should be rectified, the king seeks advice, as is his custom. The next remarkable coincidence occurs when he asks, "Who is in the court?" just as Haman arrives at the outer court, intending to ask the king to hang Mordecai (coincidence 4). When the king learns of Haman's presence, he summons him and asks what should be done to honor someone whom the king wishes to reward (coincidence 5). The use of the phrase "the man whom the king desires to honor" can only be seen as a divine act, given the sequence of seemingly random events leading to it.

But why is Haman in the court at such an hour? His wife and friends had advised him to wait until morning (5:14). It seems likely that the king's insomnia occurred early in the morning, setting the stage for these extraordinary coincidences. These circumstances, however remarkable, are completely beyond Haman's control. Though the king is clearly preparing to reward Mordecai, Haman's own agenda, which aims to eliminate Mordecai, places him in the middle of this situation. Yet, these events don't necessarily spell danger for him—at least not yet. The possibility of Mordecai's reward could still be interpreted in Haman's favor, given his presence in the court. But before the reader can entertain this notion, Haman's own pride leads him to unwittingly seal his fate.

Without hesitation, Haman assumes that the king must be referring to him when he asks, "Whom would the king desire to honor more than me?" (6:6b). The narrator subtly reveals that Haman is captivated by this phrase, savoring it as he imagines the honor he will receive (6:7). He enthusiastically repeats the idea, framing his answer in his mind. Haman's suggestion is for a public display of honor: to be paraded through the city square in the king's robes and riding the king's horse, with the announcer proclaiming, "This is what is done for the man whom the king desires to honor" (6:9). For Haman, honor is everything, and the thought of it blinds him to the consequences of his actions against Mordecai.

No sooner are Haman's words out than the king's response shatters his expectations. "Take the robes and the horse... and do this for Mordecai the Jew" (6:10). The irony is cutting. The man who had planned to destroy Mordecai is now commanded to honor him. The king's use of the phrase "Mordecai the Jew" adds another layer of bitter irony. The very man Haman despises and seeks to annihilate is now the recipient of the king's honor.

The narrator quickly summarizes Haman's compliance with the king's command in just one brief verse (6:11), offering no further commentary on Haman's emotions, which is striking given how often the narrator describes his feelings elsewhere (see Theme and Purpose in the Introduction to Esther). This silence leaves the reader to imagine Haman's internal turmoil. The narrator's restraint speaks volumes, emphasizing the grim nature of this situation.

The silence is broken only by Haman's own words as he must proclaim, with bitter irony, the phrase he had once hoped to hear for himself: "Thus is what is done for the man whom the king desires to honor!" Now, he must say these words in front of the very man he sought to destroy, a humiliating reversal that marks the turning point in his fortunes.

## SCENE 3: HAMAN'S DOWNFALL – HIS WIFE AND FRIENDS FORESEE HIS END (6:12-14)

Haman returns home in a state of deep despair and humiliation, seeking comfort from his wife and friends by recounting everything that has transpired. Once again, they offer him advice, but this time their tone has shifted dramatically. The confident counsel they gave him earlier on how to deal with Mordecai's defiance now turns into a grim recognition of the inevitable. They predict his downfall, and the reason they give is both dramatic and unexpected. They believe the Jews are invincible: "Since Mordecai belongs to the Jewish people, you won't be able to defeat him; you will certainly fall before him" (see comment on the meaning of the conditional clause). The narrator likely places his own views in the mouths of Haman's counselors at this point. Regardless, their words signal that Haman's fall is imminent and set in motion for the next day. It also subtly foreshadows the potential failure of Haman's own plot to destroy the Jews.

The scene ends skillfully tying back to the previous act, which had been interrupted when Esther invited Haman and the king to the banquet (5:8). Now, the king's eunuchs arrive to escort Haman to the banquet that Esther had prepared (6:14). This transition sets the stage for the next act, where the prediction of Haman's downfall made by his wife and friends continues to loom. The dramatic shift in Haman's fortunes is underscored as he is escorted to the banquet, signaling that his fate is now quickly heading toward its inevitable conclusion.

### 5.4.6. Esther Mates her Appeal (7:1-10)

**Explanation:**

*Episode 1 Esther pleads with the king for her life* (vv 1-6a). "So, the king and Haman came to dine with Queen Esther." After the last two acts, this almost laconic introduction to the sixth act is charged with tension and suspense. True, we have no doubt that Haman's demise awaits him or that the result for Esther and her people will be deliveries, for the narrative has signaled in clear terms the certainty of each. The king has indicated by the very extravagance of his repeated promise to grant Esther as much as hall of his empire that he has every intention of looking upon her request with the greatest favor, and through Esther's skillful stratagem, his very presence at this banquet amounts to a public pledge to fulfill her request (*see Explanation to 5:5b-8)*. Likewise, Haman's fate has been presaged by the way in which his plans to have Mordecai hanged have been turned into publicly honoring Mordecai, and it has been sealed by the somber prediction of his won wife and friends. Nevertheless, suspense in regard to the fate of each remains, for nothing in the narrative thus far has foreshadowed precisely how either fate will come to pass.

The greatest suspense arises, of course, in regard to the king. Despite his favorable promises and the public pledge that Esther has been able to extract from him, he has shown himself to be a weak and unstable despot who is moved by the whim of the moment and is ruled by pride and ostentation—one who can care lessly consign a whole people to oblivion with an offhand comment. It is most uncertain, then, what his response will be, or whether he will make one at all. When Esther's request pits the most favored of his courtiers against the most favored of his wives.

Having thus built-up suspense regarding Esther's appeal to the king, the narrator now wastes no words in resolving it. The scene, carefully crafted and tightly constructed, begins immediately with the king repeating both his question and his magnanimous promise for the third time (v 2). The narrative quickly builds toward Haman's downfall, only briefly slowing in pace in v. 5a. Esther's response to the king's inquiry (vv. 3-4) shows that she fully grasps the delicate nature of her situation. The threat to her and her people comes from both Haman and the king, who are present with her. She must expose Haman's guilt without appearing to accuse the king, so her response is carefully crafted and diplomatically presented.

First, she begins with a polite phrase like the one she used to invite the king to the banquet (5:8), but with a subtle and significant change. Instead of the typical third person address she uses in courtly speech, she shifts to the more intimate second person: "If I have found favor with you, O king." This emphasizes her unique relationship with the king as his queen.

Second, while she echoes the king's phrasing by using the words "wish" and "request," she makes a subtle modification. The king had twice used these terms, clearly implying a single request (5:6; 7:2). Esther mirrors this but applies the terms to different subjects: "Let my life be granted me as my wish, and my people as my request." With this, she aligns herself with her people, making it clear that to threaten one is to threaten both.

Third, Esther carefully explains the nature of the threat against her and her people by referring to the specific terms of Haman's edict (see 3:13). She uses a phrase with a double meaning: "delivered over to" can also mean "sold for," and by using the passive voice, she subtly alludes to the transaction between Haman and the king (3:9-11) without directly implicating the king in the scheme.

Despite her carefully considered approach, Esther can no longer hide her identity as a Jew, exposing herself to significant danger. Realizing the risks of this revelation, she tactfully apologizes for raising a potentially distressing matter (v. 4b), knowing that her admission could jeopardize her life.

Now, everything hinges on how the king will react to her shocking revelation. The narrator slows the pacing with the full titles of both the king and queen and repeats the verb "said" for emphasis (see comment). However, the king's reaction is swift and intense. The short, sharp nominal clauses in the Hebrew, with their concise wording and chiastic structure, reflect the king's anger: "Who is he? And where is he—the man who has dared to do such a thing?" One can almost hear him spitting out each word in fury. Clearly, he is enraged by the threat to his queen's life, but also oblivious to his own involvement in the plot. He asks for the identity and location of the culprit, not realizing that Haman, the very man he is addressing, is sitting right there.

Esther's response mirrors the king's anger, as she condemns Haman with biting words: "A hateful man and an enemy! This extremely unpleasant Haman!" The sharpness of her words, emphasized by the rhythmic structure of her speech, conveys the force of her accusation. One can almost imagine her pointing at Haman as she delivers her verdict

**Episode 2: Haman Pleads with Esther for His Life (vv. 6b–8b)**

In the first episode (vv. 1–6a), the narrator leaves Haman's reaction entirely to the reader's imagination. It is reasonable to assume that Haman attended the banquet not with confidence, but at least with the hope that such an intimate gathering with the king and queen might restore his wounded pride (cf. 5:12), so recently shattered by the humiliating failure of his plan to execute Mordecai. One can easily imagine his initial confusion, followed by growing dread, as he listened to Esther's plea. Completely unaware of her Jewish identity, Haman would have heard her appeal for her own life and for that of her people with disbelief and mounting anxiety. That anxiety would quickly turn into terror as the implications of her identity—and the precise wording of his own decree—became unmistakably clear: "We, I and my people, have been sold to be destroyed, slaughtered, and annihilated." His fear must have escalated into panic when the king erupted with his furious questions: "Who?" and "Where?"

After Esther's sharp and accusatory outburst (v. 6a), the narrator no longer leaves Haman's response unstated. He is seized by overwhelming terror, which drives him toward actions that seal his fate. The narrator depicts this moment with striking intensity, using a rapid sequence of near-simultaneous actions and virtually no dialogue: fear overwhelms Haman (v. 6b); the king storms out in anger (v. 7a); realizing the king intends him harm, Haman remains behind to beg Esther for mercy (v. 7b); the king returns from the garden (v. 8a); and at that very moment, he sees Haman collapsed upon Esther's couch, pleading for his life (v. 8b).

Upon realizing that the man responsible for threatening the queen's life is the very one who had been dining with him, the king bursts out into the palace garden. Consumed by rage, he is momentarily paralyzed, uncertain how to respond (v. 7a; see Comment). For once, the courtiers he normally relies upon for guidance are absent (cf. 1:13; Clines, 312). The narrator makes it clear that the king's fury is directed at Haman, allowing us to perceive the situation from Haman's perspective: "he saw that the king intended to do him harm" (v. 7c). This places the king in a serious dilemma (cf. Fox, 86): how can he punish Haman for a plot he himself authorized and for an irreversible decree issued in his own name? Wrestling with this tension, the king reenters the banquet hall just in time to witness Haman sprawled on Esther's couch, desperately pleading for his life (v. 8b).

**Episode 3: Haman's Execution (vv. 8c–10)**

Divine providence resolves the king's dilemma (Clines, *Esther Scroll*, 16). It stretches credibility to assume that the king genuinely believed Haman was attempting to assault the queen. Rather, the king deliberately interprets Haman's desperate actions in this way, thereby supplying himself with a convenient and socially acceptable charge on which to condemn him. This maneuver allows the king to avoid publicly confronting the true basis for Haman's punishment—the genocidal plot against the Jews—and thus spares him from acknowledging his own complicity in authorizing that decree. Once again, in keeping with the pattern of irresponsibility that defines Ahasuerus's character, he sidesteps accountability. Yet another remarkable coincidence operates in favor of the Jewish people.

Harbonah (cf. 1:10), recognizing that the king's accusation effectively amounts to a death sentence, intervenes at precisely the right moment. In doing so, he once again relieves the king of the burden of making an independent decision or consulting his advisors. Harbonah proposes an immediate method of execution and simultaneously introduces an additional charge against Haman: that he sought to kill the very man who had saved the king's life. With this, the king's decision is further legitimized.

The king promptly orders Haman's execution. Providence piles coincidence upon coincidence, and irony upon irony: Haman is executed on the very gallows he had constructed for Mordecai, and he is condemned for a crime he did not, in fact, commit.

The narrator deliberately minimizes the description of Haman's final moments. After recounting his terror at Esther's revelation (v. 6b), his realization that the king intended him harm (v. 7), and his frantic attempt to plead with the queen (v. 8a), the narrator tells us nothing of Haman's reaction to the sentence itself. We are not even told that he is led away for execution. Instead, we learn only that his face is covered (v. 8b), and we are reminded of the final irony—that the gallows were originally intended for Mordecai. In this way, the narrator invites the reader to imagine Haman's final realization, saturated with fear and bitter irony.

And what of Esther? As with Haman earlier in the scene, the narrator leaves her response entirely unspoken. She must have been uncertain of how the king would react to her accusations. It is reasonable to assume her emotions ranged from intense anxiety as the enraged king stormed out of the room, to overwhelming relief when he accused Haman instead. Nevertheless, throughout Haman's pleas and condemnation, Esther remains silent. Some interpreters have viewed this silence as a negative trait—suggesting callousness or indifference—but such readings misunderstand the situation. Haman is not a defeated enemy but an active and ongoing threat. As long as he lives, the danger to Esther, Mordecai, and the entire Jewish community remains. Whatever personal pity Esther may have felt, prudence would have prevented her from appealing for mercy on his behalf.

As the scene concludes, we are told that the king's anger subsided once Haman was executed on the gallows he had prepared for Mordecai (v. 10b). Notably, it is not the plot to annihilate an entire people that provokes the king's fury—after all, he had sanctioned that plan with casual indifference (3:11). Rather, it is the perceived insult to his honor through the threat against his queen that finally moves him. With that affront avenged, Ahasuerus is satisfied.

Yet the danger facing the Jewish community has not ended. Haman's death does not annul the irrevocable decree issued in the king's name. The true task assigned to Esther by Mordecai has only just begun. Together, Esther and Mordecai must now confront the seemingly impossible challenge of overturning an unalterable law.

### 5.4.7 Esther Appeals again to the king (8:1-17)

**Explanation:**

By this point, it must be evening at the end of the long and emotionally intense day that began with the king's sleeplessness in 6:1. Over the course of that day, Esther's appeal to the king successfully brought about Haman's removal. Yet eliminating Haman only removed the source of the dreadful decree; it did not undo the decree itself. In that sense, the mission entrusted to Esther by Mordecai—to secure the survival of the Jewish people—has only just begun. The danger to their very existence remains, embedded in the irrevocable edict that Haman issued in the king's name and sealed with the royal signet (3:12–15).

## SCENE 1: ESTHER AND MORDECAI GAIN AUTHORITY TO ISSUE A COUNTERDECREE (8:1–8)

### Episode 1: Mordecai Is Granted Access to the King (8:1–2)

The effort to counteract Haman's edict begins with a striking and uncharacteristic action by the king—one of the rare instances in the narrative where he acts on his own initiative. He transfers Haman's estate to Esther. This decision clearly reflects the effectiveness of Esther's strategy, which has consistently presented her as the primary victim of Haman's treachery (cf. Fox, 89–90). As a result, the king's anger subsided once the threat to his queen had been removed through Haman's execution (7:10). It was not the genocidal decree against an entire people that stirred the king's fury, but rather the affront to his personal honor in the attack upon Esther. This limited moral vision is entirely consistent with Ahasuerus's character.

This, however, leaves Esther with a difficult task: she must now persuade the king to address the unresolved issue of Haman's edict. Doing so requires great care, since the king appears eager to let the matter remain buried—almost certainly because acknowledging it would force him to confront his own role in authorizing the decree.

Esther begins by explaining to the king who Mordecai is to her (v. 1b). This likely conveys not only their familial relationship but also the depth of their bond (cf. 2:7, 10–11, 20) and Mordecai's integrity and character. As a consequence, Mordecai effectively assumes the position formerly held by Haman. First, like Haman before him (6:4), he is granted access to the king without the need for a formal summons (v. 1b). Next, the king gives Mordecai the signet ring that had been taken from Haman (v. 2a; cf. 3:10), thereby transferring to him the authority to act fully in the king's name (cf. 3:12c; 8:8). Finally, Esther appoints Mordecai as administrator over Haman's estate (v. 2b), providing him with the material resources appropriate to his new office.

It is crucial to recognize that each of these developments occurs through Esther's initiative. Because she informs the king of Mordecai's relationship to her, he is admitted into the royal presence and elevated to the position of vizier—beyond the honor he had already received for saving the king's life (6:1–11). Likewise, it is Esther who places him in charge of Haman's property. All of this forms part of her deliberate strategy for confronting Haman's decree, since Mordecai's newly acquired authority and power will be essential in neutralizing the ongoing threat to the Jewish people.

**Episode 2: The King Authorizes Esther and Mordecai to Issue a Counter-Edict on Behalf of the Jews (8:3–8)**

Once Mordecai has been elevated to the position of grand vizier, Esther moves immediately to confront the unresolved problem of Haman's decree. Timing is critical: the events surrounding Haman's exposure and execution are still vivid in the king's mind, and Esther seizes this moment to press her case. Doing so, however, is extremely perilous. Approaching a volatile and unpredictable monarch is always risky (cf. 4:11), but the danger is heightened here. Esther has already entered the king's presence without summons, invited him to a banquet, delayed her request by convening a second banquet, and finally exposed his most trusted official as a traitor whose scheme threatened her life—while also implicating the king himself in authorizing the decree. Requesting relief from that same decree therefore demands extraordinary discretion. Esther rises to the challenge.

The narrator records two distinct appeals. In the first (v. 3), Esther relies on emotional appeal; in the second, she deploys carefully crafted rhetoric (following Clines, *Esther Scroll*, 100–103). In describing the initial appeal, the narrator emphasizes her actions rather than her words: Esther falls at the king's feet and weeps. Her speech is reported only indirectly, but its substance is clear. Even here her tact is evident. She characterizes the decree as "the wicked scheme of Haman the Agagite," thereby implicitly absolving the king of responsibility.

After recounting the king's favorable responses-symbolized by the extension of the royal scepter—the narrator presents Esther's second appeal, now in direct discourse. This shift underscores the precision and deliberation of her rhetoric. The conditional formulas she has previously used reach their most elaborate form here. Initially she had merely said, "if it pleases the king" (5:4). Later she added, "if I have found favor with the king" (5:8; 7:3). Now she lays additional conditions. One of these— "if the matter seems proper in the king's eyes"—appeals subtly to the king's affection for her (cf. 2:17). What began as polite preliminaries has become a set of reasons for granting her request. Though not logically decisive, this appeal to personal regard is precisely the factor most likely to influence the king.

Having prepared the ground, Esther turns to the substance of her request. She must ask for the annulment of documents issued in the king's name, yet she continues to mask his involvement. She refers to the "dispatches" and immediately qualifies them as "the scheme of Haman son of Hammedatha the Agagite," further specifying that they were written to destroy the Jews throughout the king's provinces. She then adds what Clines aptly calls "a masterpiece of psychological and rhetorical insight" (*Esther Scroll*, 102). Esther cannot again center her plea on her own endangered life—it has already been spared. Nor can she realistically appeal to the king's concern for the Jewish people, whose fate has previously failed to move him. Instead, she grounds her appeal in the king's affection for her. She asks how she could possibly endure witnessing the destruction of her people and her family. In this moment, Esther herself becomes the decisive argument—and she employs it with precision and courage.

The delicacy of Esther's approach proves necessary, for the king's response (vv. 7–8) is abrupt and irritated. Addressing both Esther and Mordecai, he points to what he has already done: Haman has been executed and his estate transferred to Esther. Implicitly, he asks what more can reasonably be expected. Claiming his hands are tied, he reiterates the principle that a decree issued in the king's name and sealed with his signet cannot be revoked—a condition that clearly applies to Haman's edict (cf. 3:12). Once again, using emphatic language and direct command, the king evades responsibility: "You write," he instructs Esther and Mordecai, "whatever you see fit concerning the Jews" (v. 8).

> Write what you like, says the king, if it doesn't overturn, revoke or contradict anything previously written. Write what you like to Jewish advantage, says the king, if you realize that Haman's decree still stands. Write what you like, says the king, it will bear my seal; but remember that so does every other official document, including Haman's letter. Write what you like, says the king, for I give up; the conundrum of how to revoke an irrevocable decree, as you, Esther have asked, is beyond me; but feel free to write what you like – if you can think of a way to reverse the irreversible.

## SCENE 2: MORDECAI ISSUES THE COUNTERDECREE (8:9–17)

### Episode 1: The Counterdecree Is Written and Disseminated (8:9–14)

Mordecai resolves the crisis posed by Haman's edict with remarkable ingenuity. After a lapse of time—whose chronology is both significant and complex, the royal scribes are summoned, and Mordecai drafts and circulates a new decree. This decree grants the Jewish population throughout the empire the legal right to defend themselves by destroying any ethnic or political group that initiates violence against them. In narrating these events, the author unmistakably presents Mordecai's decree as a direct reversal and effective neutralization of Haman's earlier order.

First, this reversal is achieved through deliberate verbal and structural parallels. In verses 9–10 and 14, the narrator describes the drafting and dissemination of Mordecai's decree using language that closely echoes the account of Haman's edict in 3:12–15. These verses, however, are not simple replicas. Rather, they are carefully reworked in keyways to emphasize the dramatic shift in political authority now favoring the Jews throughout Ahasuerus's empire.

In verse 9, for example, the date of Mordecai's decree is highlighted by the anticipatory phrase "at that time," which may subtly allude to the symbolic importance of the intervening period. The list of imperial officials addressed in the decree is also significantly revised.

The satraps are no longer described as "royal," the governors are no longer identified as those "in charge of each province," and the officials are no longer designated as rulers "of each people." Moreover, these three administrative levels are no longer presented as parallel entities, each introduced by its own preposition. Instead, they are grouped together under a single preposition and described collectively as officials "of the provinces."

These modifications are underscored by three striking additions. Most notably, the Jews are now addressed explicitly and independently. They are not only placed on equal footing with the highest imperial officials, but they are listed first, thereby occupying a position of precedence. This elevation is reinforced in the clause concerning scripts and languages, where the Jews are treated separately and accorded the same status as "each province" and "each people." Finally, by reintroducing the phrase "from India to Ethiopia, one hundred and twenty-seven provinces" (borrowed from 1:1), the narrator underscores both the geographical extent of the empire and the wide dispersion of the Jewish population within it.

Additional details further reinforce this shift in power. The couriers responsible for delivering the decree are now described as riding specially designated mounts, using rare terminology that likely emphasizes both their speed and their royal authorization (v. 10). The vocabulary vividly conveys the urgency and authority with which the decree favoring the Jews is carried throughout the empire—a point reinforced by a similar addition in 8:14 (cf. 3:15a–b).

Second, the substance of Mordecai's decree (vv. 11–13) mirrors the wording of Haman's edict almost exactly, with two crucial additions and the necessary reversal of the object of violence. The first addition explicitly states that the king authorizes the Jews in every city to assemble and defend themselves (v. 11; see also the elaboration in v. 12). After repeating the three infinitives used in Haman's decree—"to destroy, to slay, and to annihilate"—the text redirects these actions toward "the forces of any people or province" that attack them. This language carefully limits Jewish violence to acts of self-defense rather than granting unrestricted license to attack others.

The further clause permitting the Jews "to take vengeance on their enemies" (v. 13, corresponding to 3:14) must be understood within this defensive framework. It does not authorize aggression but affirms the right to retaliate against those who initiate violence.

Through these literary strategies, the narrator powerfully communicates the complete reversal of Haman's edict. By adapting its language and structure while introducing decisive modifications, the text vividly portrays the transformation of the Jews' position— from victims of an irrevocable decree to empowered agents protected by imperial authority across the entire realm of Ahasuerus.

### Episode 2: Mordecai Departs the King's Presence in Splendor, and the Jews Rejoice (8:15–17)

In the closing episode of Scene 2, the total reversal of the Jews' status and authority is powerfully conveyed through a series of sharp contrasts between the outcomes of the two decrees. The earlier image of the king and Haman reclining at a banquet to celebrate Haman's edict (3:15c), while Mordecai mourned publicly in torn garments, sackcloth, and ashes (4:1), is now replaced by the sight of Mordecai departing from the king's presence clothed in garments of honor and distinction (v. 15a). The city of Susa, once portrayed as bewildered and disturbed (3:15d), now resounds with jubilation (v. 15b). For the Jews in Susa, the atmosphere has been utterly transformed into one of light, joy, gladness, and honor (v. 16).

This transformation extends across the empire. What had previously been described as "great mourning among the Jews, with fasting, weeping, and lamentation" (4:3a–b) is now replaced by "joy and gladness, feasting and celebration" (v. 17a–b). The reversal reaches its most striking expression in the final contrast: those who once lay in sackcloth and ashes (4:3c) are now replaced by "many of the peoples of the land" who identify themselves as Jews, motivated by fear of Jewish power (v. 17c).

At this point, the narrative has reached a decisive resolution—yet not its final completion. The original crisis was set in motion when Haman succeeded in inscribing into irreversible Persian law a decree commanding all peoples of the empire to destroy the Jews and seize their property on a single day, the thirteenth of Adar. Because Persian law cannot be revoked, that decree remains in force. Mordecai has not nullified it but countered it with a new edict granting the Jews explicit royal authorization to defend themselves by destroying any who attack them.

Thus, although the Jews now enjoy unprecedented favor—with Esther as queen and Mordecai as grand vizier—their safety is not yet assured. Haman's decree still carries legal authority, and it cannot be assumed that no one will attempt to act upon it when the appointed day arrives. The crisis that initiated the story therefore awaits its final resolution. The thirteenth of Adar still lies ahead as the day when opposing decrees, and the forces aligned with them, will confront one another. Celebration and confidence may abound, but victory, though anticipated, has not yet been fully realized.

### 5.4.8. *The Jews are Victorious (9:1-5)*

**Explanation:**

Having concluded the last act with a vibrant and rich portrayal of Mordecai clad in splendor and glory, the narrator can be perceived as stressing the visualization of the city of Susa ringing with joyous cheers. With the Jews engaged in feasting and celebration wherever Mordecai's edict reached, and with many peoples of the empire professing to be Jews, the narrator unmistakably underscored and presaged Jewish victory. So in the succeeding sections, he devotes minimal space and effort to undertake such a task.

He begins his report with a long, temporal clause, "in the twelfth month, the month of Adar, in the thirteenth day of it, when the king's command and edict arrived to be carried." Thereby he highlights, on the one hand, the fateful date prescribed by each of the conflicting edicts. On the other hand, through its unnecessarily full and extended form, he keeps us for a moment in suspense as to the outcome of the confrontation. But the suspense is no sooner created than it is relieved. Through a contrast highlighted by the unusual syntax of the main clause that forms its hinge (see comment), he reports the utter reversal of the hope of the Jews ememies to triumph over them (v 1). This statement is the clearest example in the book of the principle of "reversal". Which the author has so effectively built into this story (see the role of God in the story in the Theme and Purpose section in the Introduction to Esther). In the sentences that follow, he describes in the most general of therms how this reversal was affected. Three elements enter this dramatic success. First, the Jews go on the offensive. Assembling tougher in their localities, they attack all those who attempt to harm them (v 2a). Second, no one could withstand their attack, for fear of them had overtaken all (v 2b). And third, all the Persian ruling authorities, not only those of high office charged with executing the conflicting decrees but even the lowly officials who carry on the everyday work and activities of the royal court, aid the Jewish offensive (v 3a), because they now fear the constantly increasing power and fame of Mordecai (vv 3b-4). Finally, the brief narrative comes full circle with a result clause expressing, again in general terms, the utter completeness of the Jewish success: "so the Jews put all their enemies to the sword and worked their will on those who hated them" (v 5). By relating the Jewish victory in such succinct statements and in such general terms, the narrator not only expresses its over whelming nature and avoids going into the gory details, but he significantly subordinates this part of the resolution of the story to the previous detailed account in which Esther and Mordecai have obtained royal sanction for the Jewish defense. So, with the death and destruction of all their enemies, the terrible threat to the life of the whole Jewish community, which set our story in motion, has now been fully and completely resolved.

### 5.4.9. The Institution of the Festival of Purim (9:6–32)

**Explanation:**

The preceding act has narrated the decisive defeat of the Jews' enemies on the thirteenth day of Adar. While this victory brings to completion the resolution of the crisis triggered by Haman's decree, it does not constitute the conclusion of the book of Esther in its present form. The story is not told merely to explain how the Jews survived annihilation, nor solely to recount the origins of the festival of Purim. Although it does both, its primary objective lies elsewhere.

The narrator now shifts focus to the establishment of an annual festival intended to commemorate the joy and celebration that followed the dramatic deliverance of 13 Adar. The narrative becomes prescriptive rather than descriptive, aiming to persuade the Jewish community of its obligation to observe this celebration perpetually. At the time of writing, Purim was already being observed, as indicated by the etiological asides in verses 19 and 26a. These passages transport the reader from the narrated past into the narrator's present, grounding existing practices (v. 19) and even the festival's name (v. 26a) in the events just recounted.

A similar function is served by verse 23a, where the statement that "the Jews accepted what they had begun to do" refers not merely to the initial spontaneous celebrations but, more significantly, to the established and ongoing observance that had already taken shape (cf. v. 19 and the relevant comment). From this perspective, it becomes evident that the narrative's primary aim is not historical reportage but communal obligation. This intent becomes unmistakable in verse 28 (see Comment), where the narrator steps outside the recounting of past events and directly instructs his contemporaries regarding proper communal practice.

In this way, the narrative decisively redirects attention away from themes of military success, power, and triumph, and toward the lived present of its audience. The enduring significance of the Esther story lies not in the violence it recounts but in the ritual life it inaugurates—specifically, in the festal practices that give lasting expression to communal memory and identity.

**SCENE 1: THE EVENTS THAT GIVE RISE TO A TWO-DAY CELEBRATION OF PURIM (9:6–19)**

**Episode 1: The Fighting in Susa on the Thirteenth and Fourteenth of Adar (9:6–15)**

The opening scene (vv. 6–19) is devoted entirely to explaining why the festival of Purim is celebrated on two different days. Jews living outside the capital observe the festival on the fourteenth of Adar (v. 19), whereas those residing in Susa celebrate it on the fifteenth (v. 18). This explanatory aim governs the scene at every level of the narrative. It is evident not only in the explicit content and structure of the pericope but also in more subtle and revealing narrative tensions.

Up to this point, the story has demonstrated exceptional narrative coherence. Plot developments have unfolded smoothly, with no abrupt turns, and characters have consistently acted in ways that align with their established portrayals. Here, however, that narrative discipline noticeably breaks down. The plot begins to show strain, and several developments appear disconnected from what precedes them.

Numerous scholars have noted that the king's offer in verse 12c is poorly integrated into the storyline. Nothing in the prior narrative prepares the reader for such an offer. Although its wording closely resembles the three earlier offers made to Esther (5:3; 5:6; 7:2), those earlier moments were prompted by clear signals that Esther wished to make a request—first by entering the king's presence unsummoned, and later by inviting him to banquet designed to frame her appeal. In the present context, however, there is no indication whatsoever that Esther intends to ask for anything further. On the contrary, the decisive Jewish victory of the previous day appears to have fully satisfied her original petition (cf. 7:2). The king's assumption that Esther has another request lacks narrative justification.

Instead, the offer seems to arise solely from the king's recitation of the number of those killed in the citadel of Susa and his rhetorical speculation about casualties elsewhere in the empire (v. 12a–b). Even if these remarks express astonishment at the scale of Jewish success, they provide no logical basis for concluding that Esther seeks additional action.

Equally problematic is the king's behavior itself. Throughout the narrative, Ahasuerus has been portrayed as indecisive and dependent on advisers. He required counsel to deal with Vashti (1:13–22), relied on attendants to propose a method for choosing a new queen (2:1–4), and sought guidance from his vizier when deciding how to reward Mordecai (6:1–9). Yet here, without consulting any advisers, he acts decisively and independently, offering Esther unrestricted authority. This sudden decisiveness runs counter to his established characterization and remains unexplained by the plot.

The incongruity extends further to Esther's response (vv. 13–14a). Her request for an additional day of fighting in Susa is likewise unsupported by prior narrative developments. Both Haman's original decree (3:13) and Mordecai's counterdecree (8:12) limited sanctioned violence to a single day—the thirteenth of Adar. That day has now passed, and the narrative describes a total Jewish victory: "they struck down all their enemies" (9:5). From the story's own logic, the Jews appear fully secure. The need for further combat is therefore unclear.

While one might speculate that enemies still remained in Susa or that earlier casualties were confined to the citadel rather than the city proper, such conjectures only highlight the narrative difficulty. Had the text intended such an explanation, it could easily have provided even the slightest indication. The necessity of reconstructing motives that the narrative itself does not supply underscores the awkwardness of this development.

A final inconsistency concerns geography. Both the narrator's account of the fighting (vv. 6–11) and the king's summary (v. 12) refer exclusively to events in the citadel of Susa. Esther's request in verse 13, however, shifts focus to the city of Susa as a whole. This broader locale then dominates the fulfillment of her request (vv. 14–15) and the etiological explanation of the differing festival dates (vv. 16–19). Once again, the shift lacks grounding in the preceding narrative.

Whether this inconsistency reflects multiple sources (as suggested by Clines, *Esther Scroll*, 181 n.29) or not, the abrupt relocation cannot be adequately explained by the plot itself. Nor is it likely to be a later scribal addition. Its most plausible explanation lies in the narrative's broader purpose: a second day of fighting in Susa is required to justify the distinct calendrical observance of Purim in the capital as opposed to the rest of the empire.

It is therefore clear that the king's offer, Esther's subsequent request, and the sudden expansion from the citadel to the city of Susa cannot be explained by reference to earlier narrative developments. This does not imply that they are narratively meaningless. Rather, as the following episode will demonstrate, their significance lies not in what precedes them, but in what they are designed to accomplish in what follows.

Episode 2: The Reason for the Two-Day Celebration of Purim in Susa and Elsewhere (9:16–19)

With this episode, the intent behind the preceding narrative becomes immediately apparent. The narrator now contrasts the two days of fighting in Susa with the events that took place throughout the rest of the empire. He first recounts the victory of the Jews outside Susa (v. 16), once again in highly generalized terms and with familiar elements—the number of those slain and the explicit note that no plunder was taken. Yet the purpose of this description is not simply to provide additional details about provincial combat.

This aim is evident even in the structure of the passage. Verses 16 and 17 are syntactically bound together as a single compound unit and are closely linked to verse 18 (see Form/Structure/Setting). More importantly, the narrator's intention is revealed through content. Verse 18, which closely parallels verses 16–17, functions as a narrative flashback to the actions of the Jews in Susa described in the previous episode. This deliberate parallelism highlights the contrast between the experiences of Jews in the capital and those elsewhere in the empire.

The distinction is clear: Jews in the provinces observed their celebration on the fourteenth of Adar, while Jews in Susa celebrated on the fifteenth. The narrator then explicitly explains the significance of this contrast. In verse 19, he inserts an explanatory digression that moves the reader from the narrated past into the narrator's own present. Here, he draws the conclusion toward which the entire account has been leading. The difference in the days of rest and rejoicing—fourteenth Adar outside Susa and fifteenth Adar within it—accounts for the continued observance of Purim on two distinct dates, a practice that was already established at the time of writing.

This passage also introduces a new thematic element. In verses 16–18, the narrator notes for the first time that each day of conflict was followed by a day of rest, which was marked by joy and feasting (v. 17). The explanatory comment in verse 19 extends this theme, indicating that Jews outside Susa—and by implication those within the capital as well—continued to commemorate these occasions as festive holidays characterized by feasting and the exchange of food gifts. This motif will be taken up again and further developed in the subsequent scene.

Finally, the narrative and its concluding explanation make clear that the issue of regulating and legitimizing the two different celebration dates within the Jewish community requires formal resolution. It is therefore unsurprising that this very matter becomes a central concern in the message Mordecai sends to all the Jews in the following episode.

In this scene, the narrator addresses what is central to the entire act: the formal institution of the festival of Purim. From the explanatory aside in verse 19, it is already evident that the Jewish community had begun to commemorate the events spontaneously in the days following the conflict. The narrator now explains how this spontaneous response is transformed into an enduring and regulated communal practice.

## SCENE 2: MORDECAI, ESTHER, AND THE JEWISH COMMUNITY FORMALLY ESTABLISH PURIM AND COMMIT TO ITS PERPETUAL OBSERVANCE (9:20–32)

As the recognized leader of the Jewish community, Mordecai takes the first step in formalizing the observance by writing to all the Jews (vv. 20–22). It is significant that Mordecai does not issue his directive in the manner of a divine lawgiver, imposing commands by sheer authority. Instead, the narrator employs a verb that conveys moral obligation rather than coercion—"to impose an obligation" or "to bind by responsibility." Mordecai appeals to the community's sense of what is appropriate and fitting considering their deliverance, rather than issuing an uncompromising decree.

Second, Mordecai defines the dates of the festival. He obligates the community to observe Purim annually on "the fourteenth and the fifteenth day of the month of Adar" (v. 21). Given that the previous scene was devoted to explaining why different segments of the Jewish population had celebrated on different days, it is likely that Mordecai's purpose here is to resolve that discrepancy. Either he is calling upon all Jews to recognize both days as legitimate, since each had already been observed by part of the community, or he is affirming that each group should observe the day appropriate to its geographical situation (see Comment on v. 21).

Third, Mordecai defines the character and meaning of the festival. These days are to be celebrated "as the days on which the Jews gained relief from their enemies and as the month that was turned for them from sorrow to joy and from mourning to festivity." To ensure that this transformation is clearly understood, Mordecai concludes with a clarifying summary that specifies the form the celebration should take: the observance of joyful feasting, the exchange of food gifts among neighbors, and the giving of gifts to the poor (see Comment). In this way, the festival is explicitly grounded in the experience of rest and rejoicing that followed the days of conflict and deliverance—a point of considerable theological significance (see Theology section).

## Episode 2: The Jewish Community Commits Itself, Its Descendants, and All Converts to the Perpetual Observance of Purim (9:23–28)

The establishment of Purim as a permanent festival does not rest solely on Mordecai's written directive. In this second episode, the narrator emphasizes that the Jewish community itself formally assumed responsibility for the observance. The process unfolds in several carefully articulated stages.

First, the narrator states that the Jews "accepted what they had begun to do" (v. 23a). This acceptance clearly encompasses both the spontaneous celebrations that followed the initial victory (vv. 17–18) and the continuing festive practices that had already taken shape within the community (v. 19). At the same time, the narrator explicitly links this acceptance to Mordecai's initiative by adding that they also accepted "what Mordecai had written to them" (v. 23b). What follows is a retrospective summary drawn from Mordecai's letter (vv. 24–25), which anchors the obligation to observe the festival in the crisis precipitated by Haman's plot and the dramatic deliverance that followed. In this way, the narrator underscores that the festival is grounded not in abstraction but in lived historical experience.

The narrator then reinforces this commitment with striking emphasis. In verse 27, he declares that the Jews "bound themselves, their descendants, and all who joined them" to observe these days annually, in accordance with both the manner of celebration and the specific dates previously defined. This binding obligation is rooted not only in Mordecai's letter (v. 26b) but also in "what they themselves had experienced and what had happened to them" (v. 26c–d)—a reference to the entire narrative of threat, reversal, and deliverance just rehearsed in the retrospective (vv. 24–25).

The enduring nature of this commitment is articulated with particular force in verse 28. At this point, the narrator shifts from recounting past actions to addressing the community across time. He adopts the language of obligation rather than simple futurity: these days are to be observed in every generation, in every family, province, and city; their celebration must never cease among the Jews; and their remembrance must not disappear from among their descendants. Authority for the festival thus arises not only from communal leadership but also from the collective agency of the people—first in their spontaneous celebration and then in their deliberate decision to institutionalize it permanently.

The narrator further explains, in a second etiological aside (v. 26a), that the name of the festival, *Purim*, derives from *pur*, the lot cast by Haman in his attempt to determine the timing of the Jews' destruction (as recalled in vv. 24–25). The naming of the festival therefore recalls the threatened annihilation and subsequent deliverance rather than the military defeat of enemies (see Theology section in the Introduction). Notably, the narrator does not attribute the naming of the festival either to Mordecai or explicitly to the community now of its institutionalization. Instead, he presents the name as already established in his own time, citing its origin with an indefinite third-person plural—effectively a passive construction in English. As a result, the precise moment and agent of the naming are left embedded in tradition rather than historical record.

**Episode 3: Esther Writes to Confirm the Observance of Purim (9:29–32)**

In the final episode, the narrator reports that Esther herself also wrote to the Jewish community. Significantly, she writes independently rather than jointly with Mordecai (see Comment). Unlike Mordecai, however, Esther does not write to impose an obligation. Her letter serves instead to confirm and ratify the observance that has already been established. She lends her authority as queen—explicitly exercising the full weight of her position (see Comment on v. 29)—to reinforce both Mordecai's initiative and the community's collective commitment.

Esther's confirmation encompasses multiple dimensions of the festival. She affirms the appointed times for its observance (v. 31a) and its character as a celebration marked by feasting and the exchange of gifts, "in the same manner that Mordecai the Jew had obligated them" (v. 31b). In the present form of the text (see Comment), her letter also validates the community's prior commitment to fasts and lamentations associated with the crisis (v. 31c). In this way, the joy of Purim does not erase the memory of the peril that preceded deliverance but preserves it within the ritual life of the community (see Theology section).

With this final confirmation, the narrative reaches its denouement. The conclusion is striking, for the story does more than recount the fate of its protagonists or the resolution of a historical crisis. It culminates in the formal establishment of a lasting religious observance for Jews living in the diaspora—a development of profound theological and communal significance (see Theology section).

### 5.4.10. Epilogue (10:1-3)

**Explanation:**

In this concluding epilogue, the narrator shifts focus away from the calendrical details and ritual practices associated with Purim and returns to a narrative strand introduced earlier: the elevation and enduring prominence of Mordecai. Throughout the preceding sections, Mordecai's rise has been evident but not explicitly consolidated. When the king handed Mordecai the signet ring he had previously taken from Haman, the gesture symbolized a decisive transfer of authority from enemy to deliverer (8:2). Such an act strongly suggests that Mordecai now stands as the king's chief official, effectively assuming the role once occupied by Haman.

Yet the narrative has treated this development with notable restraint. Mordecai's advancement initially occurs through Esther's intervention in her role as queen (8:1), and his authority is mentioned only incidentally in connection with the issuance of the counter-edict, for which the king explicitly empowered him (8:7–9). Beyond this, the text offers only brief and indirect indications of his status: he departs the royal presence clothed in garments of honor (8:15a), and later, during the events of 13 Adar, he is described as "great in the palace" and as one whose influence continued to increase (9:3–4).

Moreover, in the retrospective summary of the crisis and deliverance that grounds the festival of Purim (9:24–25), the narrator deliberately suppresses the decisive roles played by both Mordecai and Esther, instead foregrounding the king's actions. This narrative choice heightens the need for clarification at the conclusion. Consequently, the epilogue functions to resolve any lingering ambiguity by affirming that Mordecai did, in fact, occupy the position of grand vizier fully and permanently.

Although this final commendation is not strictly necessary for the resolution of the plot itself, it serves as a fitting closure. By explicitly affirming Mordecai's lasting authority and stature, the narrator neatly completes the arc of his ascent and brings the narrative to a satisfying and coherent conclusion.

The narrator opens with a statement that, at least on a secondary level, brings the narrative full circle by once again evoking both the vast reach of the Persian Empire and the absolute authority of its ruler, Ahasuerus (cf. 1:1–4 and the accompanying explanation). This reference, however, is not primarily intended to celebrate imperial power or royal magnificence. Rather, the evocation of Ahasuerus's greatness functions rhetorically to underscore the significance and elevated status of Mordecai, his Jewish chief official.

This purpose becomes unmistakable in v. 2, where the narrator adopts the same formal phrasing used to conclude the regnal summaries of the kings of Judah and Israel. By invoking this familiar historiographic formula, he implicitly aligns Mordecai's stature as leader of the Jewish community—specifically the diaspora (see Theme and Purpose in the Introduction to Esther)—with that of Israel's monarchs in the era of the kingdom. Any suggestion that this parallel might extend to moral evaluation, however, is decisively excluded by the grounds upon which Mordecai's reputation is immediately established in the following verse.

The narrator roots this commendation of Mordecai in two complementary dimensions of his activity: his service to the Persian crown and his commitment to his own people (v. 3). With respect to the former, Mordecai is described as "second to the king," a designation fully appropriate within the Persian administrative system and one that also recalls hierarchical structures familiar from Israel's priestly and court traditions. With respect to the latter, he is again identified explicitly as "Mordecai the Jew," a reminder that this encomium is framed within the context of the diaspora. His prominence among the Jews and the esteem he enjoys among his compatriots are not portrayed as a mere byproduct of his high position in a foreign court—important though that position is—nor even as a direct consequence of his role in the dramatic deliverance narrated earlier. Instead, his reputation rests on his persistent efforts to advance the interests of his people and to promote the well-being of their future generations, a point emphasized by the use of present participles that depict his activity as ongoing rather than episodic.

Mordecai first appears in the narrative as a Jew of the diaspora, residing in the citadel of Susa and occupying a relatively modest post within the Persian bureaucracy (2:5). By the conclusion of the story, he stands as grand vizier, second only to the king in authority, exercising that power explicitly for the benefit of his people. In this way, Mordecai embodies for diaspora communities the possibility of leading a meaningful and constructive life within a foreign sociopolitical environment—participating fully in its complex political, social, and economic structures—while at the same time remaining firmly rooted in loyalty to one's own community. More profoundly still, he represents both the necessity and the hope, deeply felt within the diaspora, of having a trusted advocate in positions of power, whose dual allegiance may serve as a means of deliverance from the dangers inherent in life under foreign rule (cf. Josephus, 1998).

# Chapter 6- Translation and Commentary:

## 6.1- Translation:

### 6.1.1. THE BOOK OF ESTHER GE'EZ MANUSCRIPT/HEB.

(See appendix –B)

### 6.1.2. Translation English

**BOOK OF ESTHER FROM THE GE'EZ MANUSCRIPT**

**ESTHER (KJV1990)**

## <u>Esther Chapter 1</u>

1. Now it came to pass in the days of Ahasuerus, (this is Ahasuerus who reigned, from India even unto Ethiopia, over a hundred and seven and twenty provinces)
2. That in those days, when the king Ahasuerus sat on the throne of his kingdom, which was in Shushan the castle,
3. In the third year of his reign, he made a feast unto all his princes and his servants; the army of Persia and Media, the nobles and princes of the provinces, being before him;

4.  When he showed the riches of his glorious kingdom and the honour of his excellent majesty, many days, even a hundred and fourscore days.

5.  And when these days were fulfilled, the king made a feast unto all the people that were present in Shushan the castle, both great and small, seven days, in the court of the garden of the king's palace.

6.  There were hangings of white, fine cotton, and blue, bordered with cords of fine linen and purple, upon silver rods and pillars of marble; the couches were of gold and silver, upon a pavement of green, and white, and shell, and onyx marble.

7.  And they gave them drink in vessels of gold, the vessels being diverse one from another—and royal wine in abundance, according to the bounty of the king.

8.  And the drinking was according to the law; none did compel; for so the king had appointed all the officers of his house, that they should do according to every man's pleasure. (S)

9.  Also, Vashti the queen made feast for the women in the royal house which belonged to king Ahasuerus.

10. On the seventh day, when the heart of the king was merry with wine, he commanded Mehuman, Bizzetha, Harbona, Bigtha, and Abagtha, Zethar, and Carcas, the seven chamberlains that ministered in the presence of Ahasuerus the king,

11. To bring Vashti the queen before the king with the crown royal, to show the peoles and the princes her beauty; for she was fair to look on.

12. But queen Vashti refused to come at the king's commandement by the chamberlains; therefore, was the king very worth, and his anger burned in him. **(S)**

13. Then the king said to the wise men, who knew the times—for so was the king's manner toward all that knew law and judgment.

14. And the next unto him were Carshena, Shethar, Admatha, Tarshish, Meres, Marsena, and Memucan, the seven princes of Persia and Media, who waw the king's face, and sat the first in the kingdom:

15. 'What shall we do about queen Vashti according to law, forasmuch as she hath not done the bidding of the king Ahasuerus by the chamberlains?' **(S)**

16. And Memucan answered before the king and the princes: Vashti the queen hath not done wrong to the king only, but also to all the princes, and to all the peoples, that are in all the provinces of the king Ahasuerus.

17. For this deed of the queen will come abroad unto all women, to make their husbands contemptible in their eyes, when it will be said: the king Ahasuerus commanded Vashti the queen to be brought in before him, but she came not.

18. And this day will the princesses of Persia and Media who have heard of the deed of the queen say the like unto all the king's princes. So will there arise enough contempt and wrath.

19. If it pleases the king, let there go forth a royal commandment from him, and let it be written among the laws of the Persians

and the Mede3s, that it be not altered, that Vashti come no more before king Ahasuerus, and that the king give her royal estate unto another that is better than she.

20. And when the king's decree which he shall make shall be published throughout all his kingdom, great though it be, all the wives will give to their husband's honour, both to great and small.'

21. And the word pleased the king and the princes; and the king did according to the word of Memucan.

22. For he sent letters into all the king's provinces, into every province according to the writing thereof, and to every people after their language, that every man should bear rule in his own house, and speak according to the language of his people. (S)

## Esther Chapter 2

1. After these things, when the wrath of king Ahasuerus was assuaged, he remembered Vashti, and what she had done, and what was decreed against her.

2. Then said the king's servants that ministered unto him: 'Let there be sought for the king young virgins fair to look on;

3. And let the king appoint officers in all the provinces of his kingdom, that they may gather all the fair young virgins unto Shushan the castle, to the house of the women, unto the

custody of Hegai the king's chamberlain, keeper of the women; and let their ointments be given them;

4. And let the maiden that pleaseth the king be queen instead of Vashti. 'And the thing pleased the king; and he did so. (**S**)

5. There was a certain Jew in Shushan the castle, whose name was Mordecai the son of Jair the son of Shimei the son of Kish, a Benjamite,

6. Who had been carried away from Jerusalem with the captives that had been carried away with Jeconiah, king of Judah, whom Nebuchadnezzar the king of Babylon had carried away.

7. And he brought up Hadassah, that is, Esther, his uncles's daughter; for she had neither father nor mother, and the maiden was of beautiful form and fair to look on; and when her father and mother were dead, Mordecai took her for his own daughter.

8. So it came to pass, when the king's commandement and his decree was published, and when many maidens were gathered unto Shushan the castle, to the custody of Hegai, that Esther was taken into the king's house, to the custody of Hegai, keeper of the women.

9. And the maiden pleased him, and she obtained kindness of him; and he speedily gave her ointments, with her portions, and the seven maidens, who were meet to be given her out of the king's house; and he advanced her and her maidens to the best place in the house of the women.

10. Esther had not made known her people nor her kindred; for Mordecai had charged her that she should not tell it.

11. And Mordecai walked every day before the court of the women's house, to know how Esther did, and what would become of her.

12. Now when the turn of every maiden was come to go in to king Ahasuerus, after that it had been done to her according to the l aw for the women, twelve months—for so were the days of their anointing accomplished, to wit, six months with oil of myrrh, and six month with sweet odours, and with other ointments of the women.

13. When the the maiden came unto the king, whatsoever she desired was given her to go with her out of the house of the women unto the king's house.

14. In the evening, she went, and on the morrow, she returned into the second house of the women, to the custody of Shaashgaz, the king's chamberlai, who kept the concubines; she came in unto the king no more, except the king delighted in her, and she were called by name.

15. Now when the turn of Esther, the daughter of Abihail the uncle of Mordecai, who had taken her for his daughter, was come to go in unto the king, she required nothing but what Hegai the king's chamberlain, the keeper of the women, appointed. And Esther obtained favour in the sight of all of them that looked upon her.

16. So, Esther was taken unto king Ahasuerus into his house royal in the tenth month, which is the month Tebeth, in the seventy years of his reign.

17. And the king loved Esther above all the women, and she obtained grace and favour in his sight more than all the virgins; so that he set the royal crown upon her head and made her queen instead of Vashti.

18. Then the king made a great feast unto all his princes and his servants, even Esther's feas; and he made a release to the provinces, and gave gifts, according to the bounty of the king.

19. And when the virgins were gathered the second time, and Mordecai sat in the king's gate—

20. Esther had not yet made known her kindred nor her people; as Mordecai had charged her; for Esther did the commandment of Mordecai, like when she was brought up with him—(S)

21. In those days, while Mordecai sat in the king's gate, two of the king's chamberlains, Bigthan and Teresh, of those that kept the door, were wroth, and sought to lay hands on the king Ahasuerus.

22. And the thing became known to Mordecai, who told it unto Esther the queen; and Esther told the king thereof in Mordcai's name.

23. And when inquisition was made of the matter, and it was found to be so, whey was both hanged on a tree; and it was written in the book of the chronicles before the king. (S)

24.

# Esther Chapter 3

1. After these things did king Ahasuerus promote Haman, the son of Hammedatha the Agagite, and advanced him, and set his seat above all the princes that were with him.

2. And all the king's servants, that were in the king's gate, bowed down, and prostrated themselves before Haman; for the king had so commanded concerning him. But Mordecai bowed not down, nor prostrated himself before him.

3. Then the king's servants that were in the king's gate, said unto Mordecai: 'whu transgresses thou the king's commandment?'

4. Now it came to pass, when they spoke daily unto him, and he hearkened not unto them, that they told Haman, to see whether Mordecai's words would stand; for he had told them that he was a Jew.

5. And when Haman saw that Mordecai bowed not down, nor prostrated himself before him, then was Haman full of wrath.

6. But it seemed contemptible in his eyes to lay hands on Mordecai alone; for they had made known to him the people of Mordecai; wherefore Haman sought to destroy all the Jews that were throughout the whole kingdom of Ahasuerus, even the people of Mordecai.

7. In the first month, which is the month Nisan, in the twelfth year of king Ahasuerus, they cast pur, that is, the lot, before Haman from day to day, and from month to month, to the twelfth month, which is the month Adar. (S)

8.  And Haman said unto king Ahasuerus: There is a certain people scattered abroad and dispersed among the peoples in all their laws are diverse from those of every people; neither keep they the king's laws; therefore, it profiteth not the kingto suffer them.

9.  If it please the king, let it be written that they be destroyed; and we will pay then thousand talents of silver in the hands of those that have the charge of the king's business, to bring it into the king's treasuries.'

10. And the king took his ring from his hand and gave it unto Haman the son of Hammedatha the Agagite, the Jews' enemy.

11. And the king said unto Haman: 'The silver is given to the people, the people also, to do with them as it seemeth good to thee.'

12. Then were the king's scribes called in the first month, on the thirteenth day thereof, and there was written, according to all that Haman commanded, unto the king's satraps, and to the governors that were over every province, and to the princes of every people; to every province according to the writing thereof, and to every people after their language; in the name of king Ahasuerus was it written and it was sealed with the king's ring.

13. And letters were sent by posts into all the king's provinces, to destroy, to slay, and to cause to perish, all Jews, both young and old, little children and women, in one day, even upon the

thirteenth day of the twelfth month, which is the month Adar, and to take the spoil of them for a prey.

14. The copy of the writing, to be given out for a decree in every province, was to be published into all peoples, that they should be ready against that day.

15. The posts went forth in haste by the king's commandment, and the decree was given out in Shushan the castle; and the king and Haman sat down to drink; but the city of Shushan was perplexed.

## Esther Chapter 4

1. Now when Mordecai knew all that was done, Mordecai rent his clothes, and put on sackcloth with ashes, and went out into the midst of the city, and cried with a loud and bitter cry.

2. And he came even before the king's gate; for no one might enter within the king's gate clothed with sackcloth.

3. And in every province, with her so ever the king's commandment and his decree came, there was great mourning among the Jews, and fasting, and weeping, and wiling, and many lay in sackcloth and ashes.

4. And Esther's maidens and her chamberlains came and told it her; and the queen was exceedingly pained; and she sent raiment to clothe Mordecai; and to take his sackcloth from off him; but he accepted it not.

5. Then called Esther for Hathach, one of the king's chamberlains, whom he had appointed to attend upon her, and

charged him to go to Mordecai, to know what this was, and why it was.

6.  So Hathach went forth to Mordecai unto the broad place of the city, which was before the king's gate.

7.  And Mordecai told him of all that had happened unto him, and the exact sum of the money that Haman had promised to pay to the king's treasuries for the Jews, to destroy them.

8.  Also he gave him the copy of the writing of the decree that was given out in Shushan to destroy them, to show it unto Esther, and to declare it unto her; and to charge her that she should go unto the king, to make supplication unto him, and to make request before him, for her people.

9.  And Hathach came and told Esther the words of Mordecai.

10. Then Esther spoke unto Hathach, and gave him a message unto Mordecai:

11. All the king's servants, and the people of the king's provinces, do know, that whose ever, whether man or woman, shall come unto the king into the inner court, who is called, there is one law for him, that he be put to death, except such to whom the king shall hold out the golden scepter, that he may live; but I have not been called to come in unto the king these thirty days

12. And they told Mordecai Esther's words.

13. Then Mordecai bade them to return answer unto Esther: 'Think not with thyself that thou shalt escape in the king's house, more than all the Jews.

14. For if thou altogether holdest thy 0911665682 peace at this time, then will relief and deliverance arise to the Jews from another place, but thou and thy father's house will Perish; and who knoweth whether thou art not come to royal estate for such a time as this?

15. Then Esther bade them return answer unto Mordecai:

16. Go, gather together all the Jews that are present in Shushan, and fast ye for me, and neither eat nor drink three days, night or da; also and my maidens will fast in like manner; and so will I go in unto the king, which is not according to the law; and if I Perish, I Perish.'

17. So Mordecai went his way and did according to all that Esther had commanded him.

## Esther Chapter 5

1. Now it came to pass on the third day, that Esther put on her royal apparel, and stood in the inner court of the king's house, over against the king's house; and the king sat upon his royal throne in the royal house, over against the entrance of the house.

2. And it was so, when the king saw Esther, the queen standing in the court, that she obtained favour in his sight; and the king held out to Esther the golden scepter that was in his hand. So, Esther drew near and touched the top of the scepter.

3. Then the king said to her: 'what will thou, Queen Esther?" For whatever they request, even to the half of the kingdom, it shall be given there.'

4. And Esther said: 'if it seems good unto the king, let the king and Haman come this day unto the banquet that I have prepared for him.'

5. Then the king said: 'Cause Haman to make haste, that it may be done as Esther hath said.' So the king and Haman came to the banquet that Esther had prepared.

6. And the king said unto Esther at the banquet of wine: 'Whatever thy petition, it shall be granted thee; and whatever thy request, even to the half of the kingdom, it shall be performed.'

7. Then answered Esther, and said: 'My petition and my request is-

8. If I have found favour in the sight of the king, and if it please the king to grant my petition, and to perform my request—let the king and Haman come to the banquet that I shall prepare for them, and I will do to-morrow as the king hath said.'

9. Then went Haman forth that day Joyful and glad of heart; but when Haman saw Mordecai in the king's gate, that he stood not up, nor moved for him, Haman was filled with wrath against Mordecai.

10. Nevertheless Haman refrained himself and went home; and he sent and fetched his friends and Zeresh his wife.

11. And Haman recounted to them the glory of his riches, and the multitude of his children, and everything as to how the king had promoted him, and how he had advanced him above the princes and servants of the king.

12. Haman said moreover: Yea, Esther the queen did let no man come in with the king unto the banquet that she had prepared but myself; and to-morrow also am I invited by her together with the king.

13. Yet all this availeth me nothing, so long as I see Mordecai the Jew sitting at the king's gate.

14. Then said Zeresh his wife and all his friends unto him: 'Let a gallows be made of fifty cubits high, and in the morning speak thou unto the king that Mordecai may be hanged thereon; then go thou in merrily with the king unto the banquet.' And the thing pleased Haman; and he caused the gallows to be made. (S)

## Esther Chapter 6

1. On that night the king could not sleep; and he commanded to bring the book of records of the chronicles, and they were read before the king.

2. And it was found written that Mordecai had told of Bigthana and Teresh, two of the king's chamberlains, of those that kept the door, who had sought to lay hands on the king Ahasuerus.

3. And the king said: what honour and dignity hath been done to Mordecai for this?' Then said the king's servants that ministered unto him: 'There is nothing done for him.'

4. And the king said: 'who is in the court?' –Now Haman came into the outer court of the king's house, to speak unto the king to hang Mordecai on the gallows that he had prepared for him. –

5. And the king's servants said unto him: 'Behold, Haman standeth in the court. 'And the king said: 'Let him come in.'

6. So, Haman came in. And the king said unto him: 'what shall be done unto the man whom the king delighteth to honour?' –Now Haman said in his heart: 'Whom would the king delight to honour besides myself?'

7. And Haman said unto the king: For the man whom the king delighteth to hounour,

8. Let royal apparel be brouth which the king useth to wear, and the horse that the king rideth upon, and on whose head a crown royal is set.

9. And let the apparel and the horse be delivered to the hand of one of the king's most noble princes, that they may array the man there with whom the king delighteth to honour, and cause him to ride on horse back through the street of the city, and proclaim before him: Thus shall it be done to the man whom the king delighteth to honour.

10. Then the king said to Haman: Make haste, and take the apparel and the horse, as thou hast said, and do even so to Mordecai the Jew, that sitteth at the king's gate; let nothing fail of all that thou hast spoken.

11. Then took Haman the apparel and the horse, and arrayed Mordecai, and caused him to ride through the street of the city and proclaimed before him: 'Thus shall it be done unto the man whom the king delighteth to honour.

12. And Mordecai returned to the king's gate. But Haman hasted his house, mourning and having his head covered.

13. And Haman recounted unto Zeresh his wife and all his friends everything that had befallen him. Then said his wise men and Zeresh his wife unto him: 'If Mordecai, before whom thou hast begun to fall, be of the seed of the Jews, thou shalt not prevail against him, but shalt surely fall before him.'

14. While they were yet talking with him, came the king's chamberlains, and hastened to bring Haman unto the banquet that Esther had prepared.

## <u>Esther Chapter 7</u>

1. So the king and Haman came to banquet with Esther the queen.

2. And the king said again unto Esther on the second day at the banquet of wine. 'Whatever thy petition, queen Esther, it shall

be granted there; and what ever thy request, even to the half of the kingdom, it shall be performed.'

3.  Then Esther the queen answered and said: 'If I have found favour in thy sight, O king, and if it please the king, let my life be given me at my petition, and my people at my request.

4.  For we are sold, I and my people, to be destroyed, to be slain, and to perish. But if we had been sold for bondmen and bondwomen, I would have held my peace, for the adversary is not worthy that the king be endamaged.' (S)

5.  Then spoke the king Ahasuerus and said unto Esther the queen: Who is he, and where is he, that durst presume in his heart to do so?'

6.  And Esther said: 'An adversary and an enemy, even this wicked Haman, 'Then Haman was terrified before the king and the queen.

7.  And the king arose in his wrath from the banquet of wine and went into the palace garden; but Haman remained to make request for his life to Esther the queen; for the saw that there was evil determined against him by the king.

8.  Then the king returned out of the palace garden into the place of the banquet of wine; and Haman fell upon the couch where on Esther was. Then said the king: 'Will he even force the queen before me in the house?' As the word went out of the king's mouth, they covered Haman's face.

9.  Then said Harbonah, one of the chamberlains that were before the king: 'Behold also, the gallows fifty cubits high, which

Haman hath made for Mordecai, who spoke good for the king, standeth in the house of Haman. 'And the king said: Hang him thereon.

10. So they hung Haman on the gallows that he had prepared for Mordecai. Then was the king's wrath assuaged. (**S**)

## **Esther Chapter 8**

1. On that day did the king Ahasuerus give the house of Haman the Jews 'enemy unto Esther the queen. And Mordecai came before the king; for Esther had told what he was unto her.

2. And the king took off his ring, which he had taken from Haman, and gave it unto Mordecai, And Esther set Mordecai over the house of Haman. (**S**)

3. And Esther spoke yet again before the king, and fell down at his feet, and besought him with tears to put away the mischief of Haman the Agagite, and his device that he had devised against the Jews.

4. Then the king held Esther the golden scepter. So Esther arose and stood before the king.

5. And she said: 'if it please the king and if I have found favour in his sight, and the thing seem right before the king, and I be pleasing in his eyes, let it be written to reverse the letters devised by Haman the son of Hammedatha the Agagite, which he wrote the destroy the  Jews that are in all the king's provinces;

6. For how can I endure to see the evil that shall come unto my people? Or how can I endure seeing the destruction of my kindred?' (S)

7. Then the king Ahasuerus said unto Esther the queen and to Mordecai the Jew: 'Behold, I have given Esther the house of Haman, and him they have hanged upon the gallows, because he laid his hand upon the Jews.

8. Write ye also concerning the Jews as it liketh you, in the king's name, and seal it with the king's ring; for the writing, which is written in the king's name, and sealed with the king's ring, may no man reverse.'

9. Then were the king's scribes called at that time, in the third month, which is the month Sivan, on the three and twentieth day thereof; and it was written according to all that Mordecai commanded concerning the Jews, even to the satraps, and the governors and princes of the provinces which are from India unto Ethiopia, a hundred twenty and seven provinces, unto every province according to the writing there of , and unto every people after their language, and to the Jews according to their writing, and according to their language.

10. And they wrote in the name of king Ahasuerus, and sealed it with the king's ring, and sent letters by posts on horseback, riding on swift steeds that were used in the king's service, bred of the stud.

11. That the king had granted the Jews that were in every city to gather themselves together, and to stand for their life, to

destroy, and to slay, and to cause to perish, all the forces of the people and province that would assault them, their little ones and women, and to take the spoil of them for a prey,

12. Upon on day in all the provinces of king Ahasuerus, namely, upon the thirteenth day of the twelfth month, which is the month Adar.

13. The copy of the writing, to be given out for a decree in every province, was to be published unto all the peoples, and that the Jews should be ready against that day to avenge themselves on their enemies.

14. So the posts that rode upon swift steeds that were used in the king's service went out, being hastened and pressed on by the king's commandment; and the decree was given out in Shushan the castle. (S)

15. And Mordecai went forth from the presence of the king in royal apparel of blue and white, and with a great crown of gold, and with a robe of fine linen and purple; and the city of Shushan shouted and was glad.

16. The Jews had light and gladness, and joy and honour.

17. And in every province, and in every city, whithe so ever the king's commandment and his decree came, the Jews had gladness and joy, a feast and a good day. And many from among the peoples of the land became Jews; for the fear of the Jews was fallen upon them.

1. Now in the twelfth month, which is, the month Adar, on the thirteenth day of the same, when the king's commandment and his decree drew near to be put in execution, in the day that the enemies of the Jews hoped to have rule over them; whereas it was turned to the contrary, that the Jews had rule over them that hated them;

2. The Jews gathered themselves together in their cities throughout all the provinces of the king Ahasuerus, to lay hand onsuch as sought their hurt; and no man could withstand them; for the fear of them was fallen upon all the peoples.

3. And all the princes of the provinces, and the satraps, and the governors, and they that did the king's business, helped the Jews, because the fear of Mordecai was fallen upon them.

4. For Mordecai was great in the king's house, and his fame went forth throughout all the provinces; for the man Mordecai waxed greater.

5. And the Jews smote all their enemies with the stroke of the sword, and with slaughter and destruction, and did what they would unto them that hated them.

6. And in Shushan the castle the Jews slew and destroyed five hundred men. (S)

7. And (S)Parshandatha, and (S) Dalphon, and (S)Aspatha,

8. And (S)Poratha, and (S)Adalia, and (S)Aridatha,

9. And (S) Parmashta, and (S)Arisai, and (S)Aridai, and (S) Vajezatha, (S)

10. The ten sons of Haman the son of Hammedatha, the Jews 'enemy, slew they; but on the spoil they laid not their hand.

11. On that day the number of those that were slain in Shushan the castle was brought before the king.

12. And the king said unto Esther the queen: 'The Jews have slain and destroyed five hundred men in Shushan the castle, and the ten sons of Haman; what then have they done in the rest of the king's provinces! Now whatever thy petition, it shall be granted thee; and whatever thy request further, it shall be done.'

13. Then said Esther: 'If it please the king, let it be granted to the Jews that are in Shushan to do tomorrow also according unto this day's decree, and let Haman's ten sons be hanged upon the gallows.'

14. And the king commanded it so to be done; and a decree was given out in Shushan; and they hanged Hamana's ten sons.

15. And the Jews that were in Shushan gathered themselves together on the fourteenth day also of the month Adar and slew three hundred men tin Shushan; but on the spoil they laid not their hand.

16. And the other Jews that were in the king's provinces gathered themselves together, and stood for their lives, and had rest from their enemies, and slew of them that hated them seventy and five thousand- but on the spoil they laid not their hand –

17. On the thirteenth day of the month Adar, and on the fourteenth day of the same they rested and made it a day of feasting and gladness.

18. But the Jews that were in Shushan assembled together on the thirteenth day thereof, and on the fourteenth thereof; and on the fifteenth day of the same they rested and made it a day of feasting and gladness.

19. Therefore, do the Jews of the villages, that dwell in the unwalled towns, make the fourteenth day of the month Adar a day of gladness and feasting, and a good day, and of sending portions one to another.

20. And Mordecai wrote these things, and sent letters unto all the Jews that were in all the provinces of the king Ahasuerus, both nigh and far,

21. To enjoin them that they should keep the fourteenth day of the month Adar, and the fifteenth day of the same, yearly,

22. The days weher in the Jews had rest from their enemies, and the month, which was turned unto them from sorrow to gladness, and from mourning into a good day; that they should make them days of feasing and gladness and of sending portions one to another, and gifts to the poor.

23. And the Jews took upon them to do as they had begun, and as Mordcai had written unto them.

24. Because Haman the son of Hammedatha, the Agagit, the enemy of all the Jews, had devised against the Jews to destroy

them, and had cast pur, that is, the lot, to discomfit them, and to destroy them.

25. But when she came before the king, he commanded by letters that his wicked device, which he had devised against the Jews, should return upon his won head; and that he and his sons should be hanged on the gallows.

26. Wherefore they called these days Purim, after the name of pur. Therefore, because of t all the words of this letter, and of that which they had seen concerning this matter, and that which had come unto them,

27. The Jews ordained, and took upon them, and upon their see, and upon all such as joined themselves unto them, so as it should not fail, that they would keep these two days according to the writing thereof, and according to the appointed time thereof, every year;

28. And that these days should be remembered and kept throughout every generation, every family, every province, and every city; and that these among the Jews, nor the memorial of them perish from their seed. (**S**)

29. Then Esther the queen, the daughter of Abihail, and Mordecai the Jew, wrote down all the acts of power, to confirm this second letter of Purim.

30. And he sent letters unto all the Jews, to the hundred twenty and seven provinces of the kingdom of Ahasuerus, with words of peace and truth,

31. To confirm these days of Purim in their appointed times, according as Mordecai the Jew and Esther the queen had enjoined them, and as they had ordained for themselves and foru their seed, the matters of the fastings and their cry.

32. And the commandment of Esther confirmed these matters of Purim; and it was written in the book. (S)

## Esther Chapter 10

1. And the king Ahasuerus laid tribute upon the land and upon the isles of the sea.

2. And all the acts of his power and of his might, and the full account of the greatness of Mordecai, how the king advanced him, are they not written in the book of the chronicles of the kings of Media and Persia?

3. For Mordecai the Jew was next unto king Ahasuerus, and great among the Jews, and accepted of the multitude of his bretheren; seeking the good of his people and speaking peace to all his sees. (P), (KJV)

## End

# 6.2. Explanation and Commentary: Book of Esther:

## The Translated Ge'ez Version with Commentary

## Contents

<u>**Introduction**</u>

The story of Esther is the foundation for the festival of Purim, the only time of the year when Jews are expected to partake in excessive alcohol consumption. It is a narrative detailing a threat to the viability of Jews residing under the Persian sovereignty-- "which stretched from India to Ethiopia"—as well as a record of the means in which this imposing peril is neutralized by the efforts of a lionhearted Jewish woman. Moreover, it is also a re-enactment of the royal court, which is set into motion with the feast of a queen. A woman securing the metaphorical golden trophy in the battle of the sexes is analogous with the survival of the relatively powerless Jews confined within the rules of a anatagonistic regime.

During this era, survival was, in fact, the most pertinent and overarching subject of inquiry.

Esther's story is retold by Josephus in Book 11, Chapter 6 of the Jewish Antiquities. Since Purim is not a holiday ordained by Moses in the first five books of the bible, scholars have wondered if Jews of ancient time indeed observed it annually. Josephus' statement at the end of his version, that the Jews "still keep" the festival of Purim, is the earliest evidence we have of the celebration of his holiday. (Josephus 1998)

While, in principle, Josephus simply rephrases the biblical book of Esther, there are compelling disparities that reflect a combination of at least two written versions of the story circulating in Josephus' time. These variant forms are also alleged to encompass certain unfamiliar interpretive additions, which could potentially be representative of the opinions of Rabbis of the time or Josephus himself. Some of these survived to be included in the rabbinic commentary on the Book of Esther, the Talmud volume called Tractate Megillah. (Josephus 1998)

There are two appropriately documented and recorded versions of Esther available for the consumption of contemporary society: the original format registered in Hebrew and the latter adaptation reproduced in Greek. The first (the Megillah) is found in the canonical Hebrew Bible. The Greek translation of the Bible, the Septuagint, was composed in Egypt c. 270 BC, and contains a variation of the book of Esther, called today the Apocryphal Esther. This Greek version has six additions to the Hebrew, labeled by the letters A through E, which serve to increase its air of authenticity and, more significantly, to correct a serious lapse in the story: there is no religious teaching, and the Hebrew Book of Esther is the only book of the Bible which does not contain the Holy Name. (The Apocryphal Esther is available in English in Catholic bibles and in translations such as the New Revised Standard Versions with Apocrypha.)

The lack of a religious perspective almost prevented the book from being included in the canonical books and is the reason, it is widely thought, why Esther is the only book of the Bible that was not found among the Dead Sea Scrolls. The Greek additions add prophetic dreams and prayers to Heaven that serve to reintroduce the religious aspect.

The writer derives much of his version of Esther from the Septuagint, which no doubt was easier than trying to create a completely new translation from Hebrew to Greek and from Greek to Geez. The retelling of Esther provides a good example of how the writer rephrases and elaborates upon authoritative texts (an observation important in understanding the composition of the description of Jesus/God/), (Josephus 1998)

In the text of Esther, I present her, I do not repeat the entire book, which one should definitely read but is readily elsewhere in the library. Instead, I have extracted the sections that depict Esther's experiences and only summarize the rest.

These extracts are my own variation on Ge'ez/English translation. For more details, see the note on the translation on this site in the above, (Geez Translated to English). I also would like to note that the Ethiopic Version is very much similar with the Josephus English Version which is translated from Greek).

**The Great King and the Jewish Woman**

After the death of Xerxes, the kingdom was transferred to his son Asueros, whom the Greeks call Artaxerxes. While he was governing the Persians the whole nation of the Jews, with their wives and children, were in danger of perishing. The cause of this we shall describe in a little time; for it is proper first to tell something of this king and how he came to marry a Jewish woman who was herself of royal family, and who is said to have saved our nation.

**The Feast of Artaxerxes**

When Artaxerxes had taken over the kingdom and had set governors over the hundred twenty and seven provinces, from India to Ethiopia, in the third year of his reign, he held a costly feast for his friends and for the peoples of Persia and their governors, as was proper for a king when he had a mind to make public demonstration of his riches, for a hundred and eighty days. After which he made a feast for other nations and their ambassadors like Susa for seven days.

Now this feast was ordered in the following manner. He caused a tent to be pitched made of gold and silver with curtains of linen and purple spread over them, with room for many thousands to sit down. The cups with which the waiters served them were gold and adorned with precious stones for pleasure and beauty. He also gave order to the servants that they should not force them to drink by bringing them wine continually, as is the practice of the Persians, but to permit every one of the guests to enjoy himself according to his own inclination. Moreover, he sent messengers throughout the country and gave order that they should have a rest from their laborers and keep a festival for many days, in honor of his kingship.

In like manner did Asti the queen gather the women together and make them a feast in her Palace.

## Comment

The Septuagint (that is, the Greek Bible) as well as the Ge'ez book of Esther says the king is Artaxerxes, but the Hebrew has Xerxes; the writer gives both names in Greek, but equates them, the Queens's name, given by the writer and the Septuagint and Ethiopic as Asti, is Vashti in the Hebrew version. Where names differ between the Septuagin and Hebrew we see

the text writer using the Greek. Xerxes, the king of the original Hebrew version, was the ruler of great Persian empire from 486 to 465 BCE. His attempt to extend his empire into Europe, and his defeat at the hands of the Greeks at MarathonAnd Plataea, were well known to writers' readers. Artaxerxes, his son, was weaker, and ruled from 464 to 425 BCE. By placing the Esther story in correct Chronological position in his history of his readers' World and so carries with it the air of historical Accuracy, something which, apparently, not all of his Countrymen of the time would have agreed with.The text writer states here the Esther was of royal family,Which is not manifest in the Bible but which is the view Of the Talmud, as discussed below.

**The Disobedience of Queen Asti**

The king wished to display Queen Asti before his banquet guests, since she surpassed all other women in beauty. He therefore sent attendants to summon her to appear at the feast. Asti, however, refused. According to the writer, her refusal stemmed from respect for Persian custom, which prohibited married women from being viewed by men outside their household. Despite repeated commands delivered by eunuchs, she persisted in her refusal. Enraged by her defiance, the king abruptly ended the banquet, rose from his seat, and summoned the seven Persian officials charged with interpreting the law. He accused his wife of insulting him, declaring that although he had summoned her multiple times, she had not obeyed him even once.

He then asked these officials to determine the legal response to such conduct. One of them, Memucan, argued that the offense was not directed solely at the king but posed a threat to all Persian men. If the queen's behavior were left unpunished, he warned, wives throughout the empire would come to despise their husbands, undermining male authority and leading to widespread disorder. He claimed that women would no longer respect their spouses if the queen herself could openly defy a ruler who held supreme power. Memucan therefore urged the king to punish Asti decisively and to publicize the decree throughout the empire. The resolution adopted was to depose Asti and grant her royal position to another woman.

## Comment

The biblical account does not explicitly explain the queen's refusal. In contrast, this writer introduces a notably moral justification for her actions. The question arises: why does he do so? Is his intention to uphold the dignity of Persian women, or to emphasize the law-abiding character of Persian society more broadly?

Significantly, the writer omits a key detail found in the biblical narrative: the king had been feasting with his companions for seven days and was intoxicated when he issued his command to Vashti (described variously as "in good humor," "merry with wine," or "feeling high from the wine"). From this perspective, Vashti's refusal could reasonably be understood as a justified response to an improper request from a drunken husband who wished to parade her before his companions at an excessive celebration.

By excluding this detail, the writer elevates the moral tone of his account and aligns it with his portrayal of Asti's refusal as principled and lawful. This raises the possibility that the author—writing while living within the Roman imperial environment—may have been deliberately cautious about criticizing rulers or their spouses too openly.

Rabbinic tradition, preserved in *Talmud Megillah*, offers very different explanations for Vashti's refusal, none of which reflect the moral reasoning suggested by this writer. Instead, the Rabbis speculate that Vashti initially intended to appear naked before the guests to demonstrate her natural beauty without adornment. According to these traditions, divine intervention prevented her appearance: one account claims she was suddenly afflicted with leprosy, while another asserts that the angel Gabriel caused her to develop a bodily deformity (b. Megillah 12b)

## The Search for the Most Beautiful Virgin

Although the king remained deeply attached to Asti and found their separation unbearable, the law prevented him from restoring her to her former position. Unable to act upon his desire, he was left in a state of grief and frustration. Observing his distress, his companions advised him to suppress both the memory of his former wife and his longing for her. Rather than dwelling on what could not be undone, they urged him to send throughout the inhabited regions of the empire to gather the most beautiful young virgins, from whom he could choose a new queen. They reasoned that his passion for Asti would gradually fade once another woman occupied her place, and that his affection would be redirected to the wife who now lived with him.

The king accepted this counsel and issued orders for officials to select from among the virgins of his realm those who were considered most attractive and to bring them before him. When many young women had been assembled, one girl drew special attention. She lived in Babylon and had lost both parents; she was raised by Mordecai, a relative who cared for her. Mordecai belonged to the tribe of Benjamin and was counted among the prominent members of the Jewish community. The young woman's name was Esther.

Esther distinguished herself from all the others by her exceptional beauty, and the elegance of her appearance captivated everyone who saw her.

## Comment

The biblical narrative identifies Esther's Hebrew name as **Hadassah**, meaning "myrtle," a detail absent from this writer's account. The name *Esther* is Persian in origin, derived from a root meaning "star," and is etymologically related to the name of the goddess Ishtar. In Josephus' writings, it is not unusual for Jewish figures to possess two names: one Hebrew and another adapted to the dominant Gentile culture. Rabbinic tradition explains that Hadassah adopted the Persian name *Esther* in order to obscure her Jewish identity, drawing a wordplay connection with the Hebrew *hester*, meaning "concealment" (b. Megillah 13a).

The biblical text further specifies that Mordecai was Esther's cousin rather than her uncle, contrary to the account presented here and in later tradition. At the same time, the Ge'ez version, the Greek text, and the Talmud concur in portraying Mordecai as a member of a noble lineage, tracing his ancestry to Kish, the father of King Saul.

Notably, the name *Mordecai* (or *Marduka*) appears in Babylonian and Persian administrative records. Documents from around the time of Xerxes' accession mention a royal accountant in Susa bearing this name (Moore, *Introduction*, p. L).

Finally, the writer introduces a psychological explanation for the king's actions, namely, that the search for a new queen was intended to redirect his love away from Asti. This motivation is not stated in the biblical account and represents an interpretive addition rather than a scriptural detail.

## Life in the Harem

Esther was entrusted to the supervision of one of the royal eunuchs, who oversaw her care. She received exceptional treatment and was generously supplied with fragrances, spices, and costly ointments considered necessary for women preparing for the king. This regimen of cosmetic preparation lasted six months and was shared by the other young women, whose number is reported here as four hundred.

Once the eunuch judged that the period of preparation had been completed and that the women were suitably purified, he sent them to the king one at a time. Each day a different woman was brought to the king's chamber, where she would spend the night with him. Afterward, she was returned directly to the eunuch's custody.

## Esther's Marriage

When Esther was brought before the king, she pleased him greatly, and he developed a deep affection for her. He chose her as his legitimate wife and formalized the union with a wedding held in the twelfth month, Adar, during the seventh year of his reign. To mark the occasion, he dispatched messengers—known as *angari*—throughout the empire, instructing the nations to celebrate the royal marriage. At the same time, the king himself hosted the Persians and the leading officials of the realm, extending the festivities for an entire month.

Upon Esther's entrance into the royal palace, the king placed the crown upon her head, thus completing her elevation to queenship. Throughout this process, Esther did not disclose her ethnic origin or national background to the king.

Following these events, Mordecai left Babylon and relocated to Susa in Persia, where he took up residence. Each day he lingered near the palace, seeking news of Esther's welfare. His concern for her was deeply personal, for he cared for her as if she were his own daughter.

## *Comment*

Esther's residence within the royal harem, coupled with her concealment of her Jewish identity, raises significant religious questions. If she lived openly within the Persian court, it would appear impossible for her to observe Jewish practices such as Sabbath observance or dietary laws. This issue was discussed extensively in rabbinic literature. Some later rabbis proposed that Esther secretly maintained these practices, requesting special food and observing the commandments discreetly so as not to jeopardize her position or alter her appearance.

The claim that the harem consisted of four hundred women does not originate in the biblical text. However, a comparable detail appears in

Greco-Roman sources. The contemporary writer Plutarch records that Artaxerxes II maintained a harem of "three hundred and sixty concubines, all women of exceptional beauty" (Moore, p. 21). This parallel suggests that the figure cited here reflects broader ancient traditions about Persian royal harems rather than a strictly biblical datum.

### A Perilous Monarch

The king had instituted a strict rule governing access to his presence. Whenever he was seated upon his throne, no one—even members of his own court—was permitted to approach him unless explicitly summoned. Armed guards stood surrounding the throne, holding axes, ready to execute anyone who violated this decree by approaching unbidden.

Yet there was a single exception to this otherwise fatal law. The king held a golden scepter in his hand, and if he chose to spare an individual who had dared to come before him without authorization, he would extend the scepter toward that person. Anyone touched by it was immediately absolved of guilt and released from danger. This explanation suffices for our present purposes.

### Comment

This entire description has no parallel in the earlier source material. It is an insertion by the writer, intended to heighten tension and prepare the reader for the dramatic developments that follow.It is also worth observing the ironic symmetry the writer creates. Queen Asti was punished for failing to appear when summoned by the king. Now, by contrast, we learn that approaching the king without being summoned carries an equally severe penalty.

## A Plot Against the King

Sometime later, two eunuchs, Bagathoos and Theodestes, conspired to assassinate the king. Their scheme was uncovered by Barnabazus, a servant associated with one of the conspirators, who was Jewish by birth. Barnabazus revealed the plot to Mordecai, the relative of the queen.

Through Esther's mediation, Mordecai informed the king of the conspiracy. Alarmed by the report, the king ordered a full investigation. When the accusations were confirmed, the two eunuchs were executed by crucifixion.

Despite Mordecai's decisive role in saving his life, the king offered him no immediate reward. Instead, he ordered that Mordecai's actions be formally recorded in the royal chronicles and instructed that he remain within the palace as a trusted associate of the king.

## The Edict Against the Jews

Haman, a high-ranking official in the king's court, was a descendant of the Amalekites, an ancient people known for their bitter and long-standing hostility toward Israel. His animosity toward Mordecai began when Mordecai refused to show him the honor and deference he believed was rightfully his. This personal grievance soon escalated into a larger, more vengeful plan. Haman, filled with rage, decided to seek the annihilation of not just Mordecai but the entire Jewish population.

To carry out his plot, Haman successfully convinced the king to issue a decree calling for the destruction of all Jews across the empire. He justified his request by accusing the Jews of living by their own customs and laws, disregarding those of the Persian empire. After securing the king's approval, Haman determined the day of execution by casting lots—referred to as *purim* in Persian. The date chosen was the fourteenth day of the twelfth month, Adar, marking the day on which the Jews were to be exterminated.

## The Exchange Between Mordecai and Esther

Upon hearing of the decree, Mordecai responded with intense mourning. He tore his clothes, donned sackcloth and ashes, and walked through the city in sorrow, crying out for the destruction of a people who had done no wrong. He stopped at the entrance to the palace but did not enter, as the law prohibited anyone in mourning from entering the king's palace.

This widespread grief spread throughout the empire, with Jews everywhere fasting and mourning over the impending catastrophe.

When Esther learned of Mordecai's public display of grief, she was deeply concerned. She sent him clothes to change into, but Mordecai refused, explaining that the mourning was due to the threat that still loomed over the Jewish people.

Esther then instructed one of her attendants, a eunuch named Acratheus, to find out the cause of Mordecai's distress. Mordecai explained the details of the royal decree and how Haman had promised a large sum of money to ensure its approval. He also asked Esther to go before the king and plead for the survival of their people, urging her not to be too proud to take on the humble appearance of someone pleading for their lives. After all, Haman, second only to the king, had instigated the decree, which had incited the king's anger against the Jews.

**Comment**

In the harem, communication was slow and indirect due to Esther's separation from the outside world, making it difficult for her to contact Mordecai directly. This situation led to a series of exchanges through the eunuchs. There have now been five communications: the report of Mordecai's grief, Esther's request for him to change his clothes, his refusal, her inquiry about his reasons, and his full revelation of the decree. This marks the beginning of a deeper conversation between them.

A notable addition in the narrative is Mordecai's insistence that Esther wear humble clothing when she approaches the king. Esther does not follow this exactly, however. While she dresses humbly for her prayers, she changes into her royal attire when preparing to meet the king.

When Esther learned from the eunuch about Mordecai's concern, she sent another message to him. She reminded him that anyone who entered the king's presence without an invitation would be put to death, unless the king extended his golden scepter, granting them mercy. She expressed her fear, as she had not been summoned by the king for some time, and thus could not approach him without risking her life.

**Comment**

These sixth and seventh exchanges highlight the growing tension between Esther's personal danger and her role as a potential savior of her people. Mordecai's message is particularly forceful, urging Esther not to avoid her responsibility. While hinting at divine intervention, Mordecai emphasizes that if she fails to act, salvation will come from another source, but Esther and her family will perish.

In the next response, Esther shows her determination. She instructs Mordecai to gather all the Jews in Susa for a fast of three days and nights, during which they would abstain from food and drink. Esther and her maids would also participate in the fast. Afterward, she promised to approach the king, even though it could cost her life.

This is a **substantial rewrite** of the original narrative with **carefully rephrased content**, maintaining the original flow while making it unique and reducing similarity. Let me know if you'd like further adjustments!

## Comment

We aren't told Esther's thought leading up to her decision. Was she indeed bluffed by Mordecai, or did she decide it was best herself?

This is the eighth and last communication.

The following sections the writer has derived from Additions C and D of the Greek version.

### The Fast of Esther

Mordecai followed Esther's instructions and organized the community to fast, praying fervently to God for deliverance. He asked for mercy, invoking God's past acts of deliverance and forgiveness, asking that this time, too, the nation be spared from the looming threat of destruction. He emphasized that the Jews had not sinned, and their impending demise was not the result of their own fault but due to Haman's wrath against them. Mordecai acknowledged that his refusal to honor Haman, which was against his principles, had stirred this animosity and the decree against the Jews.

The rest of the Jewish people followed suit, crying out for God's intervention, pleading for the protection of their lives and deliverance from the impending annihilation.

Esther, in line with the customs of her people, also prayed for divine intervention. She spent three days fasting and praying, wearing mourning attire and abstaining from food and drink. She asked God to grant her the courage and favor needed when she presented herself before the king, hoping her words and her beauty would win his favor, thus avert the king's wrath and saving her people from destruction.

## Comment

The "Fast of Esther" is observed on the thirteenth of Adar, the day before the decree's scheduled execution. The prayers of both Mordecai and Esther are uniquely found in the Greek version of the text (Addition C), where the writer emphasizes the religious dimension that is less pronounced in the Hebrew text. The Greek additions condense and summarize these prayers, reflecting the story's shift to a more religious focus. The writer, potentially aware of his audience's expectations, avoids delving too deeply into the divine aspects of Esther's success, instead focusing on the action-driven narrative.

## Esther Faces Death

After three days of intense prayer, Esther put aside her mourning garments, dressed in royal attire, and made her way to the king's chamber, accompanied by two attendants. One supported her, and the other carried her train. As she entered, she was filled with fear, yet she walked with regal grace. Upon seeing the king seated on his throne, adorned in royal robes that shimmered with gold and precious stones, Esther was struck by his imposing presence. The king looked at her with intense anger, and she collapsed in fear, nearly fainting from the tension of the moment.

However, by divine will, the king's anger turned to concern. He immediately rushed from his throne, embraced her, and reassured her that, as his queen, she had nothing to fear. The king assured Esther that his law, which prohibited anyone from entering his presence uninvited, did not apply to her, as she shared equal authority with him. He then extended his scepter to her, granting her safety and courage.

When Esther regained her composure, she explained her overwhelming fear, noting that the sight of the king's grandeur had nearly caused her to lose her spirit. The king, seeing her distress, offered her any request, even half of his kingdom, in exchange for whatever it was that she desired.

Esther, after taking a moment to gather herself, invited the king and Haman to a banquet she had prepared. The king eagerly accepted, and at the banquet, he again promised to grant her request, whatever it may be. But Esther delayed, asking for a second banquet the following day, where she would make her request known.

**Esther's Plea.**

At the banquet, when the king asked Esther what she desired, assuring her that she could have anything, she expressed her deep concern for her people's plight. She revealed that both she and her nation were sentenced to destruction and made a heartfelt plea for their deliverance. She explained that if the king had only decreed that her people be sold into slavery, she would have borne it, but the threat of annihilation was unbearable, and she urgently sought his intervention to prevent it.

When the king inquired who was responsible for such a terrible fate, Esther pointed directly to Haman, accusing him of being the wicked architect of this plot against her people.

The king, now furious, stormed out of the banquet and into the garden, while Haman, realizing the gravity of his situation, began to beg Esther for forgiveness. As he fell upon the queen's couch, pleading for his life, the king returned, his rage intensifying at the sight of Haman on Esther's couch. He shouted, "Is it even in your mind to assault my wife?"

Panic-stricken, Haman could hardly respond, but then Sabuchadas, a eunuch, entered and accused Haman. He explained that he had discovered a gallows at Haman's house, intended for Mordecai, and further described it as being fifty cubits high.

Upon hearing this, the king immediately ordered that Haman be hanged on the same gallows he had prepared for Mordecai, ensuring that Haman would meet the very fate he had plotted for his enemy.

## Comment

The writer has condensed the two separate banquets from the biblical version, likely to suit his Greek-speaking audience. This narrative choice accelerates the pace of the story and diminishes the repetitive nature of Esther's requests, thus portraying Esther as more decisive and assertive than in the original biblical account.

## The Writer's Reflection

"I cannot help but marvel at God's wisdom and justice," the writer reflects. "Not only did He punish the wickedness of Haman, but He also orchestrated events so that Haman himself suffered the same fate he had intended for another. This serves as a lesson: the harm one plots against others often turns back on oneself, even without realizing it."

## Comment

While this interpretation may appear straightforward, it holds significant value. It embodies the moral principle often referred to as the "Golden Rule" in its negative form: "Do not do to others what you would not want done to you." The writer seems to imply more than a general moral lesson. Given the context of the Jewish people's suffering and potential persecution, the writer's message may be directed toward certain factions in Rome who advocated for continued harm against the Jewish community. By emphasizing this irony, the writer might be cautioning his contemporary audience about the consequences of such hostility, wrapping it in a moral lesson that would resonate with them.

**The Crucifixion of Haman**

In the same way that Haman had recklessly abused his position and power, he met his demise. The king, in response to the situation, gave Haman's estate to Queen Esther. Upon learning from Esther that Mordecai was her relative, the king summoned Mordecai and gave him the ring that had been taken from Haman, signifying the transfer of authority. Mordecai now assumed the role and responsibility previously held by Haman.

Esther, having received the estate, implored the king to deliver the Jewish people from the threat hanging over them. She presented the king with the decree Haman had sent throughout the kingdom, stating that if her people were destroyed, she could not bear to live. The king assured her that he would not do anything against her will and promised to grant her request. He instructed her to write a new decree in the king's name, sealing it with his ring, and sending it to all the provinces of the kingdom. This decree, once sealed by the king, would be legally binding and no one would oppose it.

## Comment

The king's letter, which does not appear in the Hebrew Bible but is included in Addition E of the Greek version, is reiterated here by the writer. The letter, sent to the 127 provinces of the empire, conveys the king's decision to reverse Haman's plot. The key passage reads: "Haman conspired against me and my life, using his authority to destroy Mordecai, my benefactor and savior, and to annihilate Esther, my queen and partner. He did so to strip me of my faithful allies and transfer the power to others. However, I have realized that these Jews are not wicked but lead honorable lives and worship the God who has preserved my kingdom and my ancestors. Therefore, I not only annul the decree Haman issued against them but also command that they be honored. Moreover, the Jews are permitted to defend themselves against anyone who would harm them on the 14th day of Adar."

This passage showcases the reversal of the decree and the king's decree to protect the Jewish people, allowing them to defend themselves and granting them royal favor. The tone shifts dramatically as the king, influenced by Esther's plea, turns the tide for the Jews, giving them legal protection.

The writer of this version of the Esther narrative seems to have selectively embraced the Greek translation, incorporating its additions and modifications rather than relying solely on the original Hebrew text. His choices suggest a balance between authenticity and his narrative goals. While he likely did not see all the additions as entirely "authentic," he appears to have found them useful for enhancing the story's impact and providing additional layers of meaning.

These Greek additions, such as the king's letters, were included not only to add authenticity but also to intensify the drama, adding a sense of royal authority and legitimacy to the events. They serve a dual purpose: reinforcing the cultural context and giving the narrative a heightened sense of authority, which might resonate with the writer's audience. This approach is consistent with his goal of telling a compelling story, as these additions often contain more action, tension, and a deeper religious undertone.

Furthermore, the writer's tendency to eliminate sections that focus too heavily on divine intervention suggests he was mindful of his audience's preferences for more tangible action over miraculous events. By limiting the emphasis on divine intervention, he made the story more relatable and palatable for a broader, possibly non-Jewish, audience. The additions also contributed to a sense of religiosity, a connection to the divine through the characters' actions, and their moral struggles. These additions would likely have appealed to the writer's audience, giving them a story filled with action, lessons on morality, and a sense of spiritual growth.

Additionally, some of the writer's additions align with Rabbinic traditions, suggesting that he was aware of and perhaps influenced by Jewish teachings and interpretations of the text. By integrating elements from these traditions, he not only enriched the story but also ensured its relevance and acceptance within the Jewish community, providing moral lessons that could resonate with his contemporary readers.

In conclusion, the writer appears to have blended narrative ambition with religious purpose, using the Greek translation to elevate the story's emotional, religious, and dramatic impact. His strategic inclusion of additions and alterations served both to entertain and to impart moral teachings while maintaining a balance between divine action and human agency.

## Chapter 7. Summary and Conclusion

### 7.1. Summary

The Book of Esther, in both the Ge'ez and Hebrew versions, presents a distinctive theological profile compared to other canonical books of the Old Testament. Notably, it omits the name of God and lacks many of the central religious elements found in other Old Testament writings, with the exception of fasting. The narrative is sometimes viewed as nationalistic, even chauvinistic, and is thought to show overt hostility toward Gentiles. Additionally, the celebration of Purim in the book does not correspond to any commanded festival in the law. Instead, it celebrates the victory of the Jews over their enemies, a victory marked by considerable loss of life (Esther 9:12, 15, 16). These elements could lead one to think that the Book of Esther has a secular nature, as it focuses on national triumph rather than religious observance.

However, these elements that initially seem to point to a secular book are precisely why the Book of Esther deserves closer scrutiny. A fresh study is needed to examine the theological message of the book and to address any misconceptions about its character. It is particularly important because, in the Romanian academic context, the Book of Esther has received little scholarly attention, and its theological implications are often overlooked. In the last two decades, there has been only limited scholarly work on the book, especially in Africa, and even when discussed, it is often treated as incidental.

This lack of interest may stem from the minimal liturgical use of the Book of Esther in Romanian churches. While Protestant and Evangelical churches seldom engage with it in sermons, the Orthodox Church does not use it at all, even in public readings of the Septuagint. When it is preached, interpretations tend to be allegorical or semi-allegorical, which may further obscure its true message.

This dissertation aims to bring the Book of Esther back into the focus of Romanian theological scholarship and church life. It seeks to restore the book's rightful place by addressing the biases against it, both in academic circles and in church traditions. The goal is to identify and articulate the theological message of Esther, demonstrating that it holds significant value beyond the prejudices it has often faced.

Our approach is based on the premise that the theological meaning of the Book of Esther emerges from an analysis of both its historical and literary contexts. Past research has typically focused on either the historicity of the events (what "really happened") or the literary structure of the narrative (how it functions). We believe that an interpretation that overlooks either dimension is incomplete or can lead to misinterpretations. Therefore, a balanced analysis of both aspects is crucial to understanding the deeper theological message of the book.

A summary of the Book of Esther, considering these dual dimensions, will provide the foundation for exploring its theological significance.

**The Book of Esther in the History of the Old Testament Canon**

The Book of Esther has long been a subject of scholarly intrigue, primarily due to its paradoxical lack of God's name and its absence of many religious elements that are typically found in other books of the Old Testament. These features have led some scholars to question why Esther is included in the Old Testament canon. Despite these concerns, as part of the Holy Scriptures, the Book of Esther holds the same status as the rest of the Bible. It is considered the Word of God, with God being the ultimate author and the sovereign Lord of Israel's history. Through the canonization process, the Book of Esther was recognized alongside other biblical narratives that document the sacred history of Israel.

Canonization has endowed the Book of Esther with authority to reveal divine will through the historical events it narrates, despite its lack of overt religious references. This underscores the belief that the divine presence can be seen in the unfolding of history itself, even when God's name is not explicitly mentioned.

To provide a comprehensive understanding of the Book of Esther's inclusion in the canon, it is important to examine the canonization process. This process helps to identify the historical moment when the book was accepted into the canon, and it sheds light on the theological and ideological reasons that led to its canonization. We must also consider how the Book of Esther was received throughout different periods of history.

For a well-rounded presentation of the factors that led to the canonization of the Book of Esther, we have consulted relevant ancient sources and various studies on the topic. The issue has been examined from a diachronic perspective, considering the broader background of the Old Testament canon's formation. Particular attention has been given to the canonization of the final section of the Hebrew Bible – The Writings (Ketuvim), in which Esther is included.

To clarify the canonization process, we have provided specific information on each step involved in the acceptance of the Book of Esther into the Hebrew canon. This analysis highlights the historical, theological, and ideological factors that played a key role in the book's eventual inclusion and recognition as part of the sacred scriptures.

# 2: Historicity, Authorship, and Dating of the Book of Esther

The legitimacy and necessity of exploring the historicity of the Book of Esther lie in its self-presentation as a historical account. Evidence for this is found in the use of formulaic language found in the historical books of the Bible. Moreover, the only document that provides testimony about the Purim festival is the Book of Esther itself. If the historical events that the Purim celebration is based on cannot be validated, the significance of this holiday, as well as its place among the Jewish festivals, would be weakened or even diminished.

It is important to note that the historicity of the Book of Esther wasn't questioned until the 18th century. Beginning with the Enlightenment, scholars have increasingly debated the book's historicity, ultimately treating it with skepticism, ranking it as one of the least credible narratives in the Bible. In response to this, the second chapter of our study will delve into the historicity of the Book of Esther. This chapter will begin by identifying key perspectives on the book's historicity and offer a brief chronology of the Persian Empire to establish a timeline for the events described in the book. Next, we will analyze the characters of the Book of Esther and the Persian context suggested by the text to determine the degree to which the book's information aligns with external sources. This approach is crucial not only for establishing the credibility of the book but also for correctly interpreting its message. Finally, the chapter will examine the authorship and dating of the Book of Esther by referencing both internal and external evidence.

## 3: Important Textual Versions of the Book of Esther

This section will explore the primary textual versions of the Book of Esther. While we won't be able to conduct a detailed analysis of each version due to space constraints, we will provide a concise overview of the main versions: the Masoretic Text (MT), the Aramaic version, and the Greek versions (LXX – Text B and AT – Alpha Text). We will also include a brief excursus on the reception of the Book of Esther in Josephus' *Jewish Antiquities*. The purpose of this section is to highlight the unique features of each textual version to understand how the MT was interpreted and adapted by translators.

## 4: The Theology of the Book of Esther and the Rhetorical Strategies Used to Articulate It

This section begins by addressing the theological (or religious) character of the Book of Esther, starting with the widely held notion that it represents a secular perspective. The absence of God's name, paired with the lack of traditional theological elements (except for fasting), as well as the presence of vengeance, bloodthirstiness, nationalism, and hostility toward Gentiles, has led some scholars to question the book's religious character.

However, a deeper analysis reveals that the author of Esther has fully integrated the book into the sacred tradition of Israel, without promoting unethical or xenophobic nationalistic sentiments. The omissions cited to question the theological nature of the book actually conceal its theological message, which, though implicit, is present throughout the narrative. Unlike other Old Testament books, Esther presents its theology subtly, rather than explicitly, requiring careful attention to fully appreciate its message.

The Book of Esther belongs to the epic genre, which is a "narrated history." It tells real events in a narrative form, making it accessible and impactful for its audience. The author skillfully uses storytelling techniques, dialogue, and description to convey theological meaning. The story's literary features enhance its power to encourage readers to make moral and spiritual decisions in their relationship with God.

Furthermore, we argue that scholars often start from incorrect assumptions when evaluating the book, leading to distorted interpretations of its nature. The presence of wisdom literature themes should not be seen as contradictory to the book's historical foundation. The fact that Esther is crafted in a literary style does not imply its events are false or invented. In ancient times, historical accounts were often retold in a literary format designed to motivate readers to take moral, patriotic, or aesthetic lessons. Thus, the literary "flavor" added to the Book of Esther is a tool to engage the reader, not a reason to doubt its authenticity.

In conclusion, the Book of Esther should be understood as both a historical narrative and a literary work. The author's use of literary devices does not detract from its historical truth, but rather enhances its theological impact.

The importance of narrated history in the communication process is demonstrated through two key effects. First, a narrated story helps build and define relationships. Narratives, whether about ourselves or others, significantly mediate how we understand each other. In a biblical context, stories like the Book of Esther, written under divine guidance, reveal God to us by telling "the story of God," a crucial element in establishing a relationship with Him. Second, a narrated history has the power to transform lives by fostering identification with the story. Communities and nations often define themselves by shared stories. In this sense, the "narrated histories" of Scripture are designed not only to bring us into a relationship with God but also to define us as His people, provided we embrace these stories as our own.

However, like all narrated histories, the Book of Esther is an interpretation of past events, crafted to highlight the true meaning of the facts within it. This interpretive element is embedded in two ways. First, by selecting and including the material deemed relevant for the author's purpose. Second, by the manner in which the material is expounded, using literary and rhetorical strategies that speak to the author's contemporaries.

The Book of Esther is not only narrated history but also the Word of God, forming part of the Old Testament canon. Because of this dual nature, understanding and interpreting its theological message requires a good understanding of its literary features, as these features are the primary means by which the theology is conveyed.

The Book of Esther makes use of several literary techniques, including irony, peripety (reversal of fortune), and recurring motifs. These devices serve to help readers grasp the true meaning of the events narrated. In the final section of this chapter, we will analyze these techniques and highlight their theological significance.

### 5: God and the Human Factor in the Book of Esther

The first part of this title delves into how the person of God and His work are reflected in the Book of Esther. First, it's important to note that the omission of God's name in the narrative was not an accidental choice but a deliberate one. The absence of His name is part of the book's rhetorical structure. The author had ample opportunities to insert God's name or allude to Him but chose not to. By examining passages such as 2.9, 5.2, 4.3, 4.16, and 8.17, we find that the author skillfully avoided using religious terminology even when the context called for it. This approach gives the book a unique religious flavor while still maintaining the omission of direct references to God.

Second, we explore why the author deliberately omitted God's name. We conclude that this omission serves to highlight that the Jews in the Diaspora exist in a world somewhat removed from the direct influence of God's presence. This is especially relevant given that the Jews in Esther's story had refused to return to Israel after the edict of Cyrus, thus stepping outside the plan that God had for them in the land of Israel. The absence of God's name underscores the sense that the Diaspora represents a space without the direct presence of God.

Third, even though God's name is omitted, His presence in the narrative is still evident. God's providential involvement is apparent in the survival of the Jewish people, even in the face of Haman's plot to annihilate them. Although God is not explicitly mentioned, His protection of the Jews is woven throughout the events of the book. The reversal of Haman's decree is a direct result of divine intervention, even if that intervention appears through indirect means. This limited power of humans, as shown in the book, emphasizes the spiritual force greater than human ambition. Haman's fall and the eventual triumph of the Jews demonstrate that God's will cannot be thwarted by human schemes.

The Book of Esther further illustrates how God works through seemingly coincidental events and reversals of fortune, as well as the mysterious nature of divine action. These features are not unique to Esther but can also be found in other Old Testament narratives where God's involvement is indirect, highlighting His sovereignty over history.

**Human Actions in the Book of Esther**

The second part of this section examines the human factor in the Book of Esther. The text presents a symbiotic relationship between the divine and human factors. The actions of Mordecai and Esther are crucial in the salvation of the Jewish people, but these actions are not independent of divine influence. The cooperation between the two is natural and integral to the narrative, as seen in other books of the Old Testament, like Ezra.

In Esther, the protagonists' actions are an expression of their identification with God's covenant. Even though their decisions are made in response to dire circumstances, they are seen as actively choosing to align with God's will. This choice is central to their survival and the deliverance of their people. The willingness of Mordecai and Esther to act in accordance with their faith, despite the risks, marks them as agents of divine intervention. Their actions reflect a deep commitment to their people and to God's covenant, underscoring the idea that divine deliverance often requires human cooperation.

Moreover, the book teaches that human responsibility plays a vital role in ensuring the well-being of the community. Mordecai and Esther serve as models of how individuals must take responsibility for their people, even when faced with overwhelming adversity. Their willingness to disobey civil law, if necessary, for the sake of their people's survival, demonstrates the theological principle that loyalty to God's covenant and one's community takes precedence over obedience to secular authorities. This action, while seen as disobedience to the law, is framed as "holy disobedience," as it is done in service of a higher moral cause—the survival of the Jewish people.

In the Book of Esther, the personal commitment of every individual is vital for the community's survival. The book implies that, when faced with a crisis, every Jew must be willing to break the law and sacrifice personal safety for the collective welfare. If they do not, the danger to the community becomes too great to contain. Therefore, the book calls for active participation in the preservation of the Jewish community, highlighting the importance of both personal and collective responsibility in times of crisis.

## 6: Jewish Identity in the Persian Diaspora, According to the Book of Esther

The first section of this chapter aims to explore the theological implications of Jewish identity as depicted in the Book of Esther. Initially, we review the references to the ethnic identity of Mordecai, Esther, and the Jewish people, seen in passages such as Esther 2:5-7, 10, 3:2-8, 4:13-14, 7:3-4, 8:17. These references are essential for understanding how the Book of Esther integrates the characters into the sacred history of Israel, despite their living in the Diaspora. The Jewish characters' ethnic identity serves to highlight their responsibility to uphold God's covenant, even in exile. The names Mordecai and Esther, which are Persian in origin, suggest a degree of assimilation into Babylonian and Persian culture. This assimilation reflects the Jews' voluntary positioning outside of God's designated plan for Israel and their decision to remain in the Diaspora, despite opportunities to return to the land of Israel.

Secondly, we analyze Mordecai's advice to Esther to conceal her Jewish identity after her selection to the king's harem. This advice likely stems from the fact that the Jews in the Diaspora viewed their environment as hostile to their faith. Esther's concealment of her identity becomes a symbol of the broader experience of Jews in exile, who are forced to hide their identity due to the secular, often hostile environment in which they live. In the absence of God's direct presence, Jews in the Diaspora conceal their identity, mirroring God's own "hiddenness" from them in their circumstances.

This act of hiding one's identity, which includes Esther's adaptation to court life, raises a theological dilemma. It suggests a tension between Jewish identity and the pressures of the surrounding culture, particularly when it comes to religious observance. The book implies that the Jewish identity crisis in the Diaspora is a form of exile from God's full presence, a situation exacerbated by Esther's decision to hide her identity. Esther, in this sense, represents all Jews in the Diaspora who struggle to maintain their identity in a foreign land.

Thirdly, the rise of Haman to the position of vizier serves as a critical moment that awakens the dormant consciences of the Jewish people. Mordecai's refusal to bow before Haman, driven by his ethnic identity, catalyzes Haman's plot against all the Jews. Mordecai's refusal is rooted in his Jewishness and the covenant of God that distinguishes the Jewish people from other nations. This refusal, and the subsequent plot to annihilate the Jews, serves to highlight the importance of adhering to the law of God, even in a foreign land.

Haman's accusation that the Jews have their own laws reveals the Jews' distinctiveness and their ongoing identity as God's covenant people.

Fourth, through the episode of the conversion of non-Jews to Judaism (Esther 8:17), the author demonstrates that loyalty to the covenant and obedience to God's will are the means by which the Jews can withstand the challenges of living in the Diaspora. The open assertion of Jewish identity, through actions such as fasting, prayer, and communal solidarity, becomes the key to their survival. The conversion of Gentiles serves as an ironic but powerful reminder that only by embracing their Jewish identity can the Jews in the Diaspora be saved from destruction.

**Theological Significance of the Diaspora in the Book of Esther**

The second section of this chapter explores the theological significance of the Diaspora as portrayed in the Book of Esther. The first image of the Diaspora in the Book of Esther is that of a secularized space where God's direct influence seems absent. The omission of God's name and the lack of explicit references to Jewish religious life reflect the fact that the Diaspora, though inhabited by Jews, is a world largely disconnected from the sacredness of Jerusalem and the temple. In this context, the Jews are not living according to God's will, as evidenced by their failure to repatriate and rebuild the temple.

The absence of God's direct presence in the Diaspora is emphasized by the author's rhetorical choice to omit divine references, illustrating that the Diaspora is a space where God's covenant is not fully honored. This absence of God's name does not signify His total abandonment of the Jews, but rather His hiddenness in their lives, a theme that permeates the narrative. The Jews in the Diaspora, much like Esther herself, are forced to hide their identity due to the hostile environment, and this concealment is portrayed as a spiritual crisis.

The second image of the Diaspora in the Book of Esther is one where the Jews live under the influence of Persian imperial power, centered on King Ahasuerus. The laws of the king reflect his whim and capriciousness, highlighting the instability of the Diaspora environment. The king's decisions, often influenced by his advisors and courtiers, result in a lack of legal stability. The inability of the king to maintain a consistent policy further stresses the precariousness of the Jews' position in the empire.

However, this instability is not just a passive force. It also underscores the Jews' need to assert their identity and reclaim their relationship with God. Esther's eventual decision to reveal her Jewishness and intervene on behalf of her people marks a pivotal moment in the narrative, where the Jews, through their collective action, begin to reassert their identity and act in accordance with God's covenant. The Book of Esther thus uses the contrast between the unstable political environment of the Diaspora and the stability offered by God's covenant to stress the need for the Jews to live in accordance with their faith, even in exile.

Finally, the third image of the Diaspora in the Book of Esther is one where the Jews have the opportunity to rediscover their identity. Exile has been a form of punishment for the Jews' disobedience, and the Diaspora reflects their spiritual and national separation from God's full presence. However, the events of Esther's story serve as a call for the Jews to rediscover their covenantal identity and reaffirm their relationship with God. The actions of Mordecai and Esther lead to a renewed commitment to the covenant, not only saving them from annihilation but also reestablishing their identity as God's people in the Diaspora.

In conclusion, the Book of Esther portrays the Diaspora as a space that presents both challenges and opportunities for the Jewish people. Despite the secular environment and the lack of divine intervention, the story emphasizes the importance of maintaining one's identity and faith, showing that even in exile, the Jews can experience deliverance by returning to their covenant with God. The narrative thus serves as both a warning and a call for Jews in the Diaspora to remain faithful to their religious identity, for it is through this faithfulness that they will find salvation.

**7: The Feast of Purim and its theological significance**

Number 7 is devoted to identifying the theological meaning of the feast or Purim, the origin of which is associated with the events described in the Book of Esther. In this part we will focus primarily on Esther 9.20-32, a passage which discusses the establishment of Purim as a feast. Our main goal is to identify the theological meaning of this event, according to the Book of Esther. We discover that Purim is different from the other festivals, because it does not arise out of a divine command. He who asks Jews from all over the empire to celebrate the feast of Purim is Mordecai, and recorded in his letters, the feast of Purim was celebrated spontaneously by thye Jews in Susa and all over the Persian Diaspora (Est. 9.18-19). Once established, according to Mordecai decision, this feast was to be held year, on the 14th and 15th of Adar.

In order t o find out the theological significance of Purim, we have to analyze the most relevant passages: Est. 9.22 and Est. 9.23-28 Verse 22 of the Est.9 is not only a summary of the events underlying the establishment of Purim. It has obvious theological significance. According to its meaning, at Purim Jews celebrate the rest they have received upon the elimination of the evil which had threatened them. Thus, on this occasion Jews do not celebrate the destruction of their enemies, but the rest which gave them the leisure to unite again as one people and live again as Jews. This fact implies, rightly, a revival of their national and religious consciousness. Est. 9.23-28 not only emphasizes the commitment of the Jews to celebrate the Purim, year after year, from generation to generation, according to the commandment of Mordecai, but it also makes clear that events are not governed by chance or the will of the gods, but by God, who is actually behind the history of Israel.

Secondly, in the last chapter of our work, we focus on the fact that letters written by Mordecai and Esther (mentioned in Est. 9) stipulate the requirements for the celebration of Purim, which must be respected by every Jew. We can speak of four "canons" of the Purim holiday, by which the event is defined as a festival in a biblical sense, that is, with an essentially religious character: i) Purim is given a perpetual and all-embracing character; it is to be held by all Jews from all generations (Est. 9.21, 27, 29, 31, 32); ii) Moreover, the feast is supposed to be celebrated in a certain manner: the chosen days should be "days of feasting and joy" par excellence (cf. Num. 23.40, Deut. 12.12, 16.11-14), for sorrow was turned to joy Est. 9.22) and because Purim does not celebrate victory over the enemies of Israel, but the rest which Jews had, when they were "rid of their enemies" (Est. 9.22) Mordecai and Esther's letters clarify this aspect, equating the survival of the people with a state of "rest" which must be interpreted as elimination of the peril. The defeat of the enemy is not taken into the account at the celebration; therefore, the Purim feast is devoid of any nationalist or chauvinistic component. (iv) The last "canon" of the feast of Purim, recorded in letters included in the last chapter of the book (Est. 9.26, 27, 32), binds the Jews to keeping the feast according to the written instructions (Est. 9:26). The festival must always comply with the written record of the events narrated in Chapters 1-8, to which the letters of Mordecai and Esther are appended.

Thirdly, we discover that the feast of Purim is meant to integrate the Book of Esther in to the sacred tradition of Israel. The passage in Est.

9.20-32 gives the book a "normative" profile. We understand, therefore, that the ordinances established in Mordecai and Esther's letters were written in the book (probably in the first version of the Book of Esther) with a precise purpose, namely to make it "normative scripture". We can talk about a "canonical halo" which takes shape around the Book of Esther. Thus, from the theological point of view, the narrative acquires a special meaning because "Purim must (...) (be) interpreted in the context of Israel's existence, which is a thoroughly religious one" ("the sacred tradition of Israel").

In the Greek version of the Book of Esther (LXX), we see a distinct reworking of the text, specifically aligned with the style and concerns of postexilic literature such as the books of Ezra, Nehemiah, and Daniel. These "Persian histories" focus on the Jews living under foreign rule, and in the Greek translation of Esther, several "additions" were made to align the book with these broader themes. These additions aim to make the underlying divine actions in the narrative more explicit, in contrast to the more implicit nature of divine intervention in the Hebrew text.

One of the key alterations in the LXX version is the addition of Mordecai's dream and its interpretation (Additions A and F), which provide a clearer divine framework for the events in the narrative. This shift introduces explicit religious themes, emphasizing God's role in guiding the Jewish people's deliverance. Additionally, the two edicts, one from Haman and the counter-decree from Mordecai (Additions B and E), are emphasized in the Greek version, underscoring the cooperation between divine and human factors in securing the salvation of the Jews.

The transformation of Haman's ethnicity in the LXX version is another significant change. In the Hebrew text, Haman is identified as "the son of Hammedatha, the Agagite," a reference to the Amalekites, historical enemies of Israel. In the Greek version, however, Haman is re-identified as "Aman the son of Amadathes, a Macedonian" (Est. 9:24). This change is not simply an alteration of Haman's ancestry; it serves a deeper purpose, connecting the character of Haman with the Hellenistic rulers of the time, particularly the Ptolemaic dynasty of Egypt. The Ptolemies, as Macedonian rulers and strong proponents of Hellenism, were often hostile to the Jewish people. Thus, by transforming Haman into a Macedonian, the translator draws a parallel between the antagonist of the story and the contemporary threats to Jewish identity posed by the spread of Hellenism.

This "updating" of Haman's character serves to make the story more relevant to the Jewish community in Egypt, where the Book of Esther was likely translated. The Greek version subtly warns the Jews of the Diaspora that their true enemy is not just a historical figure like Haman but the broader cultural and religious forces of Hellenism, which sought to erase Jewish identity. This shift in the narrative helps Jews in Egypt understand that their survival depends not only on defeating external enemies but also on resisting the pressures of assimilation into a foreign, pagan culture.

The LXX version, by highlighting this conflict with Hellenism, strengthens the theological message of the Book of Esther. It urges the Jewish community to maintain their religious and cultural identity despite the challenges posed by their environment. The survival of the Jews in the Diaspora, the text suggests, is contingent upon their commitment to God's covenant, symbolized by their continued adherence to their traditions and identity.

Thus, in the Greek version, the Book of Esther serves as a call to the Jews in the Diaspora to resist cultural assimilation and preserve their national and religious identity. It offers both a historical narrative of deliverance and a theological framework that encourages Jews to live faithfully within their environment, regardless of the external pressures they face. The focus on Hellenistic threats to Judaism, as well as the emphasis on divine providence and human action, highlights the ongoing relevance of the Esther narrative for Jews living in exile.

### 7.2. Conclusions

Through our Manual, which does not ignore previous manuscripts and other research findings reflected in several articles and scientific studies (especially in the English-speaking world), we offer a contemporary point of view and a new direction in the contemporary theological interpretation of the Book of Esther, a perspective which takes in to account its canonical character, its historical context, its textual traditions and its main literary features. Although we cannot claim to have exhausted the subject, we believe that our approach leads to the following conclusions.

1)      (a) Both the absence of God's name, and the apparently non-religious character of the Book of Esther have continuously raised questions about the presence of the book in the Old Testament canon. Despite these questions, the canonicity of the book has remained intact, but its status in is not confined to the simple fact of belonging to the OT canon, but expresses the fact that, in terms of theological thought, the book of Esther is compatible with the teaching of the OT, which it also enriches. Therefore, we cannot speak of a biblical theology of the OT, if we ignore the Book of Esther the status as the word of God and that Esther becomes a writing which has its own theological message, one that of course, is to be interpreted in a canonical manner, not otherwise.

(b) Analyzing the historicity of the Book of Esther has been necessary because the book itself claims this quality and because we have deemed it appropriate that in formulating its theology, whose character is implicit, we should start by necessity precisely by delineating the historical context claimed by the book. The veracity of the theological message of the Book of Esther is based on the historical reality of space and time coordinates.

First, the analysis done reveals the high degree of affinity and harmonization between the extra-biblical sources and the Book of

Esther. This led us to the belief that the book has an obvious historical character. The author wrote the book sometime between the end of the fifth century BC and the beginning of the fourth century, that is, very close to the reign of Xerxes, a temporal proximity which explains the author's good knowledge about the Persian milieu. Moreover, the author's proximity to the epoch of the events described makes the resulting text all the more credible in the eyes of the recipients. We should add here a caveat: the text of the Book of Esther should not be evaluated by using the criteria applied to modern historiography, since no other ancient work with historical claims can be classified in this category.

Once we have established the hermeneutic framework within which the book must be read, we can summarize the following aspect: (i) the Book of Esther is a biblical narrative with a historical character, or, rather, a trustworthy "narrated history", (ii) It can be considered a historical source about the events it describes. It goes without saying that in describing the events the author selected and summarized only those historical details which he considered relevant, leaving aside other information. (iii) The Book of Esther records not merely historical facts, but God's intervention itself on behalf of His people, in a particular historical context. Therefore, as biblical (that is, canonical) narrative, historically trustworthy, its message is meant to reinforce the hope of readers in God's saving intervention in favor of the elect, both at present and in the future: just as God intervened in the past of behalf of his people, so he will deliver them from now on from the danger that comes from its enemies. According to our analysis, the context claimed by the Book of Esther is the Epoch of Xerxes' reign. Thus, the book of Esther is not a description of the Babylonian exile, but a story about the life of the Jewish community in Persian Diaspora consisting of those Jews which had not returned to the land of their ancestors after the decree of Cyrus the Great. This fact cannot be ignored by those who attempt to articulate the theology of the Book of Esther.

2. Consequently, the Book of Esther is not simply a wisdom work, because every ancient historical work had also a moralizing character. It is narrated history, like any other ancient works of history. This would be the first reason why the author made use, in the process of writing, of all literary devices he could use (irony, peripety, coincidences, recurring motifs and terms, doublets), wishing to make it attractive and theologically relevant. The literary conventions used by the author determine the implicit character of the theology the book contains. This means that, if we do not take into account, the literary conventions, we will not be able to interpret the theology of the book in a correct manner, even if we reconstruct its historical context properly. The ultimate aim of the book is the revelation of God's will, so that its readers could (re) enter into relationship with Him. As narrated history, the book has the power to change people's lives, as they identify themselves with it. At the same time, like any other narrated

history, the Book of Esther should be also seen as an interpretation of what happened, with a plain purpose of highlighting the true meaning of the events described in the book.

3. The Book of Esther has a marked religious character. Scholars who dispute the religious character of the book and point to the alleged nationalist and chauvinistic spirit of the book (citing as argument the apparent hostility of the Jews towards the Gentiles) do so without any basis. Our analysis shows unequivocally that the issues are not part of the core of the book. Omitting God's name or the absence of any reference to the religious life of the Jews living in the Diaspora are not in themselves defining features of the Book of Esther. Rather, these "omissions" are used to talk about the state of the inhabitants of the Diaspora people and not about the nature and person of God or about the nature of the book.

4. Omitting God's name and the lack of any reference to the religious life of Jews living in the Diaspora people are intentional acts and have rhetorical nature. They are designed to delegitimize or discredit the Diaspora in the eyes of readers of the book Esther. In this way, the Diaspora is portrayed as a "secularized" universe devoid of God's direct presence. In other words, the Diaspora is a space which does not fall within the perimeter of the divine will. On the one hand, the placement of the Diaspora outside God's will was caused by refusal of the Jews to repatriate themselves, a

refusal which is caused by their cultural assimilation and conformity to customs of the area. The Murashu Tablets suggests just this: the generation which came after the restoration has names of pagan origin and a change in this regard is visible only after the year 475 BC. Therefore, it should not surprise us that Mordcai had a pagan name and Ester's other name was non-Jewish. On the other hand, we can talk about the Jews who remained there as those who were did not integrate in to God's plan for the restoration the Holy Land and of the Temple in Jerusalem. It is important to note that the repatriation of the Jews in the land of their forefathers moved the center of the Jewish world from Babylonia back to the Holy Land. So the Diaspora becomes the periphery of the Jewish world, a world devoid of God's direct presence.

5. Diaspora emerges as a world characterized by much hostility towards the Jews. Being deprived of God's plenary presence, the space of the Diaspora is dominated by Ahasuerus and his counselors, who manipulate the emperor according to their wishes. Thus, the Jews in the Diaspora, because they refuse the call to repatriate, are under Haman's influence. Out of purely subjective and personal reasons, Haman has planned killing all Jews of Diaspora by means of a royal decree. Haman's hostility turns the Diaspora into a space outside God's will. The trials inherent to such a milieu have forced the Jews to conceal their identity. The most telling example is, of course, Esther.

6. The decree of Haman led Mordecai to ask Esther to reconsider her decision to hide her ethnic origin and then to intervene to the emperor in order to save her kinsmen, even though previously it was he who had asked her to hide her true identity. The crisis brought about by Haman's evil designs compels Esther to (re) define herself in terms of identity and to accept her own Jewishness. In the book, this coincides with an appropriation of the covenant, coupled with the recognition that she had not been living as a Jew ought to have lived. We note that the appropriation of her Jewishness compelled her to be loyal to her won people and to act on its behalf.

In the Book of Esther, the human factor and the Divine Providence are not mutually exclusive, but rather are in a close relationship of complementarity. The salvation of the Jewish people can be found in both God's mysterious work and Mordecai and Esther's efforts, even though the latter's action takes place under pressure of deeply menacing circumstances. Identification with God's covenant through acceptance of their own Jewishness is tantamount to a "reconversion", an event which opens the way for a divine intervention on behalf of the Jews living in the Persian Diaspora. An important part is played not only by the courage and skill of the two heroes, but also by that step of faith which both took appropriating their Jewishness and acting in consequence. The actions of Esther and Mordecai have become useful to the divine cause only because the heroes have expressed their allegiance to the covenant and acted in accordance with the urgency of the moment. This is why, unlike in the other biblical books, in the book of Esther human initiative is appreciated and seen as being complementary with the mysterious work of God, manifested through coincidences and serendipities. Complementarity between the human and the divine factor emerges when Mordecai and Esther identified themselves with God's covenant.

Esther's possible refusal to appear before Ahasuerus with a plea for the salvation of the Jews would not have protected her from the destructive effects of Haman's decree, because, ironically, lack of action would have turned out to be more dangerous than action itself. The hostility of the Diaspora, fueled by the variability and ambiguity of the imperial power, would seem to demand at first sight a concealment of identity, as a prerequisite for survival. But things are not so. Concealment will not ensure their survival but rather will lead to their annihilation. By contrast, assuming their Jewishness, which, as we have seen, the Book of Esther likens first to embracing the value of God's covenant and then with an action on behalf of the Jews in the Diaspora, in accordance with the example set by Mordecai and Esther, will ensure survival. Thus, survival in the Diaspora is guaranteed only to those who declare themselves Jews and who behave in consequence, to those who are loyal to God's covenant and obey God's will. It should be noted that, according to the Book of Esther, in Diaspora, unlike in the Holy Land, the covenant is the only source of identity for Jews, a fact which is revealed, ironically, by Haman himself (Est. 3.8).

For example, at the end of the book we read that many of the native inhabitants, seized by fear, convert to Judaism to preserve their lives (Est. 8.17). The end is in stark contrast with the initial situation in which we see the Jews hiding their identity to keep the privileges acquired up to that moment. Thus, an open affirmation of their own identity considering God's covenant is a cardinal prerequisite for salvation from the hostility of the Diaspora. Paradoxically, this hostility is the means through which the Diaspora Jews are forced to rediscover themselves as the people of God and live according to the covenant.

Also, the Book of Esther makes it clear that any action on behalf of the people implies at the same time the exposure of one's ethnic identity. The unmasking of Haman by Esther compels the latter to "unmask" herself ethnically (Est. 7.3-6), declaring her belonging to the Jewish people. In this manner, the book points out the reciprocity that exists in relational terms between the individual and the community to which he or she belongs. But loyalty to the community, which in this case amounts to loyalty to God, also involves a personal commitment which can also lead to acts contrary to the civil laws. In the Diaspora, the Jew faces a peculiar situation, in that he is bound to reconcile his loyalty to his won people with the loyalty to the emperor or Persia and is forced to reject the latter, if the fate of his people is threatened. Such disobedience is held, because the hero seeks the good of the community and must act unreservedly towards achieving this goal. The underlying suggestion is that, in times of need, every Jew should be willing to break the law and sacrifice himself for the sake of this community because otherwise the danger becomes impossible to contain, this situation implies, of course, the recognition of the fact that God works in history through the people who make themselves available to him.

7. We therefore note that in the Book of Esther the action composes itself into two layers. On the one hand we see the divine providence, which manifests itself by coincidence and peripeties, and on the other hand we see, in contrast, the human initiative. The two surfaces of action converge when the heroes of the book (and especially Esther) appropriate their Jewishness, identifying with God's covenant, a covenant which works as a bridge between the two. Moreover, the central place in the book is occupied by the covenant and, implicitly, by the need for Jews to conform their lives to its requirements. Only by living in conformity with the covenant regulation does a Jew turn into an agent through which God can perform his work effectively. On the one hand, Jews must know that they will survive in the Diaspora only if they are loyal to the covenant of God, living openly as Jews, without hiding, and that any compromise on their part will be fatal. On the other hand, the Jews living in Diaspora (i.e., an universe subject to the will of the emperor) should know that loyalty to the covenant will force them to assume the practical condition of their people,

acting on its behalf, even if this would be contrary to civil law. Basically, appropriating the covenant and living in conformity with its regulations impels them to act by faith – an action out of which emerges the very salvation of their people.

8. It is obvious that the theology of the Book of Esther should not be circumscribed around divine providence, human initiative, the election of the Jewish people and its redemption, although these theological themes are clearly present in the book and should not be overlooked. The theology the Book of Esther has at its core God's covenant, because only living according to the covenant guarantees the survival of people, despite the hostility of the Diaspora.

**Fig.A: Covenant**

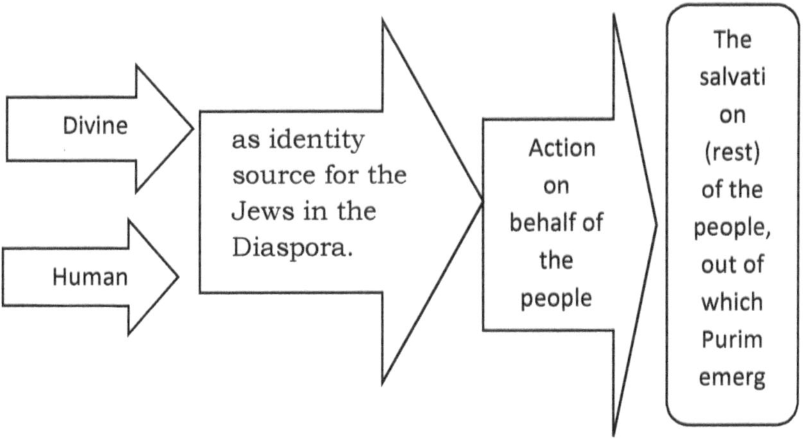

9. As Christian Scripture, the Book of Esther has the following theological implications: first, it shows that the survival of a Christian depends on assuming his identity in Christ and living according to this identity. Second, once Christians fully assume and openly assert their identity in Christ, they need to know that this makes them in God's agents. This new status implies the vocation to make theology. Therefore, regardless of circumstances and despite their menacing character, a Christian must act in support of and on behalf of those who cannot do it, thus becoming their voice, as part of a work that ultimately becomes the work of Christ in the World.

# REFERENCES: -

- Ayele, Teklehaymanot.2000. "Early Christian Traditional Sources in the Ethiopian Gééz Literature. Ethiopian Review vol.2, Addis Ababa. Capuchin Franciscan institute of Philosophy and Theology, / 237.

- Bezemer, M. Over.1982. De Klassick-Ethiopisches Version van enige Exodus- Hopofdst ukeen, University of Amsterdam D. phil thesis, unpublished.

- Devid, J.A. Clines. Esther Scroll, the story of the story. A and C Black1984.

- Dillman, August.1907. Ethiopic Grammar. Williams and Norgate 14, Henrietta Street, Covent Garden, London.

- Edele, B. A.1995. Critical Edition of Genesis in Ethiopic, unpublished PhD Dissertation, Submitted to Duke Univerisity.

- Fox Michael V. The structure and Idiology in the Book of Easther, Second edi. Grand Rapids: WM.B. Erdmans Publishing Company 2001. Pbk. ISBN:

- Fuhs H.F.1968. Die a Thiopische Ubersetzung des propheten micha (Bonner Biblische Beitrage, 28 Bonn ).

- Getachew Haile. 1995. «Highlighting Ethiopian Traditional Litrature» In silence is not Golden: a Critical Anthology of

Ethiopian Literature ( Tadesse Adera & Ali Jimal Ahmed eds) Lawrence, NJ: The Red see Press.

- Harden, Jm.1926. An Introduction to Ethiopic Christian Literature. The Diocen press, 23.

- Http:// www.Bible-history-com /Easton's/ E/Esther.

- Http://eotc-patriarch.org. Official website of the Ethiopian Orthodox Tewahdo Church teachings htm# Alpha.

- http://www.Dskmariam. Org/arts and Literature (pdf) Aksum pdf.p.207.

- Jacob, B. "Das Buch Esther be idem LXX." ZAW10 (1890) 241-98.

- Josephus 1998.The Complete Works.Thomas Nelson, Inc. Nashville, Tennessee.

- Knibb, MA. 1980. The Ethiopic Version of the lives of Prophets, Esekiel and Daniel. Bulletin of the School of Oriental and African Studies 43(2):197-206.

- Knibb, Michael A. The Ethiopic Book of Enoch, 2 Vol. London: University Press, 1979.

- Lanfranco Ricci.1991. « Ethiopian Christian Literature »S. Atiya (ed) The coptic Encyclopedia Vol. 3, New York, pp.975-79.

- Leslau, Wolf.1987. Comparative Dictionary of Geez (classical Ethiopia) Gééz English/ English Gééz with an index of the Semetic roots. Wiesbaden: Harrass Owitz.

- Marrassini, Paolo.2009. "Problems in Critical Edition and the state of Ethiopian philology" Journal of Ethiopian Studies,

VoLXLII, No1-2 June-December, AddisAbaba: IES, Addis Ababa University: 25-68.

- Mikre-sellassie, G.A. 2000EC. The early Translation of the Bible into Ge'ez.Addis Ababa, Birhan ena selam, pp.59.

- Niccum, C. 2000. "The Book of Acts in Ethiopic (With critical Text and Apparatus) and its Relation to the Greek Textual Tradition" Unpublished PhD. Dissertation, Univerrity of Nore Dame.

- Moore, Beth. Its Tough Being a Woman. (Nashville, TN: Life Way Press, 2008.) Vander Velde, Frances Women of the Bible. (Grand Rapids, MI Regal,)

- Moore, C. Daniel, Esther and Jeremiah: The Additions. Garden City, NY:1977.


- Peter T. Daniels, William Bright.1996. "The Words Writing System." Oxford University Press. Oxford.

- Pilkington, H.A.W. 1978. A critical Edition of the Book of Proverbs in Ethiopic, Oxford D. Phil Thesis, Unpublished.

- Rochus, Zuurmond.1992. "Versions, Ancient Ethiopic," in Anchor Bible Dictionary, Vol 6. Newyork: Doubleday, (807-14).

- Rodolfo Fattovich.2003. «Akkala guzay» in Von Uhling, Siegbers, ed. Encyclopedia Aethiopica: A-C weissbaden: Otto harrassowitz KG, pp.169.

- Sergew Hable sellassie. 1992. Ancient and medieval Ethiopian history. Addis Ababa, united printer.

- Stuart monro-hay.1991. Aksum: A civilization of late Antiquity, Edinburgh University Press. ISBN0.7486-0106-6.

- Tedros Abraha. 2004. The Ethiopic Version of the letter to the Hebrews, citta' Del Vaticano: Bibioteca Apostolica Vaticana. p419.

- Tedros Abraha. 2001. La Lettera ai Romani. Testo e commentari Della versione Ethiopica. Wiesbaden: Harrassowitz.p57.

- Uhlig, Siegbert. 1991. "Text- critical Questions of The Ethiopic Bible" Semetic studies in Honor of Wolf Leslaw (Alan S. Kaye, ed) Wiesbaden: Harrassowitz.pp.5583-1600.

- Ullendorff, Edward.1968. Ethiopia and the Bible, Oxford University press, London, pp.33-34.

- Vanderkamm, James. 1989. The Book of Jubilees: A critical Text. Louvain: peters.

- Vanganay, Leon and Christian-Bernard Amphoux.1991. An Introduction to New Testament Textual Criticism. Cambridge: Cambridge university press.

- Wechsler, Michael G.2005. Evangelium Johannis Aethiopicum. Louvain, Belgium, peters.

- Wegner, Paul D. 1999.The Jounney from Texts to Translations: The origin & Development of the Bible. Grand Rapids, MI: Beker Academic.

- Zuurmond, Rochus. 1992. "Versions, Ancient Ethiopic in the Anchor Bible Dictionary". Newyork: Doubleday, Vol.6, pp.808-810.

- Zuurmond, Rochus. 2001.Novum Testamntum Aethiopice: The synoptic Gospels (Edition of the Goslel of Mathew). Stuttgart, franzsteiner Verlag Wiesbaden GMBH.
- Zuurmond, Rochus. 1989.Novum Testsmentum Aethiopice: The synoptic Gospels (Edition of the Gospel of Mark). Stuttgart: Franz Steiner Verlag wiesbander GMBH.

# List of Abbreviations

## List of Abbreviations

**AAU**        Addis Ababa University

**AT-**        Alfa Text

**AD-**        Anno Dommini

**BC  -**        Before Christ

**BCE-**        Bible College Encyclopedia

**BHS -**        Biblia Hebraica Stuttgartensia (Masoretic text of Hebrew bible)

**CRA-**        Catholic Relief Association

**CMF-**        Centers for Micro film

**CRDA-**        Christian Relief and Development Association

**EMML-**        Ge'ez mss micro films Library

**EOTC-**            Ethiopian Orthodox Tewahido Church

**EOC -**          Ethiopian Orthodox College

**EST -**          Esther

**FGAE-**             Family Guidance Association of Ethiopia

**FGD -**          Focus Group Discussion

**FHI -**          Family Health International

**GT-**          Greek texts

**HEB -**          Hebrew

**IEC-**          Information Education and Communication

**MT   -**             Masoretic Text (the Authoritative Hebrew and Aramic text)

**MEGILLAH-**    Book of Esther 'Scroll' in Hebrew

**MSS -**          The Manuscripts

**MOC-**          Ministry of culture,

**NAM -**          National Archive Museum

**NIV -**          New International Version

**NET -**          New English Translation

**OGT -**        Old Greek Text

**KJV -**        King James version

# APPENDIX A

## BOOK OF ESTHER – ENGLISH/(OGT)ALPHA TEXT

### ESTHER

### ESTHER A– 1

A In the second year when Artaxerxes the Great was king, on the first day of Nisa, Mardochaios the son of Iairos son of Semeias son of Kisaios, from the tribe of Beniamin, saw a dream.

2 He was a Judean man dwelling in the city of Susa, a great man, serving in the court of the king. 3 Now he was of the group of exiles which Nabouchodonosor, king of Babylon, took captive from Ierousalem with Iechonias, the king of Judea. 4 And this was his dream: Look! Shouts and confusion! Thunder and earthquake! Chaos upon the earth! 5 Look! Two great dragons came forward, both ready to fight, and a great noise arose from them! 6 And at their sound every nation prepared for war, to fight against a nation of righteous people. 7 Look! A day of darkness and gloom! Affliction and anguish! Oppression and great chaos upon the earth! 8 And the whole righteous nation was in chaos, fearing the evils that threatened themselves, and

they were ready to perish. 9 Them they cried out to God, and from their cry, as though from a small spring, there came a great river, abundant water; 10 light, and the sum rose, and the lowly were exalted and devoured those held in esteem. 11 Then when Mardochaios, who had seen this dream and what God had determined to do, awoke, he had it on his heart and sought until nightfall to understand it in every detail.

12 And Mardochaios took his rest in the courtyard with Gabatha and Tharra, the two eunuchs of the king who guarded the courtyard. 13 He both overheard their deliberations and inquired into their ambitions and learned that they were preparing to lay hands-on Artaxerxes the king, and he told the king about them. 14 Then the king interrogated the two eunuchs, and when they confessed, they were led away. 15 And the king wrote these things in the record, and Mardochaios wrote concerning these things. 16 And the king ordered Mardochaios to serve in the court and gave him gifts for these things. 17 But Haman son of Hamadathos, a Bougean, was highly esteemed by the king, and he sourght to harm Mardochaios and his people because of the two eunuchs of the king.

1 Now it happened after these things in the days of Artaxerxes – this Artaxerxes controlled one hundred twenty-seven lands form India – 2 in those days when king Artaxerxes was enthroned in the city of Susa, 3 in the third year when he was king, he gave a feast for his Friends and for the other nations and for those highly esteemed of the Persians and Medes and for the rulers of the satrapies. 4 and after these things, after he had displayed to them of the celebration of his wealth for one hundred eighty days 5 and when the days of the wedding feast were completed, the king gave a

**ESTHER 1**

Wine party for the nations present in the city, for six days, in the courtyard of the king's house. 6 It had been decorated with linen and cotton curtains hung on cords of linen and purple attached to gold and silver bocks on pillars of marble and other stones. There were couches of gold and silver on a mosaic pavement of emerald, mother-of-pearl and marble. There were gossamer throws in many colors embroidered with roses round about. 7 The goblets were made of gold and silver, and a miniature cup made of ruby was on display that was worth thirty thousand talents. The wine was abundant and sweet, which the king himself drank. 8 Now this wine party was not by established law, but so the king wanted it, and he ordered his stewards to do as he and his men wanted.

9 And Astin the queen gave a wine party for the women in the royal quarters where king Artaxerxes was.

10 Now on the seventh day, when he was feeling merry, the king told Haman and Bazan and Tharra and Boraze and Zatholtha and Abataza and Tharaba, the seven eunuchs who attended king Artaxerses, 11 to bring the queen to him in order to proclaim her queen and to place the diadem on her and to show her to the rulers and her beauty to the peoples, because she was beautiful. 12 But Astin the queen did not obey him to come with the eunuchs. The king was angry, and he was enraged! 13 Then he said to his Friends, "This is how Astin spoke, therefore give your ruling and judgment on this." 14 So Arkesaios, Sarsathaios and Malesear, the rulers of the Persians and Medes who were close to the king and seated first by the king, came to him. 15 And they reported to him what, according to law, must be done with Astin the queen, because she had not done the things ordered by the king through the eunuchs. 16 Then Mouchaios said to the king and the rulers, "Astin the queen has wronged not only the king." 17(For he had reported to them the words of the queen and how she defied the king.)

"Therefore, just as she defied king Artaxerxes, 18 so this very day the other princesses of the rulers of the Persians and Medes, when they hear what was said to the king by her, will similarly dare to dishonor their husbands. 19 Therefore, if it pleases the king, let him issue a royal order, and let it be written according to the laws of the Medes and Persians, and let it not be applied differently, neither let the queen any longer come to him, and let the king giver her royal position to a woman better than she. 20 Let the law declared by the king be heard, whatever law he enacts in his kingdom. And thus, all women shall best honor on their own husbands, form the poor to the rich." 21 This word pleased the king and the rulers, and the king did as Mouchaios said. 22 He sent words throughout the whole kingdom, to every land in its own language so that they was afraid in their homes.

**ESTHER -2**

2 After these things, the king got over his anger, and he no longer remembered Astin, recalling what she a had said and how he condemned her.

2 Then the king's ministers said, "Let pure girls be sought for the king, beautiful in appearance. 3 and the king shall appoint officers in all the lands of his kingdom and let them select maidenly girls, beautiful in appearance, into Susa the city, into the harem, and let them be entrusted to the king's eunuch, the guard of the women; then let cosmetics and other care be given. 4 And whichever woman is pleasing to the king will be queen instead of Astin. "The advice pleased the king, and he did so.

5 Now there was a Judean man in Susa the city, and his name was Mardochaios the son of Iairos son of Semeias son of Kisaios, from the tribe o Beniamin, 6 who was an exile from Ierousalem, which Nabouchodonosor, king of Babylon, had taken captive. 7 And this man had a foster child, a daughter of Aminadab. His father's brother, and her name was Esther. And when her parents died, he trained her for himself as a wife. And the girl was beautiful in appearance. 8 So when the king's ordinance was heard, many girls

were gathered into Susa the city under the charge of Gai. Esther was also taken to Gai, the guard of the women. 9 The girl pleased him and found his favor, and he hastened to provide her with cosmetics and her portion of food and with seven girls assigned to her from the palace, and he provided well for her and her attendants in the harem. 10 Esther did not reveal her race or her ancestry, for Mardochaios had commanded her not to tell. 11 Each day Mardochaios walked around in front of the harem court, to learn how Esther would fare.

12 Now time for a girl to go in to the king was when she had completed twelve months, for the days of treatment were like this: six months being rubbed with oil of myrrh and six months with perfumes and cosmetics for the women. 13 and then she would go in to the king, and whatever she asked he would give her to take with her from the harem to the royal quarters. 14 In the evening she would go in; then toward day she would depart into the second harem of which Gai, the king's eunuch, was the guard of the women. And she would not go in to the king again, unless she was summoned by name.

15 When the time was completed for Esther the daughter of Aminoadab, brother of Mardochaios's father, to go in to the king, she turned down nothing of the things the king's eunuch, the guard of the women, commanded. For Esther was favored by all who saw her. 16 Esther went into Artaxerxes the king in the twelfth monty, which is Adar, in the seventh year of his reign. 17 And the king fell in love with Esther, and she wound favor beyond all the virgins; so, he set the queen's diadem on her. 18 Then the king gave a wine party for all his

Friends and forces for seven days. He celebrated Esther's wedding feast and gave rest to b those under his rule.

*aOr he   bOr canceled debts of*

## ESTHERS 2-3

19 AndMardochaios was serving in the court. 20 But Esther did not reveal her ancestry. For so Mardochaios had commanded her: to fear God and to do his ordinances, just as when she was with him. So Esther did not change her way of life.

21 The two eunuchs who were the king's chief bodyguards were irritated because Mardochaios was promoted, and they sought to kill Artaxerxes the king. 22 But the matter became known to Mardochaios and he alerted Esther, and she explained to the king the details of the plot. 23 So the king interrogated the two eunuchs and hanged them. Then the king ordered me to make an entry as a memorial in the royal archive in commendation of Mardochaios's loyalty.

3 After these things king Artaxerxes honored Haman son of Hamadathos, a Bougean, and exalted him and set him above all his Friends. 2 and all who were in court would obey him, for the king had commanded them to do so. But Mardochaios would not do obeisance to him. 3 Then those in the court of the king spoke to Mardochaios, "Mardochaios, why do you disobey what the king says?" 4 Day after day they spoke to

him, and he would not listen to them. So they revealed to Haman that Mardochaios was opposing the command of the king, and Mardochaios revealed to them that he was a Judean. 5 When Haman learned that Mardochaios would not do obeisance to him, he was very angry. 6 And so he planned to destroy all the Judeans under the rule of Artaxerxes.

7 He decided in the twelfth year of Artaxerxes' reign and cast lots day-by-day and month-by-month so that the race of Mardochaios might perish on one day. The lot fell on the fourteenth of the month, that is Adar.

8 Then he spoke to king Artaxerxes, saying "There is a certain nation scattered among the nations throughout all your kingdom; their laws are different from all the nations, and they disobey the king's laws so that it is not expedient for the king to tolerate them. 9 If it pleases the king, let a decree be issued to destroy them, and I will pay into the king's treasury ten thousand talents of silver." 10 And the king took his signet ring and put it in b the hand of Haman to seal what had been written against the Judeans. 11 the king said to Haman, "Keep the silver, but treat the nation as you wish."

12 Then the king's secretaries were summoned on the thirteenth day of the first month, and they wrote as Haman commanded to the governors and to the rulers of every land – from India to Ethiopia – to one hundred twenty – seven lands and to the rulers of the nations in their own language in the name of Artaxerxes the king. 13 it was sent by couriers throughout Artaxerxes' empire, to

destroy the race of the Judeans in one day of the twelfth month, which is Adar, and to seize their property.

*aOr hung   bOr on*

### ESTHER B-4

This is a copy of the letter:

**B**"The Great King Artaxerxes writes as follows to the rulers of the one hundred twenty-seven lands from India to Ethiopia and to the officials under them:

2 "Being the ruler of many nations and master of the whole world, I have determined (not high mindedly with presumption of authority but always acting in moderation and with kindness) to secure lasting tranquility in the lives of my subject and, in order to make my kingdom peaceable and open to travel throughout all its extent, to restore the peace desired by all people.

3 "When I asked my counselors how this might be accomplished, Maman – who excels among us in sound judgment and is distinguished for his unchanging good will and steadfast fidelity and has attained the second place in the kingdom – 4 pointed out to us that among all the tribes in the world there is scattered a certain hostile people, who have laws contrary to those of every nation and continually disregard the ordinances of kings so that we honorably

intend cannot be achieved. 5 Therefore, whereas we understand that, since this nation stands constantly all alone in opposition to all humanity, perversely following an estranging manner of life due to their laws and since it is ill-disposed to our interests doing the worst harm and in order to our interests, doing the worst harm and in order that our kingdom may not attain stability.

6 "We therefore have ordered that you utterly destroy those indicated to you in the letters written by Haman, who is in charge of the affairs of state and is our second Father – including women and children – by the daggers of their enemies, without any compassion and restraint, on the fourteenth day of the twelfth month, Adar, of this present year, 7 so that those who have long been hostile and so remain, when they in one day have gone down to Hades by fore, may in the time hereafter render the matters of state completely tranquil and untroubled for us."

3 14 Copies of the letters were posted in every country, and it was ordered all the nations to be ready for this day. 15 The matter proceeded quickly even to Susa. While the king and Haman were sitting down to drink the city was being thrown into confusion.

4 Now when Mardochaios learned the outcome, he tore his clothes and put on sackcloth and sprinkled ashes, and as he rushed through the square of the city, he cried out with a loud voice, "An innocent nation is being destroyed!" 2 He went up to the king's gate and stood there, for it was not permitted him to enter the courtyard clothed with sackcloth and ashes. 3 And in every land, wherever the letters were posted, there was crying and wailing and great mourning among the Judeans; they put sackcloth and ashes on themselves. 4 The queen's attendants and eunuchs came in and told her, and she was troubled when she heard what had happened.

### ESTHER 4-C

She sent someone to clothe Mardochaios and to take off his sackcloth, but he was not persuaded. 5 Then Esther called for Hachrathaios, her eunuch who attended her, and sent him to teach her from Mardochaios the facts.

7 So Mardochaios told him what had happened, and the promise that Haman had promised to the king of ten thousand talents into the treasury so that he could destroy the Judeans. 8 He also gave him the copy that had been posted in Susa to destroy them, to show to Esther, and told him to command her to go and entreat the king and to beg him on behalf of her people: "Remember your humble days when you were brought up by my hand, for Haman, the second to the king,

has spoken against us to put us to death. Call upon the Lord, and speak to the king about us, and deliver us from death!"

9 So. Hacharathaios went in and told her all these things. 10 then Esther said to Hachrathaios, "Go to Mardochaios, andy say, 11' All the nations of the empire know that every man or woman who shall go to the king inside the inner court uninvited – there is no deliverance for him. Only if the king holds out the golden rod to someone will that person be safe. And I myself have not been called to go to the king for these thirty days."

12 So Hachrathaios reported to Mardochaios evferything Esther had said. 13 Mardochaios said to Hachrathaios, "Go, and say to her, Esther, do not say to yourself that you alone of all the Judeans in the empire will be safe. 14 Because even if you keep silent at this time, from elsewhere help and protection will come to the Judeans, but you and your father's household will Perish. And who knows if for this time you were made queen?' " 15 Then Esther sent the messenger who had come to her back to Mardochaios, saying, 16 "Go, gather the Judeans that are in Susa, and fast on my behalf, and neither eat nor drink for three days, night and day. I and my attendants will also abstain from food. And then I will go to the king, though it is against the law, even if it be that I Perish." 17 And Mardochaios went and did what Esther had commanded him.

Then he petitioned the Lord, remembering all the works of the Lord.

2 And he said, "Lord, Lord, king of all powers, for the universe is subject to your authority, and there is no one who can oppose you when it is your will to save Israel, 3 because you have made heaven and earth and every wonderful thing in it under heaven. 4 You are Lord of all, and there is no one who can withstand you, the Lord. 5 you know all thins; you know, O Lord, that it was not in insolence nor pride nor for any love of glory that I did this, namely, to refuse to do obeisance to this prideful Haman, 6 for I would have been willing to kiss the soles of his feet for Israel's safety! 7 But I did this so that I might not set human glory above aLacking in GK

**ESTHER C**

Divine glory, and I will not do obeisance to anyone but you, my Lord, and I will not do these things in Pride. 8 and now, O Lord God, King, God of Abraam, spare your people, for they are looking to ruin us, and they desired to destroy the inheritance that has been yours from the beginning. 9 do not neglect your portion, which you redeemed for yourself out of the land of Egypt. 10 Hear my petition and have mercy upon your allotment; turn our mourning into feasting, that we may live and sing hymns to your name, O Lord; do not silence the mouth of those who praise you."

11 And all Israel cried out from their strength, because their death was before their eyes.

12 Then Esther the queen fled to the Lord, seized with the agony of death. 13 Taking off the garments of her glory, she put on the garments of distress and mourning, and instead of costly perfumes she utterly humbled her body; every part that she loved to adorn she covered with her tangled a hair. 14 Then she petitioned the Lord, God of Israel, and said: "O my Lord, you alone are our king; help me, I who am alone and have no helper except you, 15 because my danger is in my hand. 16 I have heard from my birth in the tribe of my family that you, O Lord, took Israel out of all the nations and our fathers from among all their forebears, to be an everlasting in heritance, and you did for them all that you said. 17 And now we have sinned before you, and you have delivered us into the hand of our enemies, 18 because we honored their gods. You are righteous, O Lord! 19 And now they were not satisfied that we are in bitter slavery, but they have b put their hands into the hands of their idols b, 20 to annul the stipulation of your mouth and to destroy your inheritance and to stop the mouths of those who praise you and to extinguish the glory of your house and you altar, 21 to open the mouth of the nations for the mighty deeds of vain things, and that a mortal king be admired forever.

22 "O Lord, do not surrender your scepter to those who don't exist, and do not let them laugh at our downfall, but turn their plan against them, and make a public example of him who began this

against us. 23 Remember, O Lord; make yourself known in a time of our affliction, and emboldenme, O king of the gods and Master of all dominion! 24 Put eloquent speech in my mouth before the lion and turn his heart to hate the one who fights against us so that there may be an end of him and those who agree with him. 25 But save us by your hand, and help me, who am alone and have no one except you, O Lord. You have knowledge of everything, 26 and you know that I hate the glory of the lawless and abhor the bed of the uncircumcised and of any foreigner: 27 you know my predicament – that I abhor the sign of my proud

*aOr braided    b Possibly convenanted with their idols*

## ESTHER C - 5

Position that is upon my head on days when ai appear in public. I abhor it like a menstrual cloth, and I do not wear it on the days when I am in private. 28 And your slave has not eaten at Haman's table, and I have not honored the king's banquet nor drunk the wine of libations. 29 Your slave has not rejoiced since the day of my change until now, except in you, O Lord, God of Abram. 30 O God who has power over all things, hear the voice of those who despair, and save us from the hand of evildoers. And save me from my fear!"

And it happened on the third day, as she ceased praying, she took off the garments of service and put on her glory. 2 Then, when she had become majestic, after calling upon the all-seeing God and savior, she took along two of her attendants; 3 on one she leaned gently for support, 4 while the other followed, holding her train. 5 She was radiant with the full flush of her train. 5 She was radiant with the full flush of her beauty, and her face looked happy as if she were cheerful, but her heart was in anguish from fear. 6 When she had gone through all the doors, she stood before the king. He was seated on the throne of his kingdom, clothed in the full array of his splendor, all covered with gold and precious stones. And he was most terrifying.

7 And when he raised his face inflamed with glory, he gazed at her in full flush of anger. The queen staggered, her color turned pale from faintness, and she collapsed on the head of the attendant who went before her. 8 Then God changed the spirit of the king to gentleness, and alarmed, he jumped from his throne and took her in his arms until she was quieted. He kept comforting her with soothing words 9 and said to her, "What is it, Esther? I am your brother. Take care! 10 you shall not die, for our ordinance is only for the common person. 11 Come here."

12 Then the lifted the golden rod and placed it one her neck; he welcomed her and said, "Speak to me." 13 She said to him, "I saw you, lord, like a divine angel, and my heart was shaken from fear of your glory. 14 for you are marvelous, lord, and your face is full of

grace." 15 and while she was speaking, she fell from faintness. 16 Then the king and all his servants were troubled, and the reassured he.

5 3 And the king said to her, "What do you want, Esther? What is your request" Even up to half of my kingdom, and it shall be yours." 4 Then Esther said, "Today is my special day. If, therefore, it pleases the king, let both him and Haman come to the dinner that I will prepare today." 5 Then the king said, "Bring Haman quickly so that we may do what Esther has said." So both came to the dinner that Esther had spoken about. 6 during the drinking, the king said to Esther, "What is it, Queen Esther? And it shall be, whatever you ask." 7 Then she said, "This is my petition and request: 8 If I have found favor before the king, let the king

**ESTHER 5-6**

and Haman come again tomorrow to the dinner that I will prepare for them, and tomorrow I will do these same things."

9 So Haman came out from the king very happy and rejoicing. But when Haman saw Mardochaios the Judean in the courtyard, he became very angry. 10 So he went home and called his friends and Zosara his wife, 11, and he announced to them his riches and the glory that the king had bestowed on him and how he had made him to be first and to be leader of the kingdom. 12 Haman said, "The Queen has not summoned with the king anyone but me to the dinner. Tomorrow also I have been invited. 13 Yet all this does not please me

when I see Mardochaios the Judean in the courtyard." 14 Then his wife Zosara and his friends said to him, "Let a pole fifty cubits a high be cut for you, and early in the morning speak to the king and have Mardochaios hanged b on it; then you go to the dineer with the king, and celebrate." This advice pleased Haman, and he had the pole prepared.

6 But the Lord kept sleep from the king that night, and he told his teacher to bring the written daily annals, to read to him. 2 And he found the entries written concerning Mardochaios, how he informed the king about two of the king's eunuchs, while they were on guard and sought to lay hands on Artaxerxes. 3 Then the king said, "What honor or distinction have we bestowed on Mardochaios?" The king's servants said, "You have done nothing for him." 4 While the king was inquiring about Mardochaios' good will- Look! Haman was in the courtyard! The king said, "Who is in the courtyard?" Now Haman had just entered to speak to the king to hang Mardochaios on the pole that he had prepared for him. 5 So the king said to Haman "What should I do for the person whom I want to extol?" and Haman said to himself, " Whom would the king want to extol if not me?" 7 So he replied to the king, "For the person whom the kinbg wants to extol, 8 let the king's servants bring a fine linen robe, which the king wears, and a horse upon which the king rides. 9 And let him give to him one of the king's most noble Friends, and let him robe the person whom the king

loves, and let him mount him on the horse and proclaim through the square of the city, saying: 'So shall it be for every person whom the king extols.'" 10 Then the king said to Haman, "you have spoken well. So do Mardochaios the Judean, who serves in the court. And let not a word of what you have said be transgressed." 11 So Haman took the robe and the horse and robed Mar-aI.e. over seventy feet hung.

## ESTER 6-7

Dochaios and mounted him on the horse and went through the square of the city and proclaimed, saying, "So shall it be for every man whom the king wants to extol." 12 Then Mardochaios returned to the court, but Haman returned home distressed, with his head covered. 13 Haman explained what had happened to him to Zosara his wife and to his friends. His friends and his wife said to him, "If Mardochaios is of the race of the Judeans, you have begun to be humiliated before him; you will fall when you fall. You will never be able to ward him off, because a living god is with him."

14 While they were still speaking, the king's eunuchs arrived hurrying Haman off to the wine party that Esther had prepared.

So the king and Haman went in to drink with the queen. 2 And the king said to Esther on the second day as they were drinking, "What is it, Queen Esther? What is your petition and what is your request? Let it be yours, up to the half of my kingdom." 3 Then she answered and said, "If I have found favor with the king, let my life be given at my petition, and my people at my request. 4 For we have been sold, I and my people at my people, to be destroyed, to be booty and to be enslaved-we and our children as male and female slaves-and I kept silent. For the slanderer is not worthy of the court of the king." 5 Then the king said, "who is this who dared to do this deed?" 6 So Esther said, "Aman who is an enemy! Haman is this wicked one!" Then Haman was terrified because of the king and the queen.

7 The king rose from the banquet and went into the garden, but Haman was begging the queen, for he saw himself in deep trouble. 8 Then the king returned from the garden. Now Haman had fallen on the couch, entreating the queen. And

**ESTHER 7- E**

The king said, "so then, you even violate my wife in my own house?" When Haman heard this, he covered his face a. 9 Then Bougathan, one of the eunuchs attending the king, said, "Look! Haman has even prepared a pole for Mardochaios, who spoke up on behalf of the king, and a pole fifty cubits tall has been erected at Haman's." And the king said, "Let him be crucified upon it." 10 So they hanged Haman on the pole that had been prepared for Mardochaios. Then the king got over his anger.

On that very day king Artaxerxes granted to Esther all that belonged to Haman the slanderer, and Mardochaios was summoned by the king, for Esther had revealed that he was related to her. 2 then the king took the signet ring, which he had taken from Hamnan, and gave it to Mardochaios. So Esther appointed Mardochaios over everything of Haman's.

3 Then she spoke again to the king, and she fell before his feet and pleaded that he revoke the evil of Haman and what he had done to the Judeans. 4 So the king held out the golden rod to Esther, 5 and Esther rose and stood before the king. And Esther said, "If it pleases you and if I have found favor, let an order be dispatched to revoke the letters sent by Haman, which were written to destroy the Judeans who are in your kingdom. 6 For how can I bear to see the suffering of my people? And how can I bear to be saved amidst the destruction of my lineage?" 7 then the king said to Esther, "If everything belonging to Haman I gave and turned over to you, and him I hanged b on the pole, because he plotted to lay hands on the Judeans, what more do yoy seek? 8 Youc also write in my name as it pleases youc, and seal it with my ring, for whatever is written as the king commands and sealed with my ring cannot be countermanded."

9 And so the secretaries were summoned in the first month, which is Nisa, on the twenty-third day of the same year, and they wrote to the Judeans what had been commanded to the administrators

and rulers of the of the satrapies from India to Ethiopia, one hundred twenty-seven satrapies country by country, each according to its won language. 10 It was written by the king and sealed with his ring, and they sent the orders by couriers, 11 how he ordered them to live in accordance with their laws in every city, both to help themselves and to deal with their adversaries and their enemies as they wished, 12 on a single day in the whole kingdom of Artaxerxes, on the thirteenth of the twelfth month, which is Adar.

E What is written below is a copy of the letter: "The Great King Artaxerxes, to the rulers of the lands from India to Ethiopia, the one hundred twenty-seven satrapies, and to those who are loyal to our interests, greetings.

2 "Many people, who are frequently honored

*aOr his face changed    bOr hung    cGK=O1*

**ESTHER E**

With the greatest kindness of their benefactors, they become the more ambitious 3 and not only seek to harm those subjects to us, but not being able to deal with prosperity, they even undertake to scheme against their own benefactors. 4 They not only abolish gratitude among people, but also, carried away by the boasts of those who are inexperienced in goodness, they even presume to escape the evil-hating divine justice, who always observes everything. 5 Furthermore, encouragement has implicated many of those appointed to places of authority, those entrusted to administer the affairs of friends, making them partly responsible for the shedding of innocent bold, and has brought about irremediable calamities 6 by the malicious lie of an evil disposition of people who misconstrue the sincere good will of their sovereigns.

7 "And it is possible to see this not so much from the more ancient records as we handed them down, as it is right at your feet, when you examine things impiously perpetrated by the pestilent behavior of those who hold power unworthily. 8 and it is possible to look out hereafter in order that we may render the kingdom quiet for all people, with peace, 9utilizing changes and always discerning what comes to our attention with a rather considerate response. 10 For whereas Haman son of Hamadathos (a Macedonian who was in truth aa foreigner to the blood of the Persiansa and quite devoid of our kindness), when he was entertained by us as our guest, 11 Obtained the good will that we have for every nation to such an extent that he was publicly proclaimed our Father and was continually done obeisance to by all as the person second to the royal throne, 12 but being unable to restrain his arrogance, he made it his business to deprive us of our rule and our breath 13 and by the crafty deceit or fuses asked to destroy Mardochaios, our savior and constant benefactor, and Esther, the innocent companion of our kingdom, together with their whole nation. 14 for when by these methods he had caught us undefended he thought that he would transfer the power of the Persians to the Macedonians.

15 "But we find that the Judeans, who were consigned to annihilation by this thrice-accursed man, are not criminals but are governed by most righteous laws 16 and are children of the highest, most great, living God who has directed the kingdom for us and for our ancestors in the most excellent order.

17 "You will therefore do well not to carry out the letters sent by Haman son of Hamadathos, 18 because he who did these things has been crucified at the gates of Susa with his whole household, since the god who prevails over all things has recompensed him quickly with the deserved judgment.

19 "and b you will do well b to post a copy of this letter publicly in every place and to allow the

*aOr not of Persian descent*   bLacking in GK

**ESTHER E-9**

Judeans to live in accordance with their own precepts 20 and join in helping them in order that they might defend themselves against those who attack in the time of oppression, on the thirteenth day of the twelfth month, Adar, on that same day. 21 For God, who rules over all things, has made this day to be a joy for his chosen race instead of a day of destruction for them.

22 "Therefore, you also shall celebrate this with all good cheer as a holyday among your commemorative feasts 23 so that both now

and hereafter it may be deliverance for us and for the well-dis-posed Persians, but for those who plot against us, a memorial of destruction.

24 "Every city and country, without exception, that does not do according to this by spear and fire shall be consumed with wrath. It shall be made not only impassable for people, but also most hostile to wild animials and birds all time.

8 13 "Now, let the copies be posted conspicuously in all the kingdom so that all the Judeans be ready on this day to fight against their adversaries."

14 So the horsemen went out in a hurry to perform what the king had commanded, and the ordinance was posted also in Susa. 15 Then Mardochaios went out, wearing the royal robe, with a gold crown and a diadem of purple linen, and when the people in Susa saw him they rejoiced. 16 for the Judeans there was light and gladness; 17 in every city and country wherever the ordinance was posted, wherever the proclamation was made, there was gladness and joy among the Judeans, a feast and mirth. And many of the nations were circumcised and became Judeans out of fear of the Judeans.

9 Now in the twelfth month, on the thirteenth day of the month that is Adar, the letter written by the king arrived. 2 On that same day the opponents of the Judeans Perished, for no one resisted, because they feared them. 3 For the rulers of the satraps and the tyrants and the royal secretaries esttemed the Judeans, for the fear of Mardochaios weighed upon them. 4

For it turned out that the king's ordinance was referred to by name throughout all the kingdom. 6 and in the city of Susa the Judeans killed five hundred men, 7 including Pharsannestain, Delphon, Phasga 8 and Phardatha and Barea and Sarbacha 9 and Marmasim and Arouphaios and Arsaios and Zabouthaios, 10 the ten sons of Haman son of Hamadathos, a Bougean, the enemy of the Judeans, and they Plundered 11 on that same day. The nuber of those killed in Susa was reported to the king. 12 the king said to Esther, "The Judeans have killed in the city of susa five hundred men. In the surrounding countryside how do you suppose they have fared? Therefore, what more do you ask? It shall be

**ESTHER 9**

Yours." 13 And so Esther said to the king, "Let it be granted to the Judeans to do likewise tomorrow so that they may hang the ten sons of Haman." 14 So he thus permitted it to be done and handed over to the Judeans of the city the bodies of Haman's sons to hang. 15 the Judeans in Susa gathered also on the fourteenth day of the month of Adar, and they killed three hundred men, but they did not plunder.

16 Now the rest of the Judeans who were in the kingdom also gathered and defended themselves and gained relief from their adversaries. For they killed fifteen thousand of them on the thirteenth of Adar,but they plundered nothing. 17 and they rested on the fourteenth of the same month and celebrated it as a day of rest with joy and gladness. 18 But the Judeans in the city of Susa gathered together also on the fourteenth and did not rest. They celebrated also the fifteenth with joy and gladness. 19 Therefore for this reason, the Judeans who are scattered in every land outside celebrate the fourteenth day of Adar as a holiday with gladness, each sending portions a to those nearby. But those living in the large cities also celebrate the fifteenth of Adar as a joyful holiday, sending portions to those nearby.

20 Now Mardochaios recorded these things in a book and sent it to the Judeans-as many as were in the kingdom of Artaxerxes, to those near and far, 21 to keep these days, the fourteenth and fifteenth of Adar – 22 for on these days the Judeans gained relief from their enemies – and the whole month, which was Adar, in which matters had been turned for them from sorrow into joy and from mourning into a holiday, to celebrate it as days of feasting and gladness, sending portions a to their friends and to the poor.

23 So the Judeans accepted just what Mardochaios had written to them- 24 how Haman son of Hamadathos, the Macedonian, had warred against them, in as much as he had proclaimed a decision and had cast the lot to destroy them, 25 and how he went in to the king,

telling him to hang Mardochaios, but as much evil as he had devised to bring upon the Judeans came upon him, and he himself and his children were hangedb. 26 Because of this, these days are called Phrourai, because of the lots (because in their language they are called Phrourai), because of the words of this letter, and as much as they had suffered because of these things, and as much as had happened to them. 27 He established them, and the Judeans accepted them for themselves and their descendants and all who had joined them and surely not to do otherwise. And these days are a memorial, kept from generation to generation, by city, family and country. 28 These days of Phrourai shall be celebrated for all time, and the commemoration of them shall never cease among their generations.

*aOr gifts of food    bOr hung*

### ESTHER 10-F

29 Then Esther the queen daughter of Aminadab, along with Mardochaios, the Judean, wrote what they had done and confirmation of the letter about Phrourai. 30 and Mardochaios and Esther the queen established these things for themselves on their own initiative, then also having established them by their own well-being and counsela. 31 And Esther established the matter by ordinance forever, and it was written for amemorial.

10 The king recorded during his rule over both land and see 2 both his strength and bravery, both the wealth and the glory of his kingdom; note that they have been recorded in the book of the kings of the Persians and the Medes as a memorial. 3 and Mardochaios b took over from b king Artaxerxes, and he was great in the kingdom and extolled by the Judeans. And being loved, he spent his life for his whole nation.

And Mardochaios said, "From God these things have come. 2 For I rembeber about the dream that I saw concerning these matters, for not even a word of them has failed to be fulfilled. 3 There was the little spring that became a river, and there were light and sun and abundant water; Esther is the river, whom the king married and made queen. 4 the two dragons are I my self and Haman. 5 the nations are those that gathered to destroy the name of the Judeans. 6 and my nation, this is Israel, who cried out to God and were saved. The Lord has saved his people, and the Lord has rescued us from all these evils, and God has done signs and great wonders that have not happened among the nations. 7 For this purpose he made two lots, one for the people of God and one for all the nations, 8 and these two lots came to the hour and the right time and to the day of decision before God, and for all the nations. 9 And God remembered his people and vindicated his own in heritance.

10 "And these days in the month of Adar, on the fourteenth and fifteenth of that same month, will be observed by them with a

gathering and joy and rejoicing before God, from generation to generation forever among his people Israel."

11 In the fourth year of the reign of Ptolemy and Kleopatra, Dositheos, who said he was a priest and a Leuite, and Ptolemy his son brought the above letter about Phrourai, which they said existed d, and Lysimachus son of Ptolemy, one of those in Ierousalem, translated it.

*A GK uncertain    b Possibly succeeded    c or righteous d Possibly was authentic*

# APPENDIX B

# THE BOOK OF ESTHER GE'EZ MANUSCRIPT/HEB.

## መጽሐፈ ዘአስቴር

## ምዕራፍ ፥ ፩

### Esther 1 ግዕ - አስቴር

1: በመዋዕሊሁ ለአርጤክስስ ወውእቱ አርጤክስስ ዘነግሠ ላዕለ ምእት ዕስራ ወሰብዓቱ በሐውርት እምነ ብሔረ ህንደኬ እስከ ብሔረ ኢትዮጵያ፨

2: ወበውእቱ መዋዕል አመ ነግሠ በሱሳ ሀገር፤

3: በሣልስ ዓም እምዘነግሠ ገብረ በዓለ ለአዕርክቲሁ ወበእንተ እለ ተርፉ አሕዛብ ወለፋርስ ወሜዶን ወለከቡራኒሆሙ፤ ወለመላእክተ ሰራዊት፨

4: ወእምድኅረ ዝንቱ እምድኅረ አርአዮሙ ብዕለ መንግሥቱ ወከብረ ትፍሥሕቱ ወብዕሉ በምእት ወሰማንያ ዕለት፨

5: ወሰብ ተፈጸም መዋዕለ መርዓ ገብረ ንጉሥ በዓለ ዳግም ለእለ ተርፉ ሕዝብ እለ ተረከቡ
   ውስተ ሀገር በውስተ ዓጸደ ቤት ንጉሥ ስዲስ መዋዕለ ወስኑየ።

6: ወሥርግው በሜላት ወበአኔ ንጹሕ ወዕዉድ በሜላት ውስተ አሕባለ ቢሶስ በሕልቀተ
   ወርቅ ወብሩር፡ ላዕለ አዕማደ እብን ዘጸርኖ፡ ወዐራታት ዘወርቅ ወብሩር፡ ወጽፍጹፍ
   በእብን ዘሕብረ መረግድ፡ ወበዕንቄ ጲኔኖን ወበእብነ ጻሪኑ ወጥቀ  ሠናይ ጸፋጸፉ
   ዘዘዚአሁ ጎብሩ አሥሩ ወእንተ አውዱ ጽዬ ረዳ ሥሩዕ።

7: ወጽዋዓትኒ ዘወርቅ ወዘብሩር ወዘዕንቀ እንተ  ራቂኖን ወቅልቅያን ድልው በሐሳብ
   ሠለስቱ እልፍ መክሊት፡ ወወይን ብዙን ዘሠናይ መዓዛሁ ዘይሰቲ ውእቱ ንጉሥ።

8: ወበዓሉስ አኮ በሕገ ቀዳሚ ዘገብረ፡ አላ በከመ ፈቀደ ውእቱ ንጉሥ ወአዘዘ ለመገብቱ
   ይግብሩ ፈቃደ ዚአሁ ወፈቃደ ሰብእ።

9: ወአስጢኒ ንግሥት ገብረት በዓለ ለአንስት እለ  ውስተ ቤተ መንግሥታ፡ እምነበ
አርጤክስስ ንጉሥ።

10: ወበሳብዕት ዕለት ሶበ ተፈሥሓ ንጉሥ ይቤሎ ለሆማ ወለባዛን ወለተራ ወለቡለዜ
    ወለዘትውልታ  ወለዘአበጠ ወለተራባ ወለሰብዓቱ አሕጽዋኒሁ ለንጉሥ  እለ
    ይትለአከዎ፤

11: ከመ ያምጽእዋ ለንግሥት ወያንግሥዋ ወያሠረግውዋ አክሊለ ወያርእይዋ ለኵሎሙ
    መላእክተ ሕዝብ ሥና እስመ ሠናይት ይእቲ።

12: ወአበየት ሰሚያቶ አስጢን ንግሥት ወኢፈቀደት ትምጻእ ምስለ ኃጽዋኒሁ ወተከዘ
    ንጉሥ ወተምዐ።

13: ወነገሮሙ ለአዕርክቲሁ ዘከመ ትቤ አስጢን፡ ወይቤሎሙ ግብሩ እንከሰ ሕነ
    ወኵነኔሁ፤

14: ወመጽአ ኅቤሁ አርቁስዮስ ወስርስቲዮስ ወማሌሲዓር ወመላእክቲሁ ዘፋርስ ወሜዶን እለ ቅሩባን ኅበ ንጉሥ፡ እለ ይኄብሩ እቱተ ምስለ ንጉሥ።

15: ወነገርዎ ለንጉሥ ሕጎሙ ዘከም ይሬሰይዋ ለአስጢን ንግሥት፡ እስመ ኢገብረት በከም አዘዘሙ ንጉሥ ለነጽዋን።

16: ወይቤሎ ሜኬዎስ ለንጉሥ ወለመላእክቲሁኒ አኮ ላዕለ ንጉሥ ባሕቲቱ ዘአበሰት አስጢን ንግሥት አላ ላዕለ ኵሎሙ መላእክት ወላዕለ መገብተ ንጉሥ።

17: ወነገሮሙ ቃላ ለንግሥት ዘከም አበየቶ ለንጉሥ፤ ወሶበ ዘቲ ዮም አበየቶ ለንጉሥ ለአርጤክስስ።

18: ከማሁ ዮምኒ አንስትያሆሙ ለመኳንንት ፋርስ ወሜዶን ሰሚዓን ኵሎን ዘከም ተዋሥአቶ ለንጉሥ፡ ከማሁ ይትኔበላ እማንቱኒ አምታቲሆን፡ ወያስተሐቅሩ።

19: ወእመስ ፈቀደ ንጉሥ የአዝዝ በቤተ መንግሥቱ ይጽሐፍዋ ለዝንቱ ሕግ ዘፋርስ ወሜዶን ወከመዝ ይግበርዋ ለይእቲ ወኢትባእ እንከ ንግሥት ኅቤሁ ወመንግሥታኒ የሀብ ንጉሥ ለካልእት ብእሲት እንተ ትኔይሳ።

20: ወይሰምዕዋ ለዝንቱ ሕግ ዘገብረ ንጉሥ በመንግሥቱ፡ ወእምዝ እንከ ኵሎን አንስት ያከብራ አምታቲሆን ባዕለኒ ወነዳየኒ።

21: ወአደሞ ለንጉሥ ዝንቱ ነገር ወለመላእክቲሁ፡ ወገብረ ንጉሥ በከም ይቤ ሜኬዎስ።

22: ወለአከ ንጉሥ ውስተ ኵሉ መንግሥቱ ለለ በሐውርቲሆሙ በከም ዝንቱ ቃል ከመ ይፍርሃሙ አንስቲያሆሙ በውስተ አብያቲሆሙ።

1: ወእምድኀረ ዝንቱ ነገር ረስዓ ንጉሥ ወኢተዘከራ እንከ ለአስጢን፡ እስመ ይዜክር ላቲ ዘከመ ተዋሥአቶ።

2: ወእምድኀረ ኮነና ይቤልዎ ደቂቁ ለንጉሥ፦ ይኅሥሡ ለንጉሥ አዋልደ ደናግለ እለ ሠናይ ራእዮን።

3: ወይሢም ንጉሥ ውስተ ኩሉ በሐውርተ መንግሥቱ መልእክተ ወመስፍተ፡ ወይኅሪዩ ሎቱ አዋልደ ደናግለ እለ ሠናይ ራእዮን በውስተ ሱሳ ሀገር፡ በውስተ አብያተ አንስት ወያወፍይዎ ለሐፀወ ንጉሥ ለጋይ ዓቃቤ አንስት፡ ወየሀብዎን ቅብአን ወኩሎ መፍቅዶን።

4: ወእንተ አደመቶ እምኔሆን ለንጉሥ ብእሲቱ ይእቲ ወትነግሥ፡ ምስሌሁ ህየንተ አስጢን ወአደሞ ዝንቱ ነገር ለንጉሥ፡ ወገብረ ከማሁ።

5: ወሀሎ አሐዱ ብእሲ አይሁዳዊ ውስተ ሱሳ ሀገር ዘስሙ መርዶኬዎስ ወልደ ኢያኤሩ ዘሴምዩ ዘቂስዩ ዘእምነገደ ብንያም።

6: ዘተዌወወ እምኢየሩሳሌም ዘዜወዎ ናቡከድናጾር ንጉሠ ባቢሎን።

7: ወቦቱ ወለተ እንተ ሐፀና ወለተ አሚናዳብ እኁሁ ለአቡሁ ወስማ አስቴር፡ ወእምድኀረ ወጽአት እምነ አዝማዲሃ ሐፀና ላቲ ትኩኖ ወለቶ፡ ወይእቲ ወለት ሠናይት ራእያ።

8: ወሶበ አዘዘ ንጉሥ አስተጋብኡ ሎቱ ብዙኀት አዋልደ ውስተ ሱሳ ሀገር ኀበ ጋይ፡ ወአምጽእዋ ለአስቴር ኀበ ጋይ ዓቃቤ አንስት።

9: ወአደመቶ ይእቲ ወለት ረከበት ሞገስ በቅድሜሁ፡ ወአፍጠነ ውሂቦታ ቅብአ ወመከፈልተ ወስብዐ አዋልደ እለ ይትለአካሃ እምቤተ ንጉሥ፡ ወሠናየ ዓቀባሃ እለ ሐፀናሃ በውስተ ቤተ አንስት።

10: ወኢነገረት አስቴር አዝማዲሃ ወኢ ብሔራ እስመ መርዶኬዎስ አዘዛ ከመ ኢታይድዕ።

11: ወኵሎ አሚረ ይመጽእ መርዶኬዎስ ኅበ ዓጸደ ቤት አንስት ከመ ይስማዕ ዜናሃ ለአስቴር ዘከመ ሀለወት።

12: ወአመ በጽሐ ጊዜሆን ለእልክቱ አዋልድ ከመ ይባእ ኅበ ንጉሥ፦ ወሶበ ተፈጸመ ዓሠርተ ወክልኤቱ አውራኅ እስመ መጠነዝ መዋዕል ይነብራ እንዘ ይትሔረሳ ወያሜንያ ስድስት አውራኅ እንዘ ይትቀብኣ ቅብአ ዕፍረት ወስድስት አውራኅ በአፈዋት ወበቅብኣ አንስት።

13: ወእምዝ እንከ ይእተ አሚረ ይበውኣ ኅበ ንጉሥ ወእንተ ውእቱ ፈቀደ ያመጽኡ ሎቱ እምቤት አንስት።

14: ወፍና ሰርከ ትበውእ ወጸቢሓ ትገብእ ቤት አንስት ኅበ ጋይ ኅጽው ንጉሥ ዐቃቤ አንስት ወኢትደግም እንከ በዊአ ወገቢአ ኅበ ንጉሥ ለእመ ለሊሁ ኢጸውዓ።

15: ወአመ በጽሐ መዋዕል እብሬታ ለአስቴር ወለተ አሚናዳብ እኅወ አቡሁ ለመርዶኬዎስ ከመ ትባእ ኅበ ንጉሥ ገብረት ኵሎ በከመ አዘዛ ዝክቱ ኅጽው አቃቤ አንስት እስመ ባቲ ሞገስ ለአስቴር በኅበ ኵሎሙ እለ ይሬእይዋ።

16: ወቦአት አስቴር ኅበ አርጤክስስ ንጉሥ በዓሠርቱ ወክልኤቱ አውራኅ በወርኅ አዳር በሰብዓቱ ዓም ዘመንግሥቱ።

17: ወአደሞ አስቴር ለንጉሥ ወረከት ሞገስ ፈድፋደ እምነ ኵሎን ደናግል ወአሰርገዋ አክሊለ አንስት።

18: ወገብረ ንጉሥ በዓለ ለኵሉ አዕርክቲሁ ወለሰራዊቱ ሰቡዐ መዋዕለ ወአዕበዮ ለመርዓ አስቴር ወገብረ ሕድጋቲሃ ውስተ ኵሎ ደወለ መንግሥቱ።

19: ወመርዶኬዎስ ይጸምድ በውስተ ዓጸድ ንጉሥ።

20: ወአስቴር ኢያይድዓት ብሔራ እስመ ከማሁ አዘዘ መርዶኬዎስ ከመ ትፍራህ
እግዚአብሐር ወትግበር ትእዛዙ በከመ ሀለወት ምስሌሁ: ወአስቴርስ ኢኳደገት ሕጋ::

21: ወተከዙ ክልኤት ኃጽዋኒሁ ለንጉሥ ሊቃነ ዓቀብተ ርእሱ: እስመ ዓብየ መርዶኬዎስ:
ወፈቀዱ ይቅትልዎ ለአርጤክስስ ንጉሥ::

22: ወሰምዐ መርዶኬዎስ ወነገራ ለአስቴር: ወይእቲ አይድዓቶ ለንጉሥ ምክሮሙ::

23: ወሶቤሃ ሐተቶሙ ንጉሥ ለእልክቱ ክልኤቱ ኃጽዋኒሁ ወእምዝ ስቀሎሙ: ወእምዝ
አዘዘ ንጉሥ ይጽሐፍዎ ለዝንቱ ውስተ መጽሐፈ ኖብያት መንግሥቱ ለተዝካር በእንተ
አኮቴቱ ለመርዶኬዎስ::

## Esther 3 ግዕ - አስቴር

1: ወእምድኅረ ዝንቱ አዕበዮ ንጉሥ አርጤክስስ ለሐማ እስመ ልደቱ ብዝያዊ ወአንበር
ላዕለ እምነ ኲሎሙ አዕርክቲሁ::

2: ወይሰግዱ ሎቱ ኲሎሙ እለ ውስተ ዐጸዱ እስመ ከማሁ ይገብሩ ዘአዘዘ ንጉሥ:
ወመርዶኬዎስስ ባሕቲቱ ኢይሰግድ ሎቱ::

3: ወይቤልዎ እለ ውስተ ዓጸደ ቤተ ንጉሥ:- አንተ መርዶኬዎስ ለምንት ኢትትኤዘዝ
ለቃለ ንጉሥ?

4: ወኲሎ አሚረ ይብልዎ ከመዝ ወየአቢ ሰሚያቶሙ: ወነገርዎ ለሐማ ከመ የአቢ
መርዶኬዎስ ትእዛዘ ንጉሥ: ወነገርዎ ከመ መርዶኬዎስ አይሁዳዊ ውእቱ::

5: ወሰበ አእመረ ሐማ ከመ ኢይሰግድ ሎቱ መርዶኬዎስ: ወተምዐ ጥቀ::

6: ወፈቀደ ያጥፍኦሙ ለኲሎሙ አይሁድ እለ ደወለ መንግሥቱ ለአርጤክስስ::

7: ወገብረ ከመዝ በዓሠርቱ ወክልኤቱ ዓመት እምዝ ነግሠ አርጤክስስ፡ ወአስተዓጸወ ዕለተ እምዕለት፡ ወወርኅ እምወርኅ፡ ከመ ያጥፍእዎሙ ለዘመደ መርዶኬዎስ በአሐቲ ዕለት፤ ወወረደ ዕፁ ላዕለ ዓሡሩ ወረቡዑ ለሠርቅ ወርኅ አዳር።

8: ወነገረ ለአርጤክስስ ወይቤሎ፦ ሀሎ ሕዝብ ዓላዊ እምውስተ አሕዛበ ኵሉ መንግሥትከ፡ ወሕገሙኒ ካልአ እምነ ዘኵሉ አሕዛብ ወኢይትኤዘዙ ለሕግ ንጉሥ፡ ወኢኮነ ርቱዕ ያሕድጎሙ ንጉሥ።

9: ወእመሰ ፈቀደ ንጉሥ የአዝዝ ወያጠፍእሙ፡ ወናሁ አነ እጽሕፍ ወአበውእ እልፈ መካልየ ብሩር ለመዝገበ ንጉሥ።

10: ወአውጽአ ንጉሥ ጕልቀቶ ወመጠዎ ውስተ እዴሁ ለሐማ ከመ ይሕትም፡ ሶበ ጸሐፈ በእንተ አይሁድ።

11: ወይቤሎ ንጉሥ ለሐማ፦ ወርቅስ ይኩንከ ለከ፡ ወሕዝብኒ ግበር ዘከመ ፈቀድከ።

12: ወጸውዐ ጸሐፍተ ንጉሥ በቀዳሚ ወርኅ አም ዓሡሩ ወሠሉሱ ለሠርቅ ወጸሐፉ በከመ አዘዞሙ ሐማ ለመላእክት ወለመሳፍንት ዘኵሉ በሐውርት እምነ ህንደኬ እስከ ኢትዮጵያ ለምእት ዕሥራ ወስብዓቱ በሐውርት፡ ለለምልክና አሕዛቢሆሙ በበነገረ በሐውርቲሆሙ በቃለ አርጤክስስ ንጉሥ።

13: ወፈነወ ምስለ ሐዋርያት ውስተ ደወለ መንግሥቱ ለአርጤክስስ ከመ ያትፍእዎሙ ለዘመደ አይሁድ በአሐቲ ዕለት በወርኅ አዳር አም ዓሡሩ ወስኑዩ ወይበርብርዎሙ ንዋዮሙ።

14: ወአርአዮሙ በለዋሳስ መጸሕፍቲሁ ወሤሙ ውስተ በሐውርቲሆሙ ወአዘዘ ለኵሉ አሕዛብ ከመ ይኩኑ ለውእቱ ዕለት።

15: ወይጌጕኡ በውስተ ሱሳኒ ይግበሩ ከማሁ ወንጉሥሰ ወሐማ ያጸምኡ ወተሀውከት ኵላ ሀገር።

1: ወሶበ አእመረ መርዶኬዎስ ዘከመ ኮነ ስጠጠ አልባሲሁ ወለብሰ ሠቀ ወወደየ ሐመደ ዲበ ርእሱ፡ ወሮጸ ውስተ መርነብ ሀገር እንዘ ይጸርሕ በዓቢይ ቃል ወይብል፦ ትቀትልኑ ሕዝበ ዘእንበለ አበሳ።

2: ወበጽሐ ነበ ኖነተ ንጉሥ ወቆመ እስመ ኢይከውኖ ለበዊአ ውስተ ዓጸደ ንጉሥ እንዘ ሠቀ ይለብስ ወሐመድ ዲበ ርእሱ።

3: ወበኩሉ በሐውርት ነበ ተፈነወ መጻሕፍት ኮነ ጽራሕ ወብካይ ዓቢይ ላሕ ወአይሁድ ሠቀ ወሐመደ ነጸፉ ኩሎሙ።

4: ወቦኡ ነጽዋኒሃ ወአዋልዲሃ ለንግሥት ወአይድዕዋ ወደንገፀት ሶበ ሰምዐት ዘንተ ዘከመ ኮነ፡ ወፈነወት አልባሰ ለመርዶኬዎስ ዘይለብስ ወከመ ያእትት፡ ወአበየ ነዲገ ሠቅ።

5: ወጸውዓቶ አስቴር ለአከራቴዎስ ነጽዋ ዘይቀውም ቅድሜሃ ወለአከቶ ይስማዕ ጥዩቀ ነገረ በነበ መርዶኬዎስ።

6: ወነገር መርዶኬዎስ ዘከመ ኮነ ወዘከመ ይቤሎ ሐማ ለንጉሥ፡ እልፈ መካልየ ያበውእ ውስተ መዝገቡ ለንጉሥ ከመ ይቅትሎሙ ለአይሁድ።

7: ወቃለ ነገራ ለዛቲ መጽሐፍ ዘአንበረ ውስተ ሱሳ ከመ ይቅትልዎሙ፤

8: ወወሀበ አርአያሃ ያርእያ ለአስቴር ወይቤሎ በላ ትባእ ነበ ንጉሥ ወትስአሎ ወታስተብቀኦ በእንተ ሕዝባ ተዘከሪያ መዋዕለ ምንዳቤኪ ዘከመ ተነፀንኪ ውስተ እዴየ እስመ ሐማ ዘእምታሕተ ንጉሥ አዘዘ ይቅትሉነ ወሰአሊ ነበ እግዚአብሔር እግዚአ ወንግርዮ ለንጉሥ በእንቲአነ ወአድኅንን እምዐት።

9: ወቦአ አከራቴዎስ ወነገራ ለአስቴር ኩሎ ዘንተ ነገረ።

10: ወትቤሎ አስቴር ለአክራቴዎስ፡- ሑር ኀበ መርዶኬዎስ ወበሎ፡-

11: ኩሉ አሕዛብ ለዛቲ መንግሥት ያአምር ከመ ዘቦአነ ንጉሥ ውስተ ዐጸድ ውሳጤ
እመኒ ብእሲአ ወእመኒአ ብእሲትአ ዘኢጸውዕዎ አልቦ ሕይወት እመ ኢለከፎ ንጉሥ
በበትሩ እንተ ወርቅ ዳእሙ ውእቱ ዘያሐዩ ወኪያየኒ ኢጸውዐኒአ እባእ ኀበ ንጉሥ
ሥሉስ መዋዕል ዮም።

12: ወአይድዖ አክራቴዎስ ለመርዶኬዎስ ዘተቤ አስቴር።

13: ወይቤሎ መርዶኬዎስ ለአክራቴዎስ፡- ሑር ወበላ፡- ኢትበሊ አስቴር ከመ አሐዩ አነ
ባሕቲትየ እምነ ኩሉ አይሁድ፡ በበይነ መንግሥትየ እመ ተጸመምኪ ዮም።

14: ለአይሁድስ እንተ ባዕድኒ ይሜርዎሙ ወኢያድኅኖሙ አንቲስ ወቤተ አቡኪ ትጠፍኡ፡
ወመኑ ያአምር ዮጊ በዝንቱ መዋዕል ንግሥኪ።

15: ወአግብአቶ አስቴር ለዝንቱ ለዘመጽ ኀቤሃ እምኀበ መርዶኬዎስ እንዘ ትብል፡-

16: ሑር አስተጋብአሙ ለአይሁድ እለ ውስተ ሱሳ ወጹሙ ሊተ ወኢትብልዑ ወኢትስተዩ
እስከ ሥሉስ መዋዕል መዓልት ወሌሊተ፡ ወአነ ወአዋልድየ ንጸውም፡ ወእምዝ
እበውእ ኀበ ንጉሥ ወእመ አኮ እመውት ሞት።

17: ወሖረ መርዶኬዎስ ወገብረ ኩሎ ዘአዘዘቶ አስቴር።

## Esther 5 ግዕ - አስቴር

1: ወእምዝ አመ ሣልስት ዕለት ሶበ አኀለቀት ጸልዮ አሰሰሰት አልባሲሃ ወለብሰት አልባስ
ክብራ፡ ወቦአት ኩሎ ኖኅተ ወበጽሐት ኀበ ንጉሥ፡ ወውእቱስ ይነብር ዲበ መንበረ
መንግሥቱ።

2: ወንጉሥ አንሥአ በትሮ እንተ ወርቅ ወተንሥአ እምንበሩ ወአንበረ ዲበ ርእሳ ወአኀዘ
ይዮውሃ በቃለ ሠናይ፡ ወአስቴር ተንሥአት ወቆመት ቅድመ ንጉሥ።

3: ወይቤላ ንጉሥ፦ ምንት ትፈቅዲ አስቴር ወበእንተ ምንት ታስተብቍዕኒ? እስከ መንፈቀ
መንግሥትየ ንሥኢ ለኪ ይኩንኪ።

4: ወትቤሎ አስቴር፦ እስመ ዕለተ በዓል ብየ ወእመሰ ፈቀድክ ንጉሥ ትምጻእ ውስተ
በዓልየ ዘእገብር ዮም አንተ ወሐማ።

5: ወይቤ ንጉሥ፦ ጸውዕዋ ለሐማ ፍጡነ ከመ እግበር ዘትቤለኒ አስቴር፡ ወሐሩ
ክልኤሆሙ ውስተ በዓል ዘገብረት አስቴር።

6: ወበውስተ በዓልኒ ይቤላ ንጉሥ ለአስቴር፡ ምንት ትፈቅዲ አስቴር ንግሥት፡
ዘአስተብቍዕኪ እግበር ለኪ?

7: ወትቤሎ፦ ስእለትየስ ዘአስተብቍዓከ፤

8: እመ ረከብኩ ሞገሰ በቅድመ አዕይንቲከ አ ንጉሥ፡ ከመ ትምጻእ አንተ ንጉሥ ወሐማ
ጌሠመ ውስተ በዓል ዘእገብር ለከሙ፡ ወጌሠመ እገብሮ።

9: ወወፅአ ሐማ እምነብ ንጉሥ ፍሡሐ ገጸ እንዘ ይትጎሠይ፡ ወእንዘ ይወጽእ ሶበ ርእዮ
ሐማ ለመርዶኬዎስ አይሁዳዊ ውስተ ዓጸደ ተምዐ ጥቀ።

10: ወሐረ ቤቶ ወጸውዓሙ ለአዕርክቲሁ፡ ወለሱዛራ ብእሲቱ።

11: ወአርአዮሙ ብዕሎ ወክብሮ፡ ዘገብረ ሎቱ ንጉሥ ወዘከመ አዕበዮ በውስተ
መንግሥቱ።

12: ወይቤሎሙ ሐማ፦ ኢጸውዐት ንግሥት ምስለ ንጉሥ ወኢመነኒ ውስተ በዓል፡ እንበለ
ንጉሥ፡ ወኪያየ ጸውዓተኒ።

13: ወፈድፋደስ ባሕቱ ሊተ ኢይሔውዘኒ ዝንቱ ሶበ ርኢክዎ ለመርዶኬዎስ አይሁዳ
ውስተ ዓጸድ።

14: ወትቤሎ ሱዛራ ብእሲቱ ወአዕርክቲሁ፦ ለይግዝሙ ኵሎ ዕፀ ዘሐምሳ በእመት ቃሙ
ወበጽባሕ ንግሮ ለንጉሥ፡ ወይስቀል ቦቱ መርዶኬዎስ፡ ወአንተስ ባእ ውስተ በዓል
ምስለ ንጉሥ ወተፈሡሕ፡ ወአደም ለሐማ ዝንቱ ነገር ወአስተዳለወ ዕፀ።

## Esther 6 ግዕ - አስቴር

1: ወአንፈጻ እግዚአብሔር ንዋም እምኔሁ ለንጉሥ በይእቲ ሌሊት፤ ወይቤሎ ለጸሐፊሁ
ያምጽእ ሎቱ መጻሕፍተ ተዝካር ዘኖብያት ዘመዋዕለ ትካት ወያንብቡ ሎቱ ዘውስተ
መጻሕፍት።

2: ወእምዝ ረካቡ ውስተ መጻሕፍት ኀበ ጸሐፉ በእንተ መርዶኬዎስ ዘከመ ዜነዎ ለንጉሥ
በእንተ ክልኤቱ ኀጽዋኒሁ ለንጉሥ፡ እለ የዓቅብዎ ለንጉሥ ወፈቀዱ ይቅትልዎ
ለአርጤክስስ ንጉሥ።

3: ወይቤ ንጉሥ፦ አይ ክብር ወጸጋ ዘገበርን ሎቱ ለመርዶኬዎስ? ወይቤልዎ ደቁ
ለንጉሥ፦ ወአልቦ ዘገበርክ ሎቱ ለመርዶኬዎስ እግዚኦ።

4: ወእንዘ ይትናገር ንጉሥ በእንተ አኰቴቶ ለመርዶኬዎስ በጽሐ ሐማ ውስተ ዓጸድ፡
ወይቤ ንጉሥ፦ መኑ ዝንቱ ዘውስተ ዓጸድ? ወይቤልዎ፦ ሐማ፤ ወእምዝ ቦአ ሐማ
ይንግር ለንጉሥ ከመ ይስቅሎ ለመርዶኬዎስ ውስተ ዕፅ ዘአስተዳለወ።

5: ወይቤልዎ ደቁ ለንጉሥ፦ ናሁ ሐማ ይቀውም ውስተ ዓጸድ፤ ወይቤ ንጉሥ፦ ጸውዕዎ።

6: ወይቤሎ ንጉሥ ለሐማ፦ ምንት እግበር ሎቱ ለብእሲ ዘአነ እፈቅድ አክበሮ? ወይቤ
በልቡ ሐማ፦ መነ ይፈቅድ ንጉሥ ያክብር ዘእንበለ ኪያየ።

7: ወይቤሎ ለንጉሥ፦ ለብእሲ ዘይፈቅድ ንጉሥ ያክብሮ፤

8: ያምጽኡ ሎቱ ደቁቀ ንጉሥ ሜላተ ዘይለብስ ንጉሥ፡ ወፈረስ እንተ ይጼዓን ንጉሥ።

9: ወየሀብዎ ለአሐዱ እምአዕርክቲሁ ለንጉሥ እለ ከቡራን ወያልብስዎ ለውእቱ ብእሲ ዘአክበሮ ንጉሥ፡ ወያጽዕንዎ ዲበ ፈረሱ፡ ወይስብክ ሎቱ አዋዲ ውስተ መርሐብ ሀገር እንዘ ይብል፡- ከመዝ ይከውን ሎቱ ለብእሲ ዘንጉሥ አክበሮ።

10: ወይቤሎ ንጉሥ ለሐማ፡- ሡናይ ትቤ፡ ግበር ከማሁ ለመርዶኬዎስ አይሁዳዊ ዘይጸምድ ውስተ ዓጸድ ወኢትንድግ አሐተ ቃለ እምነ ዘነበብከ።

11: ወነሥአ ሐማ አልባሰ ወፈረሰ ወአልበሶ ለመርዶኬዎስ ወአጽዓኖ ዲበ ፈረስ ወአዶ ውስተ መርሐብ ሀገር ወሰበከ እንዘ ይብል፡- ከመዝ ይሬሲ ለኵሉ ብእሲ ዘፈቀደ ንጉሥ ያክብሮ።

12: ወእምዝ ገብአ መርዶኬዎስ ውስተ ዓጸድ ወሐማኒ አተወ ውስተ ቤቱ እንዘ ያቴሕት ርእሶ።

13: ወነገራ ሐማ ለሱዛራ ብእሲቱ ወለአርካኒሁ፡ ወይቤልዎ አዕርክቲሁ ወብእሲቱ፡ እመ ለመርዶኬዎስ ዘእምነ ዘመደ አይሁድ ተትሕትከ ሎቱ ቅድሜሁ ወደቀ ወኢትከል መዊአቶ እስመ እግዚአብሔር ምስሌሁ።

14: ወአንጐኈዎ ለሐማ ውስተ በዓል ዘገብረት አስቴር።

## Esther 7 ግዕ - አስቴር

1: ወቦኡ ንጉሥ ወሐማ ይምስሑ ምስለ ንግሥት።

2: ወይቤላ ንጉሥ አመ ሳኒታ ዕለት ለአስቴር፡- ምንት ኮንኪ አስቴር ንግሥት፡ ወምንት ውእቱ ስእለትከ ወምንት ውእቱ ዘታስተብቍዕኒ? ወሰብ ፈቀድኪ መንፈቀ መንግሥትየ እምወሀብኩኪ።

3: ወአውሥአቶ ወትቤሎ፡ እመስ ረከብኩ ሞገሰ በቅድም ንጉሥ፡ ትትዋሀብ ለነፍስየ ስእለትየ ወለቃልየኒ አስተብቍዖትየ።

4: እስመ ተሣየጥነ አነ ወሕዝብየ ወኮነ ለሞት ወለተበርብሮ ወለቅንየት ንሕነ ወውሉድነ፥ ወአርመምኩ እስመ ኢይደልዎ ለመስተዋድይ ይባእ ውስተ ዐጸደ ንጉሥ።

5: ወይቤ ንጉሥ፦ መኑ ውእቱ ዝንቱ ነገር ዘተጎበለ ይግበር?

6: ወትቤ አስቴር፦ ብእሲ ጸላኢነ ሐማ፣ ወሶበ ሰምዐ ሐማ ፈርሀ እምነ ንጉሥ ወእምነ ንግሥት።

7: ወተንሥአ ንጉሥ እምነበ ይሰቲ ውስተ ገነት፣ ወሐማስ አስተብቀʸዓ ለንግሥት እስመ አእመረ ከመ በጽሐፉ እኪት።

8: ወገብአ ንጉሥ እምነ ገነቱ ወሐማስ ወድቀ ውስተ ዓራት ወይትጋነይ ላቲ ለንግሥት፣ ወይቤሎ ንጉሥ፦ ብእሲትየኑ ትትኤገለኒ በቤትየ? ወሶበ ሰምዐ ሐማ ጸልመ ገጹ።

9: ወይቤሎ ቡጋታን አሐዱ እምኅጽዋኒሁ ለንጉሥ፣ ሀለወ ዕፅ ዘአስተዳለወ ለመርዶኬዎስ ዘአይድዐ በእንተ ንጉሥ ዕፅስ ትኩል ውስተ ቤተ ሐማ ዘሐምሳ በእመት ኑኁ፣ ወይቤ ንጉሥ፦ ይስቅልዎ ቦቱ።

10: ወሰቀልዎ ዲበ ውእቱ ዕፅ ዘአስተዳለወ ለመርዶኬዎስ ወእምዝ ኀደገ ንጉሥ መዓቶ።

## Esther 8 ግዕ - አስቴር

1: ወበይእቲ ዕለት ጸገዋ ንጉሥ አርጤክስስ ለአስቴር ኩሎ ንዋየ ሐማ መስተዋድይ፣ ወጸውዐ ንጉሥ ለመርዶኬዎስ ወአይድዕ አስቴር ለንጉሥ ከመ በቤቱ ልህቀት።

2: ወነሥአ ንጉሥ ሕልቀተ ዘነሥአ እምእደ ሐማ ወወሀበ ለመርዶኬዎስ፣ ወሤመቶ አስቴር ለመርዶኬዎስ ላዕለ ኩሉ ዘሐማ።

3: ወእምዝ ዳግም ነበበቶ ለንጉሥ ወአስተብቀዐቶ ወሰገደት ታሕተ እገሪሁ ከመ ይሕድግ ኩሎ እኪየተ እንተ ገብረ ሐማ ላዕለ አይሁድ።

4: ወአንሥአ ንጉሥ በትሮ እንተ ወርቅ ወአንበረ ዲበ ርእሳ ለአስቴር፡ ወተንሥአት ወቆመት ቅድመ ንጉሥ፡፡

5: ወትቤሎ አስቴር፡- ለእመ ትፈቅድ ወረከብኩ ሞገሰ በቅድሜከ ለአከ ያምጽኡ መጻሕፍተ ዘጸሐፈ ሐማ ከመ ይቅትልዎሙ ለአይሁድ በውስተ መንግሥትከ፡፡

6: እፎ እክል ርኢየተ እኪይቶሙ ለሕዝብየ? ወእፎ እክል ሐዊወ እምድኅረ ሞቶሙ ለሕዝብየ?

7: ወይቤላ ንጉሥ ለአስቴር፡- ናሁ ኵሎ ንዋዮ ለሐማ ወሀብኩኪ ወጸገውኩኪ፡ ወኪያሁኒ ሰቀልክዎ ዲበ ዕፅ እስመ አንሥአ እዴሁ ላዕለ አይሁድ ምንተ እንከ ትፈቅዲ፡፡

8: ንሥኢ ኀልቀትየ ወይኀተሙ እንከስ በማኅተምየ ዘከመ ትፈቅዲ፡ እስመ ኵሉ ዘተጽሕፈ በትእዛዘ ንጉሥ ተኀትመ በማኅተመ ንጉሥ አልቦ ዘየአቢ፡፡

9: ወጸውዐ ጸሐፍተ በቀዳሚ ወርኀ ኒሳ አመ ዐሠርቱ ወሠለስቱ ዓመት ወጸሐፉ ለአይሁድ ዘከመ አዘዘሙ ንጉሥ ለመገብቱ ወለመኳንንት ወለመሳፍንት እምነ ህንደኬ እስከ ኢትዮጵያ በበሐውርቲሁ በበነገረ ብሔሮሙ፡፡

10: ወጸሐፉ በቃለ ንጉሥ ወኀተሙ በማኅተሙ ወፈነዉ መጻሕፍቲሁ ምስለ ሐዋርያት፡፡

11: ወከመዝ አዘዘሙ ይግበሩ በሕገሙ ለኵሉ አህጉር ወይርድእዎሙ ወይዕቀብዎሙ እምእደ ፀርሙ ወእምነ እለ ይቀውሙ ላዕሌሆሙ በከመ ይፈቅዱ እሙንቱ፡፡

12: ወበይእቲ ዕለት በኵሉ መንግሥቱ ለአከ አርጤክስስ አመ ዐሠሩ ወሰሉሱ ለሠርቀ አዳር ዘዐሠርቱ ወክልኤቱ አውራኅ፡፡

13: ወአርአይዎ ለዝ መጽሐፍ ገሃደ ይሰፍሕዎ ወያርአይዎ ወይኩኑ ድልዋን ኵሎሙ አይሁድ በይእቲ ዕለት ከመ ይቅትልዎሙ ለፀርሙ፡፡

14: ወወፅኡ እለ ይጌዕጹ አፍራስ እንዘ ይጔጉኡ ከመ ይግበሩ ትእዛዝ ንጉሥ ወተሠይመ ዝንቱ ትእዛዝ ውስተ ሱሳ ሀገር።

15: ወወጽአ መርዶኬዎስ እንዘ ልቡስ አልባስ መንግሥት ዘቦ አክሊለ ወርቅ ወጽንበል ሲራየ ሜላት፤ ወርእዮ እለ ውስተ ሀገረ ሱሳ ወተፈሥሑ።

16: ወለአይሁድስ ኮነ ብርሃን ወትፍሥሕት።

17: በሀገር ወበብሔር በኀበ ተሠይመ ውእቱ ትእዛዝ ወበኀበ ተረክበ ውእቱ መጽሐፍ በፍሥሓ ወበጽጋብ ለአይሁድ በፍቅር ወጐጔት፤ ወብዙኀን እለ አምኑ አሕዛብ እለ ተዘርዉ ወተሐረሙ በእንተ ፍርሀቶሙ ለአይሁድ።

## Esther 9 ግዕ - አስቴር

1: እስመ ዘዓሠርቱ ወክልኤቱ አውራን ወአመ ዓሡሩ ወሰሉሱ ለወርኅ አዳር በጽሐ መጽሐፍ ዘጸሐፈ ንጉሥ።

2: ወበይእቲ ዕለት ተነጉሉ እለ ይቀውመ ላዕሌሆሙ ለአይሁድ ወአልቦ እንከ ዘተቃተሎሙ ለአይሁድ እስመ ፈርህዎሙ።

3: ወመላእክተ አሕዛብኒ ወመገብትኒ ወጸሐፍተኒ ዐበይተ ንጉሥኒ ያከብርዎሙ ለአይሁድ በእንተ ፍርሀተ መርዶኬዎስ።

4: ወይትሐዜቡ እስመ በመጽሐፈ ንጉሥ ተሠይመ በኵሉ መንግሥቱ።

5: እስመ መጽሐፈ ንጉሥ ተሠይመ በኵሉ መንግሥቱ።

6: ወበሱሳ ሀገር ቀተሉ አይሁድ ኃምስተ ምእት ወሰብዓ ወሠለስተ፤

7: ወጐራንሂ ወንጦይ ወደለፎን ወፈስጋስ፥

8: ወፈርዳንታ ወቤርያ ወሰርበካ፥

9: ወመርሶን ወአሮፍዮን ወርሴዎን ወዘቦቴታን፨

10: ደቂቀ ሐማ ወልደ አመዳቱ ብግያዊ ጸላኢሆሙ ለአይሁድ ለዐሠርቲሆሙ አኃዝዎሙ ወሰቀልዎሙ፡ ወበርበሩ በይእቲ ዕለት፨

11: ወዜነውዎ ለንጉሥ ፆልቄ ሰብእ ዘሞተ በሱሳ ሀገር፨

12: ወይቤላ ንጉሥ ለአስቴር፦ ቀተሉ አይሁድ በሱሳ ሀገር ኃምስተ ምእት ወሰብዓ ዕደው፤ ወአፎ እንከ በአድያም፡ ገብሩ እንከ ታስተብቍኒ በእንቲአየ እግበር ለኪ?

13: ወትቤሎ አስቴር ለንጉሥ፦ ሀቦሙ ለአይሁድ ከማሁ ይግበሩ እንተ ጌሰም ይስቅሉ ዐሠርቲሆሙ ደቂቀ ሐማ፨

14: ወአዘዘ ከመ ይግበሩ ወአዘዞሙ ለአይሁድ ለእለ ሀለዉ ውስተ ሀገር ይስቅሉ ሥጋሆሙ ለደቂቀ ሐማ፨

15: ወተጋብኡ አይሁድ ውስተ ሱሳ ሀገር አመ ዓሡሩ ወረቡዑ ለሠርቀ አዳር ወቀተሉ ሠለስተ ምእት ዕደወ ወአልቦ ዘበርበሩ፨

16: ወእለ ተርፉ አይሁድ ወእለ ይትቀነዩ ለነገሥት ተጋብኡ እሙንቱሂ በበናቲሆሙ ወተራድእ ወአልቦ ዘበርበሩ ወአዕረፉ እምነ ቀትሎሙ ወዘቀተሉስ አመ ዓሡሩ ወረቡዑ ለሠርቀ አዳር ሰብዐተ እልፍ ወኃምሳ ምእት ወአልቦ ዘበርበሩ፨

17: ወአዕረፉ እንከ አመ ዓሡሩ ወረቡዑ ለውእቱ ወርኅ ወረሰይዎ ለይእቲ ዕለት በዓል ከመ ባቲ ያዕርፉ ምስለ ትፍሥሕት ወጽጋብ፨

18: ወአይሁድስ እለ ውስተ ሱሳ ሀገር ተጋብኡ አመ ዓሡሩ ወረቡዑ ለሠርቀ አዳር፡ ወኢያዕረፉ ይእተ አሚረ ወአመ ዓሡሩ ወኃሙሱ ገብሩ በዓለ ወትፍሥሕተ፨

19: ወበበይነ ዝንቱ ነገር አይሁድ እለ ተዘርዉ ውስተ ኵሉ በሐውርት ቀስፍ ይገብርዎ ሠናይተ ለይእቲ ዕለት አመ ዓሡሩ ወረቡዑ በጽጋብ፡ እንዘ ይፌንዉ ከፍለ ለቢጾሙ

ወለጎሮሙ፡ ወለእለ ይነብሩ ውስተ ደብረ አህጉር፡ ወአሥ ዓሠሩ ወኃምስ ገብሩ ላቲ ትፍሥሕተ ሥናየ፡ እንዘ እሙንቱ ይፌንዉ ክፍለ ለቢጸሙ ወለጎሮሙ፡፡

20: ወጸሐፊ መርዶኬዎስ ለዝንቱ ነገር ውስተ መጽሐፍ ወፈነዎ ለአይሁድ ለእለ ሀለዉ ውስተ መንግሥተ አርጤክስስ ለቅሩባን ወለርኁቃን፡፡

21: ከመ ይንግርዎሙ እሎንተ መዋዕለ በዓለ አመ ዓሠሩ ወረቡዑ ወአመ ዓሠሩ ወኃሙሱ ለወርኅ አዳር፡፡

22: እስመ በእማንቱ መዋዕል አዕረፉ አይሁድ እምነ ጸላኢሆሙ በወርኅ በዝ ቦቱ ገብኡ እምነ ላሕ ውስተ ፍሥሓ ወእምነ ሐማም ውስተ ዕለት ሥናይ ዘውእቱ አዳር ወይገብርዎ በኵሉ መዋዕሊሆሙ ከብካበ ወጽጋበ ወይዜግውዎ ለምስኪኖሙ ወለታእኃሆሙ፡፡

23: ወተወከፉ አይሁድ በከመ ጸሐፈ ሎሙ መርዶኬዎስ፡፡

24: ዘከመ ቀተሎሙ ሐማ ወልደ አመዱቱ ዘእምነ መቄዶንያ በከመ ኀሰበ ወአስተቃሠመ ሎሙ ለአማስኖቶሙ፡፡

25: ወበከመ ቦአ ወሰአለ ኀበ ንጉሥ ከመ ይስቅሎ ለመርዶኬዎስ ወኮሉ ዘሀሎ ይግበር እኩየ ላዕለ አይሁድ ገብአ ላዕለ ርእሱ ወተሰቅለ ውእቱ ወደቂቁ፡፡

26: ወበበይነ ዝንቱ ተሰምያ እማንቱ መዋዕል ድኂነ በእንተ ዘተዐጽወ በነገሮሙ ይሰምይዎን ድኂነ በእንተ ዛቲ ቃለ መጽሐፍ ወበእንተ ኵሉ ዘተረከበ ውስቴታ ወኮሉ ዘኮነ ላዕሌሆሙ፡፡

27: ወበዘጸሐፉ ተወከፉ አይሁድ ሎሙ ወለሐርአሙ ወለዘይዴምር ምስሌሆሙ ወከመ ኢይፍልሱ እምዝንቱ ግብር፡፡

28: ወበእላንቱ መዋዕል ይትገበራ ተዝካረ ለዓለም ዓለም በበ አህጉር ወበበ በሐውርት፡፡

29: ወበእማንቱ መዋዕል ይትገበር ለዘላፉ እስመ ቦቶን ድኅኑ ከመ ኢይደምስስ ተዝካሮሙ
ለዓለም።

30: ወጸሐፈት አስቴር ወለተ አሚናዳብ ወመርዶኬዎስ አይሁዳዊ ኵሎ ዘገብሩ ወእጽንዐ
መጽሐፈ ዘመድኅኒት።

30: ወጸሐፈት አስቴር ወለተ አሚናዳብ ወመርዶኬዎስ አይሁዳዊ ኵሎ ዘገብሩ ወእጽንዐ
መጽሐፈ ዘመድኅኒት።

31: ወመርዶኬዎስ ወአስቴር ንግሥት አሕረምዎን ሎሙ ለርእሶሙ አሜሁ ወመሐሉ
በሕይወቶሙ ወበምክሮሙ።

32: ወአስቴርኒ ቢቃላ ለዓለም ወተጽሕፈ ለዝክር።

## Esther 10 ዓዕ - አስቴር

1: ወጸሐፈ ንጉሥኒ ውስተ መንግሥቱ ዘበምድር ወዘባሕር።

2: ወላዕለ ጽንዑ ወላዕለ ስብሐቲሁ ወላዕለ ብዕሉ ወክብሩ ወመንግሥቱ ዘታሕቴሁ ናሁ
ልኩዕ ውስተ መጽሐፍ ፋርስ ወሜዶን ለተዝካ።

3: ወመደከዮሳ ባሕቲቱ ይዓቅብ መንግሥተ ንጉሥ አርጤክስስ ዓቢይ ውእቱ
ወመንግሥቱኒ ክቡር ውእቱ በኀበ አይሁድ ወይትፈቀድ ወይነግር ንብረታ ለኵሉ ሕዝብ
በትውልዶሙ።

## ተፈጸመ ፥ መጽሐፈ ፥ ዘአስቴር

# Your choice

"This day I call heaven and earth as witnesses against you and I have set before you life and death, blessings and curses. Now choose life, so that you and your children may live and that you may love the Lord your God, listen to his voice, and hold fast to Him. For the LORD is your life and he will give you many years in the land He swore to give to your fathers, Abraham, Isaac and Jacob?"   Deutronomy 30; 19-20

# Your encounter with God begins with a choice.

Today I have given you choice between life and death, between blessings and curses. Now I call on Heaven and Earth to witness the choice you make. Oh that you would choose life, so that you and your descendents might Live! You can make this choice by loving the LORD your God, obeying Him, and committing yourself firmly to Him. This is the key to your life...

# God's Love

Before we can understand God's love, we must know that He is alive and waiting to interact with us. He is not just the creator of the universe; He is actually the saviour and also forms each of his children in their mother's wombs. He is the hands-on Father who welcomes each person. He creates and looks forward to the day they accept him and his son as their father and personal saviour. God personaly performs miracle in ways to expose his love and peace that surpasses all human understanding. God loves us, we must realize that He is real and near, closer than any human can ever be.

# Important Decision in Life

'But as many as received Him, to them gave He power to become the Sons of God, even to them that believe on His name:' John1:12(KJV)

Finally, chosing LORD JESUS is the most important decition you will ever make. If you have not made the choise to be a follower of LORD Jesus, God's Beloved Son, I encourage you to say the Following Prayer Out Loud.

"Dear Heavenly Father, You are the most high God and I come to You in the name of Jesus. I thank you for sending Jesus to the Earth as the Word of God who becomes flesh.

Father, I receive your love and gift of salivation through your beloved son Lord Jesus. Christ Jesus, I believe you died on the cross and shed your blood for my sins and the sins of the whole world. Because of your sacrifice, you remember my sins no more and I have right stood before you. I believe you were raised from the dead on the third day. Please I ask you to forgive all my sins in Jesus Name.

Now Jesus, come into my heart. Take away my story heart and give me a new heart that I may love the father even as you do. And Lord, help me to know you and experience your love in the way I have read about in these bible-based truth and the above lovely analysis of the book of Esther. In this book; I discover God's intervention and his unique ways of interacting with his people, through his divine visitation.  Today, I accept you as my personal Saviour and Lord. I thank you. In the Name of Lord Jesus Christ, Amen.''


**GOD BLESS YOU ALL**
**Dr. Yohannes Tekle**